FinTech Law:

A Guide to

Technology Law

in the

Financial Services

Industry

Litigation and White-Collar Crime Titles From Bloomberg BNA

Anti-Corruption Law and Compliance: Guide to the FCPA and Beyond
Kevin T. Abikoff, John F. Wood, and Michael H. Huneke

Computer and Intellectual Property Crime
Hugh A. Scott

Criminal Tax, Money Laundering, and Bank Secrecy Act Litigation
Peter D. Hardy

False Claims Act: Whistleblower Litigation, Sixth Edition
James B. Helmer, Jr.

Federal Appellate Practice
Mayer Brown LLP

Health Care Fraud and Abuse: Practical Perspectives
ABA Health Law Section

Prosecuting and Defending Health Care Fraud Cases
Michael K. Loucks and Carol C. Lam

Responding to Corporate Criminal Investigations
Kirby D. Behre and Morgan J. Miller

Supreme Court Practice
Stephen M. Shapiro, Kenneth S. Geller, Timothy S. Bishop,
Edward A. Hartnett, and Dan Himmelfarb

BNA's Directory of State and Federal Courts, Judges, and Clerks
Catherine A. Kitchell

For details on these and other related titles, please visit our Website at **bna.com/bnabooks** or call **1-800-960-1220** to request a catalog. All books are available on a 30-day free-examination basis.

FinTech Law:

A Guide to

Technology Law

in the

Financial Services

Industry

Kevin C. Taylor

New York, New York

**Bloomberg
BNA**

Arlington, VA

Library of Congress Cataloging-in-Publication Data

Taylor, Kevin C., author.
    Fintech law : a guide to technology law in the financial services
industry / Kevin C. Taylor.
        pages cm.
    ISBN 978-1-61746-439-3
    1. Financial services industry--Law and legislation--United States.
    2. Computers--Law and legislation--United States. 3. Information
storage and retrieval systems--Law--United States. 4. Information
technology. I. Title.
    KF974.T39 2014
    346.73'08--dc23

                                                    2014036499

Published by Bloomberg BNA
1801 S. Bell Street, Arlington, VA 22202
bna.com/bnabooks

ISBN 978-1-61746-439-3
Printed in the United States of America

To Morgan and Kenneth

PREFACE

This First Edition is current through May 2014.

Because financial services technology can facilitate transactions without regard to the complex regulatory structure governing financial services, it also can generate complex legal and regulatory issues. This book explains those issues and offers excellent practical advice on how to address them, both for new technology companies entering the financial services arena and for more established financial services companies venturing into the ever-expanding world of financial technology.

It might be hard to tell, but this book has taken ten years to write. Part of the reason is that at least twice a week new legal issues in the arena of financial services technology cross my desk. To say it is a rapidly changing field is an understatement. In this electronic age, updating the book is easily enough accomplished, as the stream of new issues and legal and regulatory guidance emerge.

Consumers, and indeed society as a whole, rely on the financial services industry. Because of this, the industry has been regulated, in some form, at both the federal and state levels since the beginning of the United States. With 50 states, each with one or more applicable regulatory agencies, and at least 18 federal regulatory agencies that apply to this industry, the complexities of the relevant regulatory structure cannot be overemphasized.[1] Operating in this environment would be a challenge for any company.

Technology can facilitate transactions without regard to regulatory structure. In other words, technology is blind to regulatory or legal compliance. At the same time, technology can help solve problems such as compliance and anti–money laundering. Because of the constantly changing nature of this technology, regulators often cannot keep up with the changes.

These challenges exist across the financial services industry. For a new company entering the financial services arena (such as a start-up technology company), navigating this minefield of regulations is often formidable. And yet, even established financial services companies run afoul of these laws and regulations.

Most financial regulations focus on either consumer protection or market protection. Consumer protection regulations are designed to protect individuals, while market protection regulations are intended to protect market participants, which may be individuals or commercial entities.

Since people can do almost anything with technology, they are doing things today that were never even contemplated when the financial services regulatory structure was put into place. Therefore, the intended goals of the various regulations may be violated, as well as the regulations themselves. For instance, the goal of consumer protection could be violated by a technology such as mobile banking, which allows direct payments to individuals. The technology may not properly safeguard the individual's information. It may be subject to reporting and record-keeping requirements. It may be subject to consumer refund opportunities. Because they are not bank lawyers, inventors of these technologies often are not aware that existing regulatory structures may apply to their technology.

This book discusses issues affecting financial service companies due to the regulated nature of financial services. It also explains the legal and regulatory requirements for

---

[1] Some of the criticisms of this structure are described at the end of Chapter 2.

specific clauses required by financial services companies in their contracts.

Simply put, the use of technology overcame the existing legal framework. While the goals of financial service regulations are still important and desirable, their implementation must keep up with the changing nature of financial services or risk becoming no longer valid.

Does the regulatory structure of financial services need a major overhaul? You bet. But that would be another book.

Kevin C. Taylor

September 2014

ABOUT THE AUTHOR

Kevin C. Taylor started in technology law at Brown Raysman during the Internet boom of the late 1990s. In his career he has represented companies in all corners of the financial services industry: banking, securities, insurance, and credit card companies. He has also represented many technology companies that sell technology products and services to large financial institutions. He currently represents some of the largest financial companies in the world in the acquisition and use of technology, whether as software, services, hardware, or any combination of these.

SUMMARY TABLE OF CONTENTS

DETAILED TABLE OF CONTENTS

CHAPTER 1

TECHNOLOGY ISSUES IN FINANCIAL SERVICES

I. INTRODUCTION

Today, financial services are largely provided through some form of technology. But theirs is not always a perfect partnership: The regulatory structure of financial services developed without regard to technology, and in turn, technology continues to develop without regard to the regulatory structure. As a result, issues frequently arise that require thoughtful decisions from both technology vendors and regulators to ensure that the financial service industry operates smoothly.

Technology and the law often clash. The rate of technological change is exponentially greater than the rate at which the law changes to keep up with it. Early technology cases such as *New York Times Co. v. Tasini*[1] and *A&M*

---

[1] 533 U.S. 483 (2001) (copyrighted works, originally licensed for publication solely in nonelectronic form, could be republished online only with authors' express permission).

Records, Inc. v. Napster[2] demonstrated this. In both of these early twenty-first-century cases, existing law was applied in new contexts created by technological change. Existing law does not fully address the new situations presented by new technologies.

An analogous situation exists in the financial services regulatory context.[3] This book was written to help various professionals understand the current state of the financial services industry, to problem-solve the issues created by the gap between regulatory and technological growth, and to benefit from practical information gathered during two decades of representing financial institutions.

This book is useful for the following groups: (1) financial service professionals (lawyers, compliance officers, and chief information officers) who need to understand the regulatory environment in which they operate; (2) entrepreneurs who seek to solve challenges in the financial services industry; (3) technology vendors that need to navigate the regulatory structure to satisfy their clients; and (4) investors and venture capital groups that interact with the first two groups and seek to make investment decision that navigate the regulatory structure and solve real problems.

II. Overview of the Book

Chapters 2 and 3 address areas that are essential to understanding technology law in general and financial technology law in particular. Chapter 2 discusses the current and historical regulatory structure governing financial services. The chapter describes how this complex structure regulates industry segments. For purposes of this book, I divide

---

[2] 114 F. Supp. 2d 896 (N.D. Cal. 2000), *aff'd in part, rev'd in part*, 239 F.3d 1004 (9th Cir. 2001), 2001 U.S. Dist. LEXIS 2186 (N.D. Cal. Mar. 5, 2001), *aff'd*, 284 F.3d 1091 (9th Cir. 2002) (facilitating copyright infringement is copyright infringement).

[3] The Federal Financial Institution Examination Council (FFIEC), in fact, has issued several booklets that attempt to make regulatory compliance more "user-friendly," but even that hasn't helped. (The FFIEC is a group of many, but not all, of the federal financial institution regulators. It is discussed in more detail in Chapter 2.)

financial services into the following four industry segments: (1) traditional banking (institutions that take deposits and make loans); (2) securities and commodities trading and investment; (3) credit cards; and (4) insurance. While there is much overlap between these industry groups, it is useful to understand how each is regulated and operates. Different business models and lines of business are regulated differently, even by different regulators. The historical material reveals what policy goals drove regulatory decisions and gives clues as to how regulators will respond to future events, such as further changes in technology.

Chapter 3 presents an overview of intellectual property law for non-IP lawyers. It is not meant to be comprehensive but gives just enough information to enable readers to make sense of the rest of the book.

Chapter 4 looks at online activities of financial institutions in general and how those activities are regulated. Depending on the regulatory agency, the same activity can be subject to different regulations.

Chapter 5 addresses the use of mobile devices in the financial services industry. The rapidly changing mobile environment has made it difficult for regulators to keep up with the technological changes. We can expect some regulation in line with the policy goals of consumer protection and market protection. (These goals are discussed in Chapter 2.) One could predict that any technology that transmits money for consumers, or even facilitates the transmission of money, will be regulated. Even just transmitting information about a person's account balance could and should have some regulatory requirements around authentication, data security, and privacy, at a minimum. Therefore, it would be unwise to attempt to create a technology that does those things and not expect it to be subject to regulation. In other words, it would be prudent to build mobile technology with all of this in mind.

Chapter 6 looks at cloud computing, an area that has grown tremendously over the last few years. The chapter discusses strategies and recommendations for using cloud computing, especially in light of concerns such as data security.

Chapter 7 concerns technology licensing. The chapter explores various issues important to users of licensed technology, whether it is traditional software, software as a service, or some other business model. If a technology license is not properly drafted at the outset, by the time the user discovers a problem with the license, it may be too late to address that problem.

Chapter 8 addresses the use of third-party service providers for sourcing and outsourcing of services or technology useful for the financial services industry. Since financial institutions are usually held liable for the actions of their vendors, this chapter is extremely useful.

Chapter 9 discusses information governance. Information governance includes data security, privacy, record-keeping, and big data. This area is increasing, both figuratively and literally. Helping financial institutions manage the mountains of data they acquire is a growth industry.

Chapter 10 discusses electronic fraud, including identity theft and anti–money laundering. New technologies can give the bad guys an advantage, at least until the regulators catch up.

Chapter 11 discusses issues that arise with technology under bankruptcy law. This is especially important given that new technologies often come from small and start-up companies.

Finally, Chapter 12 looks at global developments and issues in financial services. This area is expected to grow in the future, making it an important topic to understand.

III. CONCLUSION

The financial services industry includes many types of activities and actors: retail banking (serving consumers), commercial banking (serving businesses), retail and wholesale stockbrokers, loan brokers, insurance companies, insurance brokers, insurance agents, commodities dealers, currency dealers, lenders of all types, money transmitters, and credit card issuers. This book groups financial services activities into four market segments: traditional banking (deposits and loans), securities and commodities activities, insurance activities, and credit card activities. Each of these segments faces different regulators, but within the segments, certain issues are the same.

Technologies such as e-mail and other computer applications make it difficult for financial institutions to comply with legal and regulatory requirements. The challenge for financial institutions is to remain compliant while ensuring the protection of their own customers and businesses.

Chapter 2

INTRODUCTION TO THE REGULATION OF FINANCIAL SERVICES

I. INTRODUCTION

This chapter contains a brief substantive review of the basic workings of the law and regulations governing the financial services industry, as well as a succinct historical account. The history of the financial services regulatory structure, although not comprehensive, sets the stage for later substantive discussion. One can only understand the complex structure of financial services regulation by first understanding its history.

II. OVERVIEW OF THE LEGAL AND REGULATORY STRUCTURE GOVERNING FINANCIAL SERVICES

A. Domestic History

1. Early Federal Bank Regulation

Banking regulation in the United States has a history at least as old as the country itself. However, the Founding Fathers did not have a unanimous view on the subject. In fact, prior to the American Revolution, England tried to impose the regulation of the Bank of England on the American colonies. The Currency Acts of 1751 and 1764 sought to protect English merchants from colonial currency that fluctuated in value. The Acts restricted the colonies' ability to issue their own paper money. Some money could be created, but it could be used only to pay public debts, not private obligations. Most of the American colonies viewed the Acts as unjust; indeed, the First Continental Congress labeled the 1764 Act as "subversive."

After the American Revolution, the new United States sought to set up a framework to address these issues. This effort generated strong and opposite opinions. Some leaders, led primarily by Alexander Hamilton, supported a national bank. Others, primarily southerners such as Thomas Jefferson, strongly opposed giving the federal government too large a role. The First Bank of the United States, founded in 1791, won out, but not without compromise. To gain southerners' backing, national bank supporters agreed to move the nation's capital south from New York to Washington, D.C. The new bank was responsible for a portion of the nation's money supply, with a charter that lasted until 1811. Shortly after the charter's expiration, the country had to finance the War of 1812. Without a central bank, Congress issued Treasury notes directly, resulting in high inflation.

Five years later, James Madison signed the charter creating the Second Bank of the United States, which was very similar to the prior bank's charter. When it expired in 1836, President Andrew Jackson would not renew the charter. Again, high inflation plagued the country, even sparking a depression in 1837.

The period from 1837 to 1863 is often referred to as the free banking era. During this time, some state-chartered banks provided functions of a central bank, including providing deposit insurance and acting as clearinghouses for bank notes.

2. National Banking Act of 1863

In 1863, Congress passed the National Banking Act. This legislation had several important provisions. It created a system of federally chartered banks called national banks. All of the national banks were required to accept one another's bank notes (i.e., currency) at full value, thus creating a national currency. This reduced risk in the event one bank failed. In addition, the banks were required to keep higher reserves than state banks, further reducing risk. Finally, national banks were required to secure their bank notes by purchasing U.S. Treasury bonds. This further reduced risk and helped finance the Civil War for the North. In addition, the federal government imposed a tax on state bank notes of 10 percent. This led to even more banks converting to the new system. By 1870, there were almost 1,700 national banks and only around 300 state banks nationwide.

This system was an improvement but not without flaws. The U.S. Treasury bonds used to secure bank notes fluctuated in value. When their value decreased, banks had to buy more reserves or borrow from other banks, resulting in a cash shortage. In addition, banks often had higher needs for funds at different times of the year. For instance, rural banks needed currency more during the planting season (when farmers were buying seed and planting equipment). This again created a money shortage. When these two forces combined, the result was a liquidity crisis. This often led to bank panics or runs on the bank by depositors to withdraw their money. These sometimes had severe economic consequences, including economic depressions. Severe bank panics occurred in 1873 and 1893, with one of the worst occurring in 1907.

A series of events are thought to have led to the banking panic of 1907. Several systemic weaknesses were present. There remained seasonal fluctuations in the money supply. Money was in short supply in the fall months, as it was needed to purchase harvests. Banks then would raise interest rates to attract deposits. This attracted domestic depositors, but foreign investors as well. This cycle had persisted for years.

The April 1906 San Francisco earthquake affected the money supply as insurance claims required large payouts. Starting in the fall of 1906, stock prices on the New York Stock Exchange began to decline. In late 1906, the Bank of England raised its interest rates, competing with New York for depositors and leading to a decrease in the U.S. domestic money supply with cash being moved to London.

The ultimate crisis was precipitated by the Heinze brothers' ill-fated scheme to manipulate stocks in an attempt to control the market for copper. This led to the collapse of at least one brokerage house[1] and runs on banks owned by Augustus Heinze and his business partner, Charles Morse. Within a short time, the situation spread to other banks and cities. More than a dozen banks failed. With traders unable to get money, stock prices declined even further, wiping out fortunes overnight. Values on the New York Stock Exchange fell by 50 percent or more. J.P. Morgan famously led a syndicate that stopped the slide in prices and averted further disaster.

However, J.P. Morgan and others were ultimately seen as elites who controlled and manipulated the economy. Morgan personally gained from the panic. A powerful Democratic congressman, Arsene Pujo, convened hearings to investigate the situation. The result led to further investigations and eventually the creation of the Federal Reserve.

At this time, the United States was the only large developed country without a central bank. Senator Nelson Aldrich and others traveled to Europe and saw firsthand how the British and German central banks stabilized their respective economies. Aldrich and his team developed a plan to create a U.S. central bank system, consisting of regional Federal Reserve banks that were overseen by a central board. The board was appointed by the president and confirmed by the Senate.

3. Federal Reserve Act

The Federal Reserve Act was signed into law by President Woodrow Wilson on December 23, 1913. This central bank initially functioned primarily as lender of last resort to reduce and eliminate future bank panics. After World War I, the Act was amended to allow the Federal Reserve to create and destroy money. During Franklin Roosevelt's presidency, the Federal Reserve was under the control of the executive branch. In 1951, it returned to independence in matters of monetary policy. In the 1970s, Congress mandated that it

---

[1] Ron Chernow, The House of Morgan 127 (1990).

maximize employment and keep prices and long-term inter-est rates stable.

4. Regulation Stemming from the Great Depression

The stock market crash in the fall of 1929 destroyed a massive portion of the nation's wealth. People felt poorer and subsequently drew more cash out of the banks, causing banks to fail, causing people to lose faith in banks, and caus-ing runs on banks and shortages of cash. Even greater wealth destruction followed.

The Pecora Commission investigated the crash and made recommendations for preventing or at least mitigat-ing such events in the future. Not surprisingly, these rec-ommendations took the form of new legislation aimed at protecting consumers and investors. One of the suggestions that resulted from the Pecora hearings was the separation of investment banking from commercial banking.

a. Banking Act of 1933

The Banking Act of 1933, often referred to as the Glass-Steagall Act, is best known for three main provisions: (1) the separation of investment banking and commercial bank-ing, (2) the creation of a national system of deposit insur-ance along with the Federal Deposit Insurance Corporation (FDIC), and (3) the requirement that every FDIC-insured bank become a member of the Federal Reserve System.

During the period leading up to the crash of 1929, many Wall Street investment banks created and then sold overvalued securities to their commercial and retail banking customers, many of whom were unsophisticated investors or smaller correspondent banks.

Senator Carter Glass sought to fix what he perceived as shortcomings of the Federal Reserve Act. Glass thought that unifying small single-office banks through the Federal Reserve System would make the whole banking system stron-ger. In addition, insuring deposits at all banks in the system added stability and confidence in the system and mitigated the occurrence of any bank runs. Deposit insurance was initially set at a $2,500 maximum.

In 1933, some 4,000 U.S. banks failed. It was the highest number of bank closings in one year ever. This massive amount of failures created a crisis, with depositors losing life savings. On March 6, 1933, President Roosevelt temporarily closed all banks, and soon thereafter, Senator Glass's legislation was introduced.

b. Securities Act of 1933

Prior to 1933, little, if any, securities regulation existed in the United States. There were some state-level laws, but hardly any federal supervision. The Securities Act of 1933 was enacted primarily to regulate the sale and distribution of newly issued securities. It addressed the sale of securities interstate and required that companies that wished to sell securities file a registration statement disclosing information about that company. The main goal of the legislation was timely disclosure of accurate information. All investors would have the same information and could base investment decisions on that, rather than information being concentrated in the hands of a few insiders.

c. Securities Exchange Act of 1934

The Securities Exchange Act of 1934 (Exchange Act) was intended to regulate the sale and exchange of existing securities in secondary marketplaces, including stockbrokerages and exchanges. Initially intended to regulate only stock exchanges, it was soon amended to regulate over-the-counter (OTC) securities as well.

d. Banking Act of 1935

The Banking Act of 1935 completed the financial system reforms begun during the Hoover administration. The

Act aimed "to provide for the sound, effective, and uninter-
rupted operation of the banking system."[2] This law, which
consists of three titles, codified the FDIC's role as a permanent agency, modified the operation of the Federal Reserve
System, and clarified existing banking laws through a number of technical amendments.[3]

Title I of the Banking Act of 1935 provided that the
FDIC, which was originally created as a temporary agency
by the Glass-Steagall Act in 1933, would become a permanent regulatory body.[4] National banks and state banks that
were members of the Federal Reserve System were required
to participate and carry insurance; nonmember banks with
deposits of $1 million or more were required to join the
Federal Reserve System within a matter of years.[5] Under this
law, the maximum insurance per depositor was set at $5,000
per insured institution.[6] Insured banks capitalized the FDIC
through insurance premiums amounting to one-twelfth of
one percent of total net deposits annually.[7]

Under Title II of the Banking Act of 1935, a number of
superficial changes to the Federal Reserve Board were introduced, including a change to the name of the Board's leader
(from "governor" to "chairman"), the second-in-command
(from "vice governor" to "vice chairman"), the members
of the Board (from "members" to "governors"), and even
the Board itself (from "Federal Reserve Board" to "Board
of Governors of the Federal Reserve System").[8] Additionally,
this law provided for a clearer separation of powers between
the executive branch and the Board, replacing the secretary of the Treasury and the comptroller of the currency—
both of whom had previously served on the Board—with

---

[2] Banking Act of 1935, Pub. L. No. 74-305, 49 Stat. 864.

[3] Howard H. Preston, *The Banking Act of 1935*, 43 J. POL'Y ECON. 743, 743 (1935).

[4] *Id.* at 744.

[5] *Id.*

[6] *Id.* at 747.

[7] *Id.*

[8] Gary Richardson, Alejandro Komai & Michael Gou, *Banking Act of 1935*, FED.
RESERVE HISTORY, http://www.federalreservehistory.org/Events/DetailView/26.

presidential appointees.[9] To further underscore its independence, the Board moved out of the Treasury building and into its own quarters in Washington, D.C.[10]

Comprehensive reforms to the Federal Reserve System under Title II of the Banking Act of 1935 extended to the Federal Open Markets Committee (FOMC), which up to that point had shared responsibility for open-market policymaking with the Federal Reserve Board and directors of the twelve Federal Reserve banks.[11] The new FOMC was charged with harmonizing national banking policy through, among other measures, establishment of discount rates and setting reserve requirements among its member banks.[12]

Title III of the Banking Act of 1935 originally contained 46 provisions that, for the most part, were tied together only by their general goal of enhancing clarity of existing banking laws.[13] Among the more notable of these provisions was the elimination of "double liability" for bank stock (the practice of requiring bank shareholders, typically officers of the bank, to pay an additional amount in the event of a bank's failure)[14] and the requirement that a bank must accumulate a paid-in surplus of 20 percent of capital before starting operations.[15]

e. Trust Indenture Act of 1939

The Trust Indenture Act of 1939 governed bonds and other debt securities. It modified the 1933 Act to require a

---

[9] Preston at 753.

[10] Board of the Governors of the Federal Reserve System, FED. RESERVE BANK OF N.Y. (Nov. 2008), http://newyorkfed.org/aboutthefed/fedpoint/fed46.html.

[11] Preston at 756.

[12] Id.

[13] Id. at 757.

[14] Gary Richardson, Alejandro Komai & Michael Gou, Banking Act of 1935, FED. RESERVE HISTORY, http://www.federalreservehistory.org/Events/DetailView/26.

[15] Preston at 757–58.

trustee to act as fiduciary for bondholders and required certain required clauses be put in all trust indentures.

f. Investment Company Act of 1940

The Investment Company Act of 1940 was one of the last significant pieces of federal securities legislation enacted in the aftermath of the Great Depression; it was signed in tandem with the Investment Advisers Act of 1940.[16] This law, which governs mutual funds, aims to protect investors from the unique conflicts presented by these investment vehicles.[17] It does so through a combination of information disclosure requirements and prohibitions on self-dealing behaviors.[18]

g. Investment Advisers Act of 1940

The Investment Advisers Act of 1940 (IAA), passed in conjunction with the Investment Company Act of 1940, governs investment advisers. Particularly compared with its companion legislation, the IAA is notably brief.[19] This law relies on broad principles prohibiting certain types of conduct by investment advisers to curb opportunities for fraud.[20] It is widely understood that private parties cannot sue under the IAA; instead, enforcement is left almost exclusively up to the Securities and Exchange Commission (SEC).[21]

---

[16] W. John McGuire, The Investment Company Act of 1940 (2005) (PowerPoint presentation), *available at* https://www.morganlewis.com/pubs/Investment%20Company%20Act%20Powerpoint.pdf.

[17] *Id.* at 5.

[18] *Id.* at 8.

[19] Barry P. Barbash & Jai Massari, *The Investment Advisers Act of 1940: Regulation by Accretion*, 39 RUTGERS L.J. 627, 627 (2013), *available at* http://www.davispolk.com/sites/default/files/files/Publication/3c8bafb5-6284-4fce-8f7d-571562536a9f/Preview/Publication Attachment/7fba66d7-741b-48ce-9ba9-5bd7873bde64/jmassari.rutgers.law.journal.article.may13.pdf.

[20] *Id.*

[21] *Id.* at 630.

5. Later Crises

a. Robert Vesco Theft

Robert Vesco, it was commonly agreed, "was responsible for one of the biggest frauds in history."[22] Although the exact amount was unknown, it was estimated to be well over $1 billion in 2008 dollars.[23] Vesco's infamous fraud was carried out by siphoning assets out of Investors Overseas Services (IOS)—a mutual fund conglomerate he acquired through hostile takeover in 1971—to an offshore investment vehicle named RPL, for "Rape, Plunder, and Loot."[24] After the SEC filed a complaint against Vesco and 41 other individuals and corporate defendants in November 1972, "alleging a scheme of extraordinary magnitude, deviousness, and ingenuity in violation primarily of the anti-fraud provision of the Securities and Exchange Act of 1934,"[25] Vesco fled the country and spent the remainder of his life out of reach of U.S. jurisdiction, albeit not out of the news media altogether.[26]

b. Securities Investor Protection Act

After the securities industry experienced prolific growth in the 1960s, coupled with Vesco's infamous activities and the general rise of the conglomerate, the industry faced a significant retrenchment in 1969 through 1970.[27] As a result, countless broker-dealer firms exited the market through voluntary liquidations, mergers with other firms, receiverships, and bankruptcies. Congress, fearing a domino effect aris-

---

[22] Michael Gillard, *Obituary—Robert Vesco*, GUARDIAN (London), May 20, 2008, http://www.theguardian.com/world/2008/may/21/internationalcrime.usa.

[23] Robert Vesco, ECONOMIST (London), Mar. 29, 2008, http://www.economist.com/node/11448479.

[24] *Id.*

[25] Int'l Controls Corp. v. Vesco, 490 F.2d 1334, 1338–39 (2d Cir. 1974).

[26] Robert Vesco, ECONOMIST (London), Mar. 29, 2008, http://www.economist.com/node/11448479.

[27] *SIPA. Securities Investor Protection Act*, U.S. COURTS, http://www.uscourts.gov/FederalCourts/Bankruptcy/BankruptcyBasics/SIPA.aspx.

ing from the failure of considerable numbers of brokerage houses, reacted by passing the Securities Investor Protection Act (SIPA) in 1970.[28]

SIPA vests responsibility for carrying out its goals in the SEC, assorted securities industry self-regulatory organizations, and the Securities Investor Protection Corporation (SIPC). SIPC is a nonprofit corporation, independent from the government, meant to restore funds and securities to investors in the event a broker-dealer holding those properties becomes insolvent.[29] Investors are currently protected from the failure of a broker-dealer firm up to $500,000 of their total equity investment and up to $250,000 cash.[30] Most broker-dealers registered with the SEC are required to belong to the SIPC.

c. The Savings and Loan Crisis

The savings and loan (S&L) crisis was precipitated by a number of factors, including deregulation of the banking industry in the early 1980s (which spurred S&Ls to engage in risky investment activities), an increase in the required amount of federal deposit insurance (exacerbating the moral hazard problem), and a sudden rise in interest rates in 1979 to 1981.[31] The rapid increase in rates for S&Ls were not accompanied by higher earnings on long-term residential mortgages—the main assets held by S&Ls—because those rates had been set when rates were significantly lower. Furthermore, a recession that began in 1981, coupled with a rapid decline in prices of energy and farm products, caused widespread default on S&L loans. This confluence of factors led to a monumental drop in S&L income: In 1980, net S&L income totaled $781 million; by 1982, it had plummeted to

---

[28] Securities Investor Prot. Corp. v. Barbour, 421 U.S. 412, 414 (1975).

[29] *Your Rights Under SIPC Protection,* FINRA, http://www.finra.org/Investors/Protect Yourself/AfterYouInvest/YourRightsUnderSIPCProtection/.

[30] 15 U.S.C. § 78fff-3(a) and 3(d) as amended through July 22, 2010.

[31] http://wps.aw.com/wps/media/objects/7529/7710171/appendixes/ch11apx1.pdf.

nogative $4.1 billion.[32] During that same three-year period, 118 S&L institutions, holding $43 billion in assets, failed across the country.[33] From 1983 to 1992, 747 S&L and other financial institutions failed, costing more than $90 billion to liquidate.[34]

d. The Repeal of Glass-Steagall

"The repeal of Glass-Steagall" refers to the dismantling of only one of the Act's notable accomplishments—the separation of investment and commercial banking. (For a detailed discussion of the Glass-Steagall Act, see II.A.4.a., above.) This feature of Glass-Steagall received intense criticism almost immediately after its passage, and attempts to weaken its influence continued in the decades following until its eventual repeal in 1999.[35]

By the 1990s, the Glass-Steagall provisions prohibiting affiliations between commercial and investment banks were viewed as superfluous at best and injurious to the health of financial institutions at worst.[36] Following a $300 million lobbying effort, Congress passed successor legislation, the Gramm-Leach-Bliley Act, which permitted banks to merge with insurance companies and investment firms.[37]

As then–Treasury secretary Lawrence H. Summers noted at the time, "'[t]oday, Congress voted to update the rules that have governed financial services since the Great Depression and replace them with a system for the 21st century,'"

---

[32] Fed. Deposit Ins. Corp., History of the Eighties—Lessons for the Future 168 (1997), *available at* http://www.fdic.gov/bank/historical/history/167_188.pdf.

[33] *Id.*

[34] *Two Financial Crises Compared: The Savings and Loan Debacle and the Mortgage Mess*, N.Y. Times, Apr. 13, 2011, *available at* http://www.nytimes.com/interactive/2011/04/14/business/20110414-prosecute.html?ref=business&_r=0.

[35] Lawrence J. White, *The Gramm-Leach-Bliley Act of 1999: A Bridge Too Far? Or Not Far Enough?*, 43 Suffolk U. L. Rev. 937, 940–42 (2010), *available at* http://suffolklawreview.org/wp-content/uploads/2013/01/White_Lead_Formatted.pdf.

[36] Yaron Brooke & Don Watkins, *Why the Glass-Steagall Myth Persists*, Forbes (Nov. 12, 2012, 10:04 AM), http://www.forbes.com/sites/objectivist/2012/11/12/why-the-glass-steagall-myth-persists/.

[37] *Id.*

adding that "'[t]his historic legislation will better enable American companies to compete in the new economy.'"[38]

e. The Gramm-Leach-Bliley Act

The Gramm-Leach-Bliley Act (GLBA), also known as the Financial Modernization Act, was enacted in November 1999.[39] In addition to resulting in the repeal of significant provisions in Glass-Steagall, the GLBA effected several other reforms of the financial services industry; most notably, it amended the Bank Holding Company Act of 1956 to allow financial services firms to sell insurance through nonbank subsidiaries and banned nonfinancial (i.e., commercial or industrial) companies from purchasing any unitary thrift holding companies—businesses that control S&L associations.[40]

GLBA did not just restructure the financial services industry, however; it also enacted provisions that imposed new disclosure and data protection requirements on financial institutions.[41] The disclosure requirements limit situations in which a financial institution may disclose consumer "nonpublic personal information" to unrelated third parties, provide for consumer notification of privacy practices and the ability to opt out of information sharing, and restrict reuse and redisclosure of consumer financial information.[42] The GLBA's data protection requirements, which the Federal Trade Commission (FTC) refers to as the Safeguards Rule, obligates financial institutions under FTC jurisdiction to maintain systems aimed at securing customer personal

---

[38] Cyrus Sanati, *10 Years Later, Looking at the Repeal of Glass-Steagall*, N.Y. TIMES DEAL-BOOK (Nov. 12, 2009, 3:49 PM), http://dealbook.nytimes.com/2009/11/12/10-years-later-looking-at-repeal-of-glass-steagall/.

[39] White at 937.

[40] *Id.* at 942–43.

[41] *Gramm-Leach-Bliley Act*, FED. TRADE COMM'N BUREAU OF CONSUMER PROT., http://www.business.ftc.gov/privacy-and-security/gramm-leach-bliley-act.

[42] FED. TRADE COMM'N, HOW TO COMPLY WITH THE PRIVACY OF CONSUMER FINANCIAL INFORMATION RULE OF THE GRAMM-LEACH-BLILEY ACT (2002), *available at* http://www.business.ftc.gov/sites/default/files/pdf/bus67-how-comply-privacy-consumer-financial-information-rule-gramm-leach-bliley-act.pdf.

information, "including names, addresses and phone numbers; bank and credit card account numbers; income and credit histories; and Social Security numbers."[43]

f. The Dodd-Frank Wall Street Reform and Consumer Protection Act

The Dodd-Frank Wall Street Reform and Consumer Protection Act (Dodd-Frank) was passed in 2010 in response to the financial crisis that began in the United States in 2007. This comprehensive Act represented the most sweeping overhaul of banking and markets since the Great Depression and was aimed at restoring confidence in the financial markets, decreasing the chances of a recurrence of another financial crisis and equipping the nation to better address the situation if it did recur.[44] Although the 828-page Act[45] is lengthy by any standards—J.P. Morgan Chase assigned more than 100 teams to analyze the legislation[46]—its main features can be summarized as follows.

- *Establishment of the Consumer Financial Protection Bureau (CFPB).* The CFPB is an independent agency that is funded by the Federal Reserve; its efforts are primarily aimed at protecting and educating consumers about consumer financial products such as mortgages and credit cards.[47]
- *Establishment of the Financial Stability Oversight Council (FSOC).* The new FSOC is charged with overseeing

---

[43] *Gramm-Leach-Bliley Act.*

[44] Damian Paletta & Aaron Lucchetti, *Law Remakes U.S. Financial Landscape*, WALL ST. J. (July 16, 2010, 12:01 AM EST), http://online.wsj.com/news/articles/SB10001424052748 704682604575369030061839958?mg=reno64-wsj&url=http%3A%2F%2Fonline.wsj.com% 2Farticle%2FSB10001424052748704682604575369030061839958.html.

[45] David Zaring, *Dodd-Frank Is Indeed Taking Root*, N.Y. TIMES DEALBOOK (Nov. 1, 2013, 1:04 PM), http://dealbook.nytimes.com/2013/11/01/dodd-frank-is-indeed-taking-root/.

[46] Paletta & Lucchetti.

[47] Bryan J. Noeth, *Financial Regulation: A Primer on the Dodd-Frank Act*, ECON. INFO. NEWSL. – CLASSROOM ED. 2 (Fed. Res. Bank of St. Louis), May 2011, *available at* http://research. stlouisfed.org/pageone-economics/uploads/newsletter/2011/201105_ClassroomEdition. pdf.

the U.S. financial system and identifying threats to the system's stability.[48]

- *Bestowing "Orderly Liquidation Authority" on the FDIC.* Under Title II of Dodd-Frank, the FDIC has "orderly liquidation authority" to step in when the FDIC, Federal Reserve, and Treasury agree that a nonbank financial institution is in danger of becoming insolvent. This power preempts bankruptcy law, and its goal is to minimize the effect of large institutional failures on financial markets as a whole.[49]

- *Creation of the Volcker Rule.* Named for former Federal Reserve chair Paul Volcker, the Volcker Rule was grounded in the notion that speculative trading was partially responsible for financial crisis.[50] Dodd-Frank attempts to prevent speculative trading by prohibiting banks from engaging in proprietary trading or acquiring any ownership in entities that engage in proprietary trading, such as hedge funds or private equity funds.[51]

- *Reformation of Rules Regarding Securitization.* Originators seeking to sell assets for securitization must now adhere to a number of regulations aimed at making sure they keep some "skin in the game" and accurately disclose the risk associated with securitized investment products.[52]

- *Restructuring of the Derivatives Markets.* Dodd-Frank addresses the lack of oversight in the OTC swaps markets by assigning regulatory authority to the Commodity Futures Trading Commission (CFTC) and the SEC. Under Dodd-Frank, the SEC has primary authority over security-based swaps (swaps based on only one security or loan or a narrowly defined group of securities), while the CFTC has authority over

---

[48] MORRISON & FOERSTER, THE DODD-FRANK ACT: A CHEAT SHEET 4–5 (2010), *available at* http://www.mofo.com/files/uploads/images/summarydoddfrankact.pdf.

[49] *Id.* at 22.

[50] *Id.* at 18.

[51] *Id.* at 19.

[52] *Id.* at 8–9.

energy and agriculture swaps and all other types of swaps.[53]

- *Overhaul of Executive Compensation and Corporate Governance Standards.* Among its more notable overhaul in this area, Dodd-Frank institutes a new "say-on-pay" measure in which companies are required to include in proxy statements a resolution asking shareholders to approve, through nonbinding vote, compensation of the top executives.[54]

Dodd-Frank remains a major milestone in financial services regulation. Even now, almost ten years after its passage, it is still being implemented. It will take even longer to fully understand its impact.

B. Current Structure of Financial Services Regulation

The current financial services regulatory structure is divided into two broad categories: traditional banking and securities (and commodities) trading activities.

1. Traditional Banking

a. Deposits and Loans

Traditional banking activities such as taking deposits and making loans are sometimes called core banking activities. "Banks" are herein defined as institutions that take depositors' money and then loan it out in what is called a fractional reserve system.

The primary regulators of these types of financial institutions make up the Federal Financial Institutions Examination Council (FFIEC). Some companies operate in one or

---

[53] *Derivatives*, U.S. Sᴇᴄ. & Exᴄʜ. Cᴏᴍᴍ'ɴ, https://www.sec.gov/spotlight/dodd-frank/derivatives.shtml.

[54] Mᴏʀʀɪsᴏɴ & Fᴏᴇʀsᴛᴇʀ at 22.

more of these areas, having multiple lines of business, each subject to differing regulations.

b. Federal- vs. State-Chartered Banks

Banks may be chartered at the federal level through the National Bank Act or at the state level through each individual state banking authority. Each system has advantages and disadvantages. However, state-chartered banks, which are FDIC-insured, are also subject to many federal regulations.

c. Credit Unions

Credit unions are nonprofit organizations that accept members' deposits and make loans.[55] Unlike banks, however, credit unions are owned by member-depositors and pay out dividends to their owners in the event they have surplus income.[56] Credit union membership is generally premised on membership in or association with a particular industry, geographical community, or educational institution.[57] The National Credit Union Administration (NCUA), a government-sponsored agency, is responsible for regulating federal credit unions.[58] The NCUA additionally owns and operates an insurance fund that insures the deposits of federal credit unions and the majority of state-chartered credit unions.[59]

d. Savings and Loans

S&L institutions, sometimes called thrifts, are financial organizations that provide loans primarily for home

---

[55] *How Is a Credit Union Different than a Bank?*, MyCreditUnion.gov, http://www.mycreditunion.gov/about-credit-unions/Pages/How-is-a-Credit-Union-Different-than-a-Bank.aspx.

[56] *Id.*

[57] *Id.*

[58] *About NCUA*, Nat'l Credit Union Ass'n, http://www.ncua.gov/about/Pages/default.aspx.

[59] *Id.*

purchases, renovations, and new construction.[60] In addition to providing home loans, S&Ls accept deposits and offer a variety of financial products, including consumer loans, credit cards, and savings plans such as tax-deferred annuities.[61] S&Ls may be structured as either corporations or mutuals, which are similar to credit unions in that depositors become owners of the entity.[62] The Office of Thrift Supervision previously oversaw S&Ls chartered by the federal government;[63] however, the Office of the Comptroller of the Currency (OCC) took over this role in July 2011.[64]

e. Installment Loan Companies

Installment loan companies are financial institutions that extend consumer or business loans in exchange for repayment of principal and interest, generally in equal installments over a fixed period of time. Installment lenders frequently require the borrower to assign the personal property purchased with the loan as collateral. Unlike so-called payday loans (i.e., a short-term loan for a small amount, "until payday"), installment loans are not commonly characterized by a final balloon payment; also unlike payday loans, installment loans are reported on consumers' personal credit reports.[65] Installment loan companies, despite their differences from payday loan companies, have also been criticized for their inordinately high interest rates and fees.[66]

---

[60] *Savings & Loan Association*, ENCYCLOPAEDIA BRITTANICA, *available at* http://www. britannica.com/EBchecked/topic/525776/savings-and-loan-association.

[61] *Differences Between Banks, Credit Unions and Savings Institutions*, WIS. DEP'T OF FIN. INSTS., http://www.wdfi.org/wca/consumer_credit/credit_guides/differencesbankscredit unionssavingsinstitutions.htm.

[62] *Id.*

[63] *Id.*

[64] *Banking Regulators*, U.S. SEC. & EXCH. COMM'N, http://www.sec.gov/answers/bank reg.htm.

[65] Martha C. White, *4 Dirty Secrets of So-Called Installment Loans*, TIME, May 16, 2013, http://business.time.com/2013/05/16/4-dirty-secrets-of-so-called-installment-loans/.

[66] *Id.*

f. Loan and Mortgage Brokers

A loan broker acts as an intermediary between lending institutions and borrowers. In contrast with a loan officer, a loan broker does not lend money directly to borrowers; instead, the broker assesses the borrower's financial situation and recommends financing based on the borrower's needs while passing along financial information to a lending institution to facilitate the borrowing. "Advance fee" loan brokers require up-front payment, sometimes regardless of whether the desired financing is obtained.[67] If the loan is secured by a mortgage on real estate, the loan broker is called a mortgage broker. Other brokers arrange to receive a certain percentage of the total financing.[68] State law regulates the type and manner of licensing for loan brokers; mortgage brokers, however, are required to obtain a license through the Nationwide Mortgage Licensing System and Registry.

g. Federal Financial Institutions Examination Council

The FFIEC is a collection of banking regulators that coordinate some of their activities. The FFIEC is composed of the following:

> Board of Governors of the Federal Reserve System
> Federal Deposit Insurance Corporation
> National Credit Union Administration
> Office of the Comptroller of the Currency
> Consumer Financial Protection Bureau
> State Liaison Committee

The State Liaison Committee is comprised of representatives from the Conference of State Bank Supervisors,

---

[67] Rachel Willard, *Advance Fee Mortgage and Loan Brokers*, BETTER BUS. BUREAU (Apr. 29, 2014), http://www.bbb.org/boston/industry-tips/read/tip/advance-fee-mortgage-and-loan-brokers-134.

[68] *Id.*

the American Council of State Savings Supervisors, and the National Association of State Credit Union Supervisors.

The FFIEC promotes uniformity of standards for examination and reporting for financial institutions regulated by its members.

2. Securities and Commodities Activities

a. Federal Securities Regulation

This section is devoted to issues encountered by entities whose primary regulator is the SEC and/or the CFTC. These include stockbrokers, broker-dealers, commodities brokers, and currency traders. These activities are inexorably linked to technology, with program trading, data feeds, and the like, and will continue to be into the future.

The primary regulator of securities activities is the SEC. Other regulators include the CFTC, Securities Industry and Financial Markets Association (SIFMA), Financial Industry Regulatory Authority (FINRA), and NASDAQ[69] and the other exchanges themselves.

b. Commodity Futures Trading Commission

The CFTC is the regulatory body charged with policing derivatives—specifically, its mission is to prevent "fraud, manipulation, abusive practices and systemic risk" relating to futures and swaps and to cultivate open and financially sound markets.[70] The CFTC oversees entities that range from contract markets to swap execution facilities, derivatives clearing organizations, swap dealers, swap data repositories, and various other intercessors.[71] The CFTC was designated

---

[69] There is some debate over the relevance of NASDAQ in the post-Dodd-Frank world. However, according to one author, "The importance of the NYSE and Nasdaq for secondary transactions in the United States cannot be overstated." STEPHEN J. CHOI & A.C. PRITCHARD, SECURITIES REGULATION: CASES AND ANALYSIS 14 (3d ed. 2012).

[70] Mission & Responsibilities, U.S. COMMODITIES FUTURES TRADING COMM'N, http://www.cftc.gov/about/missionresponsibilities/index.htm.

[71] Id.

as an independent agency in 1974, although it has existed in various forms since the early 1920s.[72] As discussed in II.A.5.f., above, the CFTC's role expanded in the wake of the 2008 financial crisis to include oversight and reform of the swaps market, which, at a volume exceeding $400 trillion, is about 12 times the size of the futures market.[73]

c. Securities Industry and Financial Markets Association

SIFMA is an industry trade group composed of more than 650 securities firms, banks, and asset managers.[74] The group, whose offices are in New York and Washington, D.C., aims to create policies that "strengthen financial markets and which encourage capital availability, job creation and economic growth while building trust and confidence in the financial industry."[75] Since 2006, SIFMA has maintained the SIFMA Municipal Swap Index, a short-term index that reflects activity in the variable rate demand obligation market.[76]

d. Financial Industry Regulatory Authority

FINRA is an independent nonprofit regulatory body sanctioned by Congress to oversee fair dealings within the securities industry.[77] FINRA carries out its goals by creating and enforcing rules dictating actions of securities firms and brokers, promoting market transparency, and providing investor education. One way that FINRA enforces its rules is through registration: All U.S. securities brokers must be licensed and registered by FINRA after passing an initial

---

[72] Id.

[73] Id.

[74] What Is SIFMA?, STARR AUSTEN & MILLER, LLP, http://www.starrausten.com/resources/what-is-sifma/.

[75] Mission, SIFMA, http://www.sifma.org/about/mission/.

[76] About the Municipal Swap Index, SIFMA (Nov. 1, 2010), http://www.sifma.org/research/item.aspx?id=1690.

[77] About FINRA, FIN. INDUS. REGULATORY AUTH., http://www.finra.org/AboutFINRA/.

exam and agreeing to complete continuing education.[78] Brokers who violate FINRA's rules face penalties such as fines, suspension, or even expulsion from the industry.[79]

e. NASDAQ

Founded in 1971 by the National Association of Securities Dealers, NASDAQ represented the first electronic trading market at the time. In 2006, NASDAQ became a national securities exchange and, with the change in designation, also began acting as a self-regulatory organization (SRO).[80] As an SRO, NASDAQ imposes certain requirements, such as minimal capital requirements and boards with a majority of independent directors.[81] In 2007, NASDAQ merged with Swedish-Finnish company OMX, which controlled seven European stock exchanges.[82] As of February 2014, NASDAQ-listed firms had a total valuation of $8 trillion.[83]

3. Insurance Activities

Because the insurance industry impacts the public interest, it is subject to regulation. The insurance industry is largely regulated on a state-by-state basis, although there is some federal regulatory oversight. This distributed regulatory structure creates an even greater challenge for this segment of the financial services industry.

---

[78] *What We Do*, Fin. Indus. Regulatory Auth., http://www.finra.org/AboutFINRA/WhatWeDo/.

[79] *Id.*

[80] Michele Bresnick Walsh, Andrew D. Bulgin & Abba David Poliakoff, *Nasdaq Stock Market Becomes a National Securities Exchange; Changes Market Designations*, Gordon Feinblatt (Sept. 2006), http://www.gfrlaw.com/pubs/GordonPubDetail.aspx?xpST=PubDetail&pub=109.

[81] There is some debate over the relevance of NASDAQ in the post-Dodd-Frank world. However, according to one author, "The importance of the NYSE and Nasdaq for secondary transactions in the United States cannot be overstated." Stephen J. Choi & A.C. Pritchard, Securities Regulation: Cases and Analysis 14 (3d ed. 2012).

[82] *NASDAQ OMX Corporate Timeline*, NASDAQ OMX, http://www.nasdaqomx.com/aboutus/company-information/timeline#2000-2010.

[83] *Company Information*, NASDAQ OMX, http://www.nasdaqomx.com/aboutus/company-information.

a. Insurance Activities of Banks

U.S. banks have engaged in insurance sales activities since the early twentieth century; however, the types of insurance products offered have rapidly evolved, along with other forms of financial innovation, over the past several years.[84] Oversight of bank insurance activities has kept pace with innovation as well—most recently, the Gramm-Leach-Bliley Act of 1999 affirmed federally chartered banks' authority to sell insurance products while clarifying the OCC's role in assessing risk arising from bank insurance activities.[85] Furthermore, both federally and state-chartered banks may be subject to state regulation of bank insurance activities pursuant to the McCarran-Ferguson Act of 1945, which granted states the power to regulate most aspects of the insurance industry.[86] The OCC has clarified that permissible bank insurance activities encompass, among other things, acting as insurance sales agents in some small communities (consistent with 12 U.S.C. § 92) or through a subsidiary without any geographic location, selling title insurance only to the extent allowed under Gramm-Leach-Bliley, providing insurance as a principal or underwriter, and investing in an insurance entity.[87]

b. Insurance Companies

Insurance companies' primary objective is to spread loss caused by a particular type of harm over a pool of persons who agree to share the risk of loss. Initially, regulation of U.S. insurance companies was left to the states, with New Hampshire credited as the first state to appoint an insurance

---

[84] OFFICE OF THE COMPTROLLER OF THE CURRENCY, INSURANCE ACTIVITIES: COMPTROLLER'S HANDBOOK 1 (June 2002), *available at* http://www.occ.gov/publications/publications-by-type/comptrollers-handbook/insactfinal.pdf.

[85] *Id.* at 1–2.

[86] *Id.* at 3.

[87] *Id.* at 4–7.

commissioner, in 1851.[88] Decades later, in 1945, Congress enacted the McCarran-Ferguson Act to solidify the states' primary domain over regulation and taxation of the insurance industry. State sovereignty over insurance remained largely intact until the passage of Gramm-Leach-Bliley in 1999, which, while affirming state power over insurance markets, also called for reform to enable financial institutions and insurance companies to interact more freely to respond to innovations in financial products.[89] Dodd-Frank also affected state insurance regulation by creating the Federal Insurance Office (FIO) within the Department of the Treasury. The FIO is charged primarily with an information-gathering role, but it also has limited power to join covered agreements with other countries regarding insurance regulation.[90] Other duties of the FIO include monitoring and reporting on most of the U.S. insurance industry, including risks associated with certain insurance companies; conferring with state and international insurance regulators; and engaging in other related activities. In December 2013, the FIO released a report that made several recommendations, including ways to facilitate interactions between domestic and international insurance regulators. The report suggested that domestic and international insurance regulators cooperate by drafting the following, including: uniform national standards for mortgage insurance, reinsurance, and commercial insurance; standards for capital adequacy, safety, and soundness; and a uniform approach for resolution of insolvent insurers.[91]

c. Insurance Agents

Insurance agents are salespeople who offer individuals and businesses insurance products including life, health,

---

[88] Nat'l Ass'n of Ins. Comm'nrs, State Insurance Regulation 1, *available at* http://www.naic.org/documents/topics_white_paper_hist_ins_reg.pdf.

[89] *Id.*

[90] *Id.*

[91] Fed. Ins. Office, How to Modernize and Improve the System of Insurance Regulation in the United States (Dec. 2013).

and property insurance policies.[92] Insurance agents are regulated by state insurance commissions; they are also bound
by sales and marketing rules imposed by state insurance
commissions.[93] Certain insurance agents offering products
considered securities—variable annuities or variable life
insurance policies, for example—are also required to enroll
as registered representatives under FINRA and comply with
that organization's rules.[94]

d. Insurance Brokers

Insurance brokers, similar to loan brokers, are inter-
mediaries facilitating insurance sales between providers and
parties seeking coverage. Insurance brokers are not captive
to any one insurance underwriter; instead, they have the
flexibility to offer policies from a number of companies.[95]
Insurance brokers are subject to the same licensing requirements as insurance agents.[96] Additionally, both brokers and
agents are often required to pass initial exams to become
licensed, obtain separate licenses for each line of insurance
product sold, and meet continuing education obligations.[97]

4. Credit Card Activities

Credit card activities are regulated by both federal and
state laws and regulations. These activities are distributed
over a variety of entities. Banks and even broker-dealers are
the issuers, while much of the processing is done by third-
party processing service providers. Merchants play a role
as well. The credit card industry has its own data standards

---

[92] *Selecting Investment Professionals*, FINRA, http://www.finra.org/Investors/Smart
Investing/GettingStarted/SelectingInvestmentProfessional/P117278.

[93] *Id.*

[94] *Id.*

[95] Chris Joseph, Insurance Broker v. Insurance Agent, HOUS. CHRON., http://work.
chron.com/insurance-broker-vs-insurance-agent-8199.html.

[96] *Id.*

[97] *Id.*

from the Payment Card Institute, which dovetails with the federal and state legal and regulatory framework.

a. Credit Card Issuers

A credit card issuer is a financial institution that offers credit cards to consumers. Issuers, such as MasterCard and Visa, open a revolving line of credit for consumers that enables them to spend up to a specified limit. Each time the consumer reduces the balance, he or she is re-advanced on the line of credit.

b. Credit Card Processors

Once a credit card is issued, credit card processors are necessary to process payments. Credit card processing involves both front-end authorization of payments and back-end settlements, which transfers funds from the issuing bank to the merchant's account. Some credit card companies, such as American Express, act as both the issuer and the payment processor.[98] Credit card processing is also referred to as merchant services.[99]

c. Merchants

In the credit card context, merchants are entities engaged in the sale of goods and services for a profit. Merchants choose whether to accept credit card payments; they are often influenced by the transaction fee charged by particular payment processors.

---

[98] Paul Downs, *What You Need to Know About Credit Card Processing*, YOU'RE THE BOSS, N.Y. TIMES (Mar. 25, 2013, 11:00 AM), http://boss.blogs.nytimes.com/2013/03/25/what-you-need-to-know-about-credit-card-processing/?_php=true&_type=blogs&_r=0.

[99] *What Are Merchant Services?*, FIDELITY, http://www.fidelitypayment.com/resources/what_are_merchant_services.

5. *State Law and Regulations for Financial Institutions*

Every state has an insurance regulator, a banking regulator, and a securities regulator. Some states also have a regulator addressing consumer protection issues. Each of these may affect financial services companies that do business within that particular state.

6. *Other Federal Regulators*

At the federal level, certain nonfinancial services regulators have regulations that may impact the financial services industry. These include the following:

Department of Education
Federal Energy Resources Commission
Federal Housing Finance Agency
Federal Trade Commission
Financial Stability Oversight Council
Government Accountability Office
Internal Revenue Service
Municipal Securities Rulemaking Board
Office of Financial Research
U.S. Department of the Treasury

7. *International Financial Services Regulation*

While certain global issues are discussed in Chapter 12, this section provides an overview of the larger international financial services regulators.

a. *International Monetary Fund*

The International Monetary Fund was established as World War II was coming to a close. Its purpose initially was to foster economic cooperation between countries. It has taken on a more regulatory function in recent years. It also sometimes provides forums for discussion of economic issues.

b. Organization for Economic Cooperation and Development

The Organization for Economic Cooperation and Development sets guidelines for using technology in connection with economic policy for its members. Since economic policy is implemented through the banking system, this organization has a lot of influence in the financial services industry.

c. European Central Bank

The European Central Bank, established in 1998, addresses monetary policy in the European Community, including price stability, and conducts foreign exchange functions. It replaced each member nation's central bank.

d. Basel III Accord

The Third Basel Accord, or Basel III, is a set of guidelines set by international bankers governing the adequacy of bank capital, stress testing, and market liquidity risk. Although compliance is technically voluntary, Basel III is considered best practices, and the marketplace would likely view any bank that does not meet Basel III guidelines as submarket. These ratios are implemented and calculated using technology and provide a backdrop for the environment in which financial services companies operate, making them relevant to this book.

8. Rationales for Financial Services Law and Regulation

a. Consumer Protection

The primary goal of most financial services regulation is to protect the consumer, or ordinary user of these services, as well as safety and soundness. Most of the legislation that came out of the Great Depression was based on this principle.

b. Market Protection

Another goal of financial services regulation, especially in the area of securities activities, is to protect the market. Creating a market in which the participants have equal access to the same information and are subject to the same rules ensures that the market operates efficiently.

9. Criticisms of the Regulatory Structure

The regulation of financial services has grown over time through a series of crises, each with subsequent remediation and reform. This has left us with a fractured system, whose gaps are exposed only by the next crisis.

Paul Volcker, former chair of the Federal Reserve Board of Governors, acknowledged this fragmented regulatory structure, calling it "a recipe for indecision, neglect and stalemate, adding up to ineffectiveness."[100] Volcker also criticized the fact that more than three years after passage of the Dodd-Frank Act, many of the law's intended reforms were not yet in effect. This, he claimed, was partly due to the fragmented regulatory structure of financial services.[101]

---

[100] *Volcker: U.S. Has Too Many Regulators*, The Tell: MarketWatch (May 29, 2013, 4:14 PM ET), http://blogs.marketwatch.com/thetell/2013/05/29/volcker-u-s-has-too-many-regulators/.

[101] *Id.*

INTELLECTUAL PROPERTY ISSUES

I. INTRODUCTION

Technology is bound up with intellectual property (IP). Intellectual property is inherent in any technology, no matter how it is delivered: as software, as a service, as hardware, or as some combination of these. In the history of patents, financial service patents are relatively new. In their time, they have been both helpful and disruptive. While not as glamorous as patents, other types of IP—trademarks, copyrights, and trade secrets—have left their mark on financial services. This chapter provides a brief primer on IP to better understand the issues that arise with respect to financial services technology. This foundation is needed to better understand the material in later chapters.

Infringement of another's IP can result in financial damages, damages to reputation, and even a criminal infringement conviction. It is equally important to protect one's own rights in IP. These may become income-producing assets, enhance one's competitive standing, and serve defensive purposes.

There are four types of IP: copyrights, trademarks and service marks, trade secrets, and patents. It is necessary to understand each of these to understand the implications in developing, implementing, and using technology in a business enterprise.

II. COPYRIGHTS

Copyrights are works of authorship fixed in some tangible medium. Copyright law does not protect facts or ideas. It does protect the expression of those facts or ideas. Databases[1] may be copyrighted. It is important to note that copyright vests when the work is written, not when published or registered. Publication and registration are important for their own reasons, but copyright ownership commences when the work is written.

Copyright law protects literary works including computer software, musical works, photographs, drawings,

---

[1] The selection or arrangement of data can be copyrighted, regardless of whether individual elements of data themselves are copyrighted.

movies, sculpture, and designs. The copyright owner has the exclusive right to (1) reproduce or copy the work; (2) prepare derivative works (transform or adapt the existing work, e.g., a translation); (3) distribute copies by any means; (4) perform the work publicly; (5) display the work publicly; and (6) for sound recordings, perform the work publicly by means of a digital transmission.

The performance of any of these rights with respect to a copyrighted work, without a license from the author, is an infringement of the author's exclusive copyright.

A. Copyright Ownership

Owning a copy of a copyrighted work does not equal owning its copyright. Just as an owner of one copy of a book does not have a right to make unlimited copies of the book and sell them, neither does he have a right to make derivative works of the book. He merely has the right to enjoy that one copy of the book. The same principles apply with a software program. The owner of a copy of a software program allows her the rights set forth in the software license, nothing more.

The author owns the copyright, even if he is an employee or a contractor working under a work for hire agreement. In the absence of a writing to the contrary, a contractor owns all copyrights. Copyrights can be assigned, but those assignments must be in writing.

Joint ownership of copyrights is permitted under the law, but it is not advisable in a practical business situation. Under joint ownership, both parties own the copyright equally. Each party has an independent right to make use of the copyright. However, coauthors can require the other author(s) to provide an accounting of such use. Coauthors cannot prohibit other coauthors from making use of the copyrighted work and cannot be found to be infringing the rights of coauthors. In the technology world, co-ownership can quickly become complicated, especially because technology often embodies other types of IP such as patents or trade secrets, which have different rules for co-ownership. It is advisable to get all copyrights from all authors of a work; one can never be too clear about ownership of IP.

1. Claims for Copyright Infringement

There is a presumption of infringement if a defendant had access to a work protected by copyright protection and if the allegedly copied work bears a substantial similarity to the copyrighted work.

If successful, the plaintiff in a copyright action may obtain the following remedies: a permanent injunction; destruction of the infringing items; actual damages suffered by the plaintiff and profits of the defendant; statutory damages (in lieu of actual damages as they may be hard to prove) of between $750 and $30,000 per work infringed, and up to $150,000 per work infringed if the infringement is found to be willful or intentional; plus attorneys' fees and costs. Criminal copyright infringement is also an available remedy. It requires a willful violation of a copyright.

2. Affirmative Defenses to Copyright Infringement

a. Fair Use

Certain unauthorized uses are excused from liability if deemed "fair." Note that the defendant must prove the fair use defense; it is not automatic in any sense. Courts must weigh (1) the purpose and character of the use, including whether such use is for commercial or nonprofit educational purposes; (2) the nature of the copyrighted work; (3) the amount and substantiality of the portion used in relation to the copyrighted work as a whole; and (4) the effect of the use on the potential market for or value of the copyrighted work.

b. Other Defenses

If a defendant can show she independently developed a work similar to a copyrighted work, then she may have a valid defense. However, the burden is on the defendant to make that showing.

3. Digital Millennium Copyright Act

The Digital Millennium Copyright Act of 1998 amended existing copyright law. It made it a crime to produce or disseminate technology or services that circumvent digital rights management controls, as well as the act of circumventing those controls, even if there is no infringement. It also provided an exemption for Internet service providers for the copyright activities of their customers.

4. Copyright—Practical Guidance

Some work product may constitute copyrightable subject matter. Copyright notices or registration is not required, although best practices suggest regular use of notice and appropriate use of registrations. Most third-party technology—data feeds, software, and databases—is copyrightable subject matter, even if the individual data elements are not subject to copyright protection.

III. TRADEMARKS AND SERVICE MARKS

Trademarks and service marks identify the origin of goods and services and vouch for their authenticity. They distinguish the goods and services from the goods and services of others. Trademark law developed as a consumer protection measure, and it is still analyzed along those lines.

Trademark owners have an affirmative obligation to enforce and protect their rights against uses that likely cause confusion, mistake, or deception among consumers. Owners of "famous" marks must protect them from dilution, even in the absence of confusion. This can include starting litigation to enforce those rights. Failure to do so can lead to a loss of value or even loss of trademark protection. Federal registration of a trademark lasts ten years with an unlimited number of renewals possible.[2] A valid trademark registration prevents others from using that mark in an Internet domain name.

Generally, the trademark owner has the right to domain names incorporating that trademark and to block others from using it, if such use causes confusion in the marketplace. Chapter 4 discusses some aspects of trademark law as it relates to online use of metatags and keywords.

A. Trademark Infringement and Remedies

The trademark owner has the right to prevent the use of copies or imitations of the mark, or substantially similar marks, in connection with the sale of goods and services, in a way that causes confusion to potential customers in the marketplace. Remedies for trademark infringement include injunctive relief, lost profits, costs, and damages starting at $500 to $10,000 per mark.

B. Trademarks—Practical Guidance

Consider registration of trademarks, as it is relatively cheap, Also, trademarks can build value over time. It is also important to avoid unauthorized copying of others' trademarks. Do not use a trademarked logo on a website, for example, unless you have written permission from the trademark owner.

---

[2] While state trademark rights exist, they are usually overridden by federal registration and have limited utility. At best, a state registration may give the trademark owner some protection in a small geographic area where it conducts business.

IV. TRADE SECRETS

Trade secrets are information that may create an actual or a potential commercial advantage for those who know or use them, as long as secrecy is maintained. The trade secret owner is protected against misappropriation and use of trade secrets, but not against independent development by a third party. This protection can be lost if the trade secret owner fails to take reasonable precautions to protect the trade secret. Examples of trade secrets include customer lists, marketing strategies, computer source code, algorithms, and formulas and other valuable nonpublic information. Misappropriation of trade secrets occurs when there is unauthorized use or disclosure of another's trade secret by someone under a duty of confidentiality to the owner of the trade secret or someone who obtained the secret by improper means. Successful plaintiffs can obtain injunctive relief and damages. Federal and state criminal penalties may also apply.

A. Trade Secrets—Practical Guidance

First, a company must know what its trade secrets are. An education and training campaign is crucial to developing a successful trade secret policy. Any trade secret policy must contain, at a minimum, the following:

- Don't disclose trade secrets to third parties without an adequate confidentiality agreement in place.
- Use nondisclosure/noncompete agreements for key employees.
- Any internal disclosures should be on a truly "need to know" basis only.
- Don't leave sensitive information in insecure environments.
- Don't use confidential information from prior employers.
- Beware the human element!

When dealing with suppliers of bank technology, it is therefore paramount to be clear which party owns particular data. Technology vendors may seek to use information and data learned from one client to provide services to another client. However, if that information is a trade secret of the first client, this should not be permitted.

Every agreement with a technology vendor must (1) protect the trade secrets and confidential information of the customer (i.e., the financial institution), (2) ensure that the customer owns that information and data, and (3) specify that the vendor has no right to use the data outside of providing services to that particular client. At the same time, it may be acceptable for a vendor to use and/or own certain information that is not confidential or a trade secret.[3]

V. Patents

A patent is the right to exclude others from making, using, selling, having made, or importing a patented invention or business process for a limited period of time, usually 20 years. The goal of patent law is to encourage innovation.

The first to file for an invention is the patent owner. To be patentable, the invention must be new, nonobvious, and a patentable subject matter. The rights in the patent vest in the person(s) who create the invention, but they can be assigned. Generally, employers require their employees to assign all patents to the employer. Finally, the inventor must contribute conceptually to the invention, not just execute instructions or write code.

Patent infringement is a non-owner's use of the patent during its term without permission from the owner. This could include actively and knowingly aiding another's infringement. Remedies for patent infringement include

---

[3] This structure has some flexibility. It makes almost no functional difference whether the customer owns the information and the vendor has a broad license to use it, or vice versa; however, customarily, if the customer has paid for the development of the intellectual property, then the customer generally owns the IP.

injunctive relief, lost profits, prejudgment interest, costs, and damages (including reasonable royalties).

A. Call Center Patent Litigation

Call centers are used by many financial institutions for various purposes from sales to customer service to collections. Numerous patent lawsuits have been filed by those claiming patents on certain technology used in call centers. One in particular is Ronald A. Katz Technology Licensing, LP, which claims more than 50 patents, including some on automatic call distribution, speech recognition, and voice response. While several of these patents have been reexamined by the U.S. Patent and Trademark Office, most have survived challenges. Over time, Katz has acquired a stable of blue chip clients that would rather license this technology than fight in court. Any entry into the call center market mandates a review of these patents and other publicly available information about this assertive plaintiff.

B. Software Patents

There is no legal definition of a software patent; however, it generally means a process or invention made effective through the use of software with the process embedded into it. While algorithms themselves are not patentable, business processes embedded in software sometimes are. Considerable debate exists as to whether software patents should exist, as the inventions are often fairly abstract. Examples of valid software patents include patents for data compression, trading systems, data encryption, and telecommunications.

In *Alice Corp. Pty. Ltd. v. CLS Bank International*,[4] Alice Corp. owned a patent on a computer-driven trading system. Alice sued CLS Bank International for infringement of its patent. The United States Court of Appeals for the

---

[4] No. 13-298 (U.S., 2014).

Federal Circuit found Alice's invention to be unpatentable on grounds that it was too abstract. In a unanimous decision written by Justice Clarence Thomas, the U.S. Supreme Court affirmed the lower court's decision and found the Alice patent invalid because it was based on "a patent-ineligible abstract idea."[5] The Court said that, absent some transformation, abstract ideas by themselves are not patentable. Presumably, if the use of a computer could have somehow transformed the abstract idea into a patent eligible invention, then the software patent would have passed muster. The Alice case illustrates that if a computer program merely implements an abstract idea, the result is not patentable. This decision certainly narrows the scope of, when, and under what circumstances software could be patentable.

---

[5] Alice Corp. Pty. Ltd. v. CLS Bank Int'l, No. 13-298, 2014 BL 170103 (U.S. June 19, 2014)

CHAPTER 4

ONLINE FINANCIAL SERVICES

I. Introduction

Now that we have discussed the regulatory framework
of financial services and basic IP issues, we can move on to a
discussion of how financial services companies do business
online. Because of the fractured nature of financial services
regulation, each of the sections in this chapter applies only
to particular segments of the financial services industry, as
indicated.

II. ADVERTISING; SOCIAL MEDIA; FEDERAL TRADE COMMISSION ENDORSEMENTS

A. Social Media—FFIEC Regulatory Guidance

This section applies only to entities that have one of the members of the Federal Financial Institutions Examination Council (FFIEC) as their primary regulator. The FFIEC released final guidance for the use of social media by FFIEC-regulated financial institutions in December 2013.[1] The regulators believed that banks' use of social media could increase the banks' risk profiles. These increased risks "include the risk of harm to consumers, compliance and legal risk, operational risk, and reputation risk."[2] Other concerns included lack of proper due diligence and lack of proper controls by the financial institution.

The FFIEC defined social media as "interactive online communications" including, text, images, audio, and video. Social media is more interactive than other types of online media such as advertising. Banks can use it for interacting with existing customers as well as potential customers. It can be used to market bank services, address customer complaints, or provide information. The informal nature of this communication, coupled with cybersecurity risks, generates potential issues for banks.

Because of this, the FFIEC suggested that banks adopt risk management programs specific to social media. These programs should include a structure of governance, policies, and procedures; a due diligence process; training programs; oversight, audit, and compliance programs; and a structure for evaluation and reporting to senior management.[3] Most important, social media use may be subject to different existing regulations depending on the activity taking place.

---

[1] FED. FIN. INST. EXAMINATION COUNCIL, SOCIAL MEDIA: CONSUMER COMPLIANCE RISK MANAGEMENT GUIDANCE (2013), *available at* https://www.ffiec.gov/press/PDF/2013_Dec%20Final%20SMG%20attached%20to%2011Dec13%20press%20release.pdf.

[2] *Id.* at 3.

[3] *Id.* at 6–7.

The FFIEC pointed out that certain existing regulations apply and should be kept in mind when using social media to attract and facilitate customers' accounts and loans.

1. Deposit Activities; Regulation DD; Truth in Savings

Regulation DD under the Truth in Savings Act,[4] and Part 707 applicable to federal credit unions,[5] require adequate disclosure of information, including information about fees and costs, interest rates, annual percentage yields, and certain other terms.[6] FFIEC-regulated institutions are required to solicit and advertise deposit accounts in a manner that is not misleading or inaccurate, or otherwise misrepresents the banks' terms. Advertisements that contain certain terms such as "bonus" or "APY" must also state certain specific requirements, including any minimum balance required. This additional information can be provided by means of a hyperlink.[7]

2. Lending Activities; Regulation Z; Truth in Lending

Banks and other FFIEC-regulated institutions must be careful when using social media when marketing, soliciting, and signing up loan customers. One of the primary laws governing lending is the Truth in Lending Act (TILA).[8] The primary regulation enacting TILA is Regulation Z.[9] TILA governs social media communications between FFIEC-regu-

---

[4] 12 U.S.C. §4301(1991).

[5] See Nat'l Credit Union Admin. Regs., 12 C.F.R. §§707.4(b)(4), 707.11.

[6] 12 U.S.C. §3201 et seq.; 12 C.F.R. §§230, 1030; 12 C.F.R. 707 (NCUA).

[7] Notice; Request for Comment; FFIEC Docket No. FFIEC-2013-0001 (Jan. 22, 2013), at 13, available at http://www.ffiec.gov/press/Doc/FFIEC%20social%20media%20 guidelines%20FR%20Notice.pdf [hereinafter FFIEC Notice, 2013-001].

[8] Dodd-Frank granting rulemaking authority under the Truth in Lending Act (TILA) to the Consumer Financial Protection Bureau; several amendments to TILA have since been made. CONSUMER FIN. PROT. BUREAU, CFPB CONSUMER LAWS & REGULATIONS 4 (2013), available at http://www.consumerfinance.gov/f/201301_cfpb_final-rule_loan-originator-compensation.pdf. 15 U.S.C. §1601 et seq.

[9] 12 C.F.R. §§26, 1026.

lated entities and customers and potential customers if that communication advertises loan products.[10] Note that the regulation does not apply to certain loans.[11] Reg. Z requires that loan advertisements be presented "in a clear and conspicuous manner"[12] and that disclosures about certain terms of loan products, including how costs are calculated, are disclosed in advertising. Such disclosure requirements can depend on the type of credit advertised, whether the loan is open-ended (such as a revolving home equity loan or credit card) or closed-ended (such as a mortgage with a fixed term or a car loan). In addition, within those categories, other requirements may apply for private education loans, home mortgages, and credit card facilities. Advertisements can state only the actual terms that will be offered. Links to additional information are permitted if the main advertisement makes clear that those other terms are available.

The following summarizes the main disclosures required under each subpart of Reg. Z. It does not specifically relate to online activities, although Reg. Z continues to apply whether solicitation or any other part of the loan process is carried out online. The FFIEC, in its December 2013 final guidance for the use of social media by FFIEC-regulated financial institutions, noted concerns regarding Reg. Z compliance in the social media context. For example, it stated that consumers may try to initiate billing disputes using social media, thereby triggering dispute-resolution

---

[10] FFIEC Notice, 2013-001, at 16.

[11] Reg. Z does not apply to (a) a loan for business, commercial, or agricultural purpose or to other than a natural person; (b) a loan in which the actual loan amount exceeds the applicable threshold amount or in which there is an express written commitment to lend an amount in excess of the applicable threshold amount, unless the loan is (A) secured by the principal home of the borrower, or (B) a private student loan as defined in §226.46(b)(5); (c) a loan for public utility services, if the charges for the services, such as delayed payment, or discounts for prompt payment, are regulated by another government unit, such as a state public service commission; (d) a loan in a securities or commodities trading account by a broker-dealer registered with the SEC or the CFTC; (e) an agreement for the purchase of home heating fuel with no interest or other finance charge; (f) student loans made, insured, or guaranteed pursuant to title IV of the Higher Education Act of 1965 (20 U.S.C. §1070 et seq.); (g) certain loans to participants in employer-sponsored retirement plans, tax-sheltered annuities, or certain governmental deferred compensation plans, provided that the loan complies with the Internal Revenue Code (26 U.S.C. §1 et seq.). (For further details, see 12 C.F.R. §226.3.)

[12] FFIEC Notice, 2013-001, at 16.

timelines and other obligations. Because of these concerns, the FFIEC cautioned that financial institutions with social media presence "should have monitoring procedures in place to address the potential for these statements or complaints to require further investigation."[13]

a. Open-End Credit—Regulation Z, Subpart B

Subpart B of Reg. Z[14] regulates truth in lending with respect to open-end credit, such as home equity lines of credit and credit and charge accounts.[15] Under Subpart B, lenders are required to make several disclosures prior to extending credit initially; exact disclosures vary with the type of open-end credit extended.[16] For credit cards, for example, disclosures include such things as annual percentage rate (APR), variable rate information, whether a discounted introductory rate is offered or a premium introductory rate is imposed, annual or other periodic fees, and more.[17] Subpart B also obligates lenders to

- have systems in place to correct billing errors;
- calculate APRs and credit balances;
- follow restrictions on using customer funds to offset indebtedness; and
- abide by certain rules before closing accounts or changing account terms.[18]

---

[13] Id. at 29.

[14] The Credit Card Accountability Responsibility and Disclosure Act of 2009 (Credit CARD Act) amended the TILA and established a number of new requirements for open-end consumer credit plans (those governed also by Reg. Z, Subpart B). Note also that the CFPB issued a new rule in 2013 revising the general limitation on the total amount of account fees that a credit card issuer may require a consumer to pay. CONSUMER FIN. PROT. BUREAU, CFPB CONSUMER LAWS & REGULATIONS 2 (2013), available at http://www.consumerfinance.gov/f/201301_cfpb_final-rule_loan-originator-compensation.pdf.

[15] BD. OF GOVS. OF FED. RES. SYS., REGULATION Z—TRUTH IN LENDING 1 (2006), available at http://www.federalreserve.gov/boarddocs/supmanual/cch/200601/til.pdf.

[16] See, e.g., 12 C.F.R. §§226.5a(b) (required disclosures for credit cards), 226.5b(d) (required disclosures for home equity lines of credit).

[17] Id. §226.5(b).

[18] BD. OF GOVS. OF FED. RES. SYS., REGULATION Z, at 1.

b. Closed-End Credit—Regulation Z, Subpart C

Subpart C of Reg. Z regulates closed-end credit, which are loans that distribute the full amount up front and must be fully repaid by a specified maturity date, including principal and interest.[19] Subpart C governs the same basic areas as Subpart B: disclosure, treatment of loan balances, APR calculations, rescission requirements, and advertising.[20] Residential mortgages, which fall under the definition of closed-end credit, have special disclosure requirements that require lenders to provide certain disclosures within three business days of receiving a home loan application and again three days prior to closing.[21] Lenders must provide additional disclosures if the loan has a variable interest rate and is secured by a residence.[22] Key disclosures required under Subpart C are as follows:

- Aggregate amount of finance charge
- APR, including method of calculation
- Variable rate–related disclosures such as method of calculation
- Amount financed (normally total payments minus finance charge)
- Payment schedule
- Required deposit, which represents the amount the lender requires the borrower to maintain at the institution as part of the loan agreement[23]

c. Record Retention and State Law Exemptions— Regulation Z, Subpart D

Subpart D of Reg. Z provides instructions regarding oral disclosures, disclosures made in non-English languages,

---

[19] Consumer Fin. Prot. Bureau, CFPB Consumer Laws & Regulations, at 4.

[20] *Id.*

[21] Fed. Deposit Ins. Corp., Truth in Lending Act 14 (2014), *available at* http://www.fdic.gov/regulations/compliance/manual/pdf/V-1.1.pdf.

[22] *Id.*

[23] *Id.* at 14–17.

record retention, the interaction of Reg. Z and state disclosure law, state exemptions, and the inclusion of a rate ceiling in home loans.[24] If a consumer inquires about the cost of open-end or closed-end credit, a lender responding to the inquiry orally must disclose the APR, as opposed to just an annual or period rate alone.[25] Regarding non–English language disclosures, lenders must provide English versions of the disclosures as well if a customer requests.[26]

d. Special Rules for Mortgages and Reverse Mortgages— Regulation Z, Subpart E

Subpart E of Reg. Z provides for rules and exemptions related to certain types of mortgage transactions. Specifically, this subpart imposes disclosure obligations and limitations on loans with rates or fees above a certain threshold.[27] It limits certain provisions in loans for "high-cost" mortgages and home equity loans, as well as reverse mortgages.[28] Subpart E also sets minimum standards for housing-secured transactions that are measured by ability to repay and qualified mortgage standards, among other things.[29] Additional disclosures necessitated by high-cost mortgages (loans in which the APR will exceed the average prime offer rate by a certain amount or in which the points and fees surpass a certain threshold) include

- consumer notices using language set out in 12 C.F.R. §1026.32(c)(1);
- APR;
- information regarding regular or minimum payments or amount of balloon payment;

---

[24] 12 C.F.R. §§1026.25–1026.30.

[25] Id. §1026.26.

[26] Id. §1026.27.

[27] FED. DEPOSIT INS. CORP., TRUTH IN LENDING ACT 3 (2014), available at http://www. fdic.gov/regulations/compliance/manual/pdf/V-1.1.pdf.

[28] Id. at 3.

[29] Id. at 33.

- a statement that interest rate and monthly payment may increase, if the loan is variable rate;
- total amount borrowed in a closed-end transaction or total credit limit available in an open-end credit account.

e. Loan Applications

Loan applications may be taken online or through social media; however, all Reg. Z guidelines and disclosure requirements still apply.[30]

Real Estate Closings—Real Estate Settlement Procedures Act. The Real Estate Settlement Procedures Act[31] prohibits fee splitting, kickbacks, or giving or receiving any type of value for real estate settlement services. The FFIEC makes clear that all of these prohibitions apply to online transactions, including through social media.[32]

Debt Collecting—Fair Debt Collection Practices Act. The Fair Debt Collection Practices Act (FDCPA)[33] regulates how debt collectors may attempt to collect loans and other amounts due. The Act applies to banks collecting their own debts and third parties collecting on banks' behalf. Generally, debt collectors cannot publicly disclose that a person owes a debt or otherwise harass that person or that person's family or friends, including by making false or misleading statements. These restrictions apply to social media as well (e.g., posting on a debtor's Facebook wall about amounts owed).[34] Penalties for violating the FDCPA include financial penalties and, in some cases, a lifetime ban from the industry.

Unfair and Deceptive Practices—Federal Trade Commission Act. The Federal Trade Commission Act prohibits "unfair or deceptive practices."[35] A communication can be unfair

---

[30] FFIEC Notice, 2013-001, at 17.

[31] 12 U.S.C. §§ 2601–2617.

[32] FFIEC Notice 2013-001, at 17.

[33] 15 U.S.C. §1692 *et seq.*.

[34] FFIEC Notice, 2013-001, at 17–18.

[35] 12 U.S.C. §§5531, 5536.

or deceptive even when it technically complies with other laws or regulations. FFIEC-regulated financial institutions are required to ensure that any online or social media communications are accurate, consistent, and not deceptive to consumers.[36] Nonbank entities are subject to Federal Trade Commission (FTC) regulation on unfair and deceptive practices.

3. Deposit Insurance

Both the Federal Deposit Insurance Corporation (FDIC) and the National Credit Union Association (NCUA) offer its members insurance on the funds deposited in those institutions.

a. FDIC Insurance

Advertisements for FDIC-insured products have certain requirements, regardless of whether they are online.[37] Advertisements that offer deposit products and mention the name of the bank must include a notice of FDIC membership. However, if the advertisement offers only nondeposit products or hybrid products such as sweep accounts, then the notice of FDIC membership cannot be included.[38]

b. NCUA Insurance

Advertisements from NCUA-insured credit unions must contain a notice stating "federally insured by the NCUA." The notice must be in a legible size and font and no smaller than any other font in the advertisement. NCUA-insured institutions must also display the NCUA sign on any web page where it opens accounts or accepts deposits.[39]

---

[36] FFIEC Notice, 2013-001, at 18.

[37] Id. at 19.

[38] 12 C.F.R. §328.

[39] Id. §740.

c. Nondeposit Products

When an FDIC- or NCUA-insured institution advertises nondeposit products to consumers, the institution must indicate that the products are not insured and carry risks, including the possible loss of principal.[40]

4. Electronic Payments Through Social Media

Regulators have made it clear that existing laws and regulations may apply to online activities of banks.[41] By allowing consumers to use social media or other online means to access and send funds, banks are subject to the same laws and regulations currently in place for similar offline transactions.[42]

The Electronic Fund Transfer Act[43] and Regulation E[44] govern electronic transfers of funds (EFT). These are defined as funds transfers commenced through various electronic devices, including computer terminals and telephones. It is likely that this would also be construed to apply to payments made via text messages on cell phones. As with Reg. E, the FFIEC expressed concern with compliance arising from use of social media in its December 2013 final guidance. With regard to Regulation E, the FFIEC noted that consumers may attempt to contact the financial institution about a perceived EFT error by using social media. Also similar to Reg. Z, the FFIEC recommended that institutions monitor social media to ensure compliance in this regard.[45]

Under Reg. E §205.4, financial institutions are allowed to combine disclosure information required under the regulation with disclosure required under other applicable laws, such as the Truth in Lending Act (Reg. Z) or the Truth in

---

[40] FFIEC Notice, 2013-001, at 20.

[41] *Id.*

[42] *Id.* at 21.

[43] 15 U.S.C. §1693 *et seq.*

[44] 12 C.F.R. §§205, 1005.

[45] FFIEC Notice, 2013-001, at 29.

Savings Act (Reg. DD).[46] Disclosures are required to be written in plain language and made available in a "form the consumer may keep."[47]

Before transferring funds, financial institutions must give consumers disclosures of the terms and conditions of the nature of the EFT services, which include (1) consumer liability for unauthorized EFTs; (2) contact information for the consumer to notify if he or she believes an unauthorized transfer was made; (3) types of EFTs the consumer may make, as well as dollar and frequency limits on transfers; (4) financial institution fees corresponding with EFT services; and (5) procedures for resolving errors in EFTs.[48] Section 205.7 of Reg. E provides the complete list of initial disclosures.

Reg. E additionally requires financial institutions to provide notice to consumers in the event of an adverse change in terms at least 21 days prior to the effective date of the adverse changes; furthermore, the institution must send consumers a reminder notice regarding its error-resolution processes from time to time (either through annual notice, abbreviated notice with every statement, or other means).[49] If an EFT error occurs and the consumer notifies the institution, the institution must investigate and address the complaint within a certain time frame.[50] Unauthorized EFTs, incorrect EFTs, and EFTs incorrectly omitted from an account statement fall under the mandatory resolution process; routine balance inquires, informational requests for tax or other purposes, and requests for duplicate copies of documents do not.[51]

---

[46] 12 C.F.R. §205.4; *see also* BD. OF GOVS. OF THE FED. RES. SYS., REG. E: COMPLIANCE GUIDE (Aug. 2, 2013), *available at* http://www.federalreserve.gov/bankinforeg/regecg.htm.

[47] 12 C.F.R. §205.4(a)(1).

[48] *Id.* §205.7.

[49] *Id.* §205.8.

[50] *Id.* §205.11.

[51] *Id.* §205.11(a).

5. Credit Reports

The Fair Credit Reporting Act (FCRA)[52] governs solicitations and collection of information to determine loan eligibility. The FFIEC has clearly stated that this applies when social media is used as a tool for these activities.[53] The FTC shares regulatory authority with the Consumer Financial Protection Bureau (CFPB) with respect to the FCRA.

The FCRA, passed in 1970, governs the manner in which institutions may gather consumer credit information and provides for consumer access to personal credit reports. Under the Act, any entity requesting a consumer report must show it has a legitimate purpose for accessing the information before it will be released. Consumers have a number of rights under the Act, all of which are meant to protect consumer privacy and ensure the fairness and accuracy of the information in the report. Entitlements under the Act include the consumer's right to know what is in his or her credit file; the right to access a credit report annually from each major credit bureau; the right to verify the accuracy of a report required for employment; the right to notification if information in the file has been used in a way that adversely affects the consumer; the right to challenge and rectify incomplete or inaccurate information; and the right to purge outdated negative information.[54]

6. Use of Third-Party Service Providers

Finally, the FFIEC has placed responsibility on financial institutions when using third parties to interact with consumers on social media sites, such as Facebook or Twitter.[55] Banks and other FFIEC-regulated institutions should

---

[52] 15 U.S.C. §§1681–1681u.

[53] FFIEC Notice, 2013-001, at 26.

[54] FED. TRADE COMM'N, A SUMMARY OF YOUR RIGHTS UNDER THE FAIR CREDIT REPORTING ACT, *available at* http://www.consumer.ftc.gov/articles/pdf-0096-fair-credit-reporting-act.pdf.

[55] FFIEC Notice, 2013-001, at 27.

monitor information on social media sites placed there either directly or through a third-party service provider. Financial institutions should consider the terms and conditions of the particular site and its ability to control the information on a third-party social media site.[56] Finally, these institutions should consider appropriate policies with respect to employees' use of social media, including their own social media accounts.[57] Any policies should be reviewed carefully to make sure they also comply with applicable state employment laws. The use of third-party service providers is discussed in Chapter 8.

B. Social Media—FINRA Regulatory Guidance

This section is relevant for entities regulated by the Securities and Exchange Commission (SEC), Commodity Futures Trading Commission (CFTC), and FINRA. FINRA has also issued guidance that addresses the use of social media by FINRA-regulated institutions.[58] In FINRA's view, social media do not preclude existing regulations and requirements, but merely bring them into the electronic realm. Existing rules governing customer communications apply equally to electronic communications such as blogs and social networking sites.[59] Firms are required to adequately supervise online communications with clients and to adopt policies and procedures for review of electronic communications.[60] These policies and procedures must address which persons may communicate via social media sites and ensure that they have the proper training, experience, and regulatory knowledge

---

[56] *Id.* at 28.

[57] *Id.* at 29.

[58] *See* NASD Rule 2210 (2014); FINRA Regulatory Notice 10-06 (Jan. 2010); FINRA Regulatory Notice 11-39 (Aug. 2011); and FINRA, GUIDE TO THE INTERNET FOR REGISTERED REPRESENTATIVES (2014). Available at http://www.finra.org/web/groups/industry/@ip/@comp/@regis/documents/industry/p299085.pdf.

[59] FINRA Regulatory Notice 10-06, at 6.

[60] *Id.*

to perform such communications [61] FINRA considers publicly available websites that appear in public chat rooms to be essentially advertisements.[62]

1. Investment Recommendations via Social Media

Firm employees should be careful when making investment advice via social media. FINRA may consider it a "recommendation."[63] Also, the poster must consider the audience for that advice (e.g., public, friends only, one specific person), as that advice may or may not be suitable for that audience.[64] The poster may even trigger further disclosure requirements to allow the customer or potential customer to make an adequate evaluation of the advice. Firms should have appropriate policies and procedures in place to educate personnel of these issues. Firms may even consider banning or severely restricting social media posts.

Regulated firms are allowed to use social media; however, the firms themselves must determine whether the social media platform complies with record-keeping and other regulatory requirements.[65] Record-keeping requirements are further discussed in Chapter 9.

2. Blogs

According to FINRA, blogs could be either advertisements or "interactive electronic forums" under FINRA Rule 2210. A blog with "static" content would be an advertisement, which requires preapproval by a registered principal of the firm, while a blog that permits "real-time interactive communications" does not have to be preapproved but does require

---

[61] *Id.* at 7.

[62] *See* GUIDE TO THE INTERNET FOR REGISTERED REPRESENTATIVES; *see also* NASD Rule 2210.

[63] FINRA Notice to Members 01-23, Suitability Rule and Online Communications (Apr. 2001), *available at* http://www.finra.org/Industry/Regulation/Notices/2001/P003886.

[64] *See* FINRA Rule 2310.

[65] FINRA Regulatory Notice 10-06 (Jan. 2010), at 3.

supervision.[66] Supervision of communications is covered in Chapter 9 on information governance.

3. Third-Party Posts

Posts to a regulated financial institution's website by third parties are not normally considered to be communications by that institution, but they may be attributed to the firm if the firm has either (1) somehow been involved in preparing that content or (2) somehow endorsed that content.[67] Responses to third-party questions are permitted as long as the answer does not otherwise violate the firm's policies.[68] Of course, firms are prohibited from knowingly linking to a third-party website that contains false or misleading content or other misleading materials. Under NASD Rule 2210, firms are responsible for any such misleading content if they somehow endorse it or participate in its creation.[69] If a firm co-brands its website with another website (e.g, by including the second firm's logo or some other indication of affiliation), the regulated firm is deemed responsible for the content on the entire third-party site.[70]

4. Practical Guidance

Therefore, a firm must take care when allowing third parties to post or link content to its site. It also should strongly consider including a disclaimer that states that third-party content does not represent the firm's views on any matter. Although a firm is not required to monitor third-party posts, adding such monitoring to its existing compliance program is wise, both to ensure compliance with FINRA regulations

---

[66] *Id.* at 5.

[67] *Id.* at 7.

[68] FINRA Regulatory Notice 11-39 (Aug. 2011), at 6.

[69] *Id.* at 3.

[70] *Id.* at 6.

and to manage copyright and other claims [71] A firm is not responsible for content on third-party sites to which it links if the firm does not (1) "adopt" or become "entangled" with the third-party content, and does not (2) "know or have reason to know" that the third-party content or website is misleading.[72]

C. FTC Guidelines on the Use of Endorsements Online

The use of endorsements is potentially an "unfair or deceptive practice"; therefore, the FTC regulations described in this section apply to all nonbank service providers to financial institutions that offer or provide consumer financial products or services. This includes many online service providers, such as Facebook, LinkedIn, and Google.

The FTC has issued guidelines on the use of endorsements in advertising.[73] The guidelines define "endorsements" to include any advertising message (including verbal messages or even the name or logo of an organization) that consumers would believe reflect the beliefs or opinions of a third party other than the advertiser.[74] For purposes of these rules, endorsements also include testimonials.[75] Examples of online endorsements are found in Appendix A.

Endorsements must represent the honest opinions or experiences of the endorser.[76] Advertisers must reasonably believe that any endorser, whether a celebrity, expert, or ordinary person, actually has the beliefs or opinions expressed in the advertisement.[77] Factors that determine reasonableness include new information about the product or service that affect its performance or effectiveness, a major change to the product or service, major changes to competitors' products

---

[71] *Id.* at 8.

[72] *Id.* at 6; *see also* NASD Rule 2210.

[73] *Id.* §255 *et seq.*

[74] *Id.* §255.0(b).

[75] *Id.* §255.0(c).

[76] *Id.* §255.1(a).

[77] *Id.* §255.1(b).

or services that affect their performance or effectiveness, and any relevant contractual terms or conditions.[78] Advertisers must ensure that any endorser has actually used the product or service at the time the endorsement was given and can run advertisements only as long as the endorser is a bona fide user of the product.[79] Advertisers may be liable for penalties or fines from the FTC for false or unsubstantiated claims made by endorsers, while the endorsers themselves may incur liability for such claims.[80]

1. Consumer Endorsements

Advertisers that use ordinary consumers for endorsements should be aware of specific FTC rules. These types of advertisements generally convey the message that the product or service works in the manner represented in the advertisement. The advertiser must substantiate any claims made by the consumer-endorser, even using scientific evidence when appropriate, as consumers are not considered competent and reliable scientific evidence.[81] Note that if an advertiser lacks evidence that the consumer-endorser's claims are typical of consumers' experience generally, then the advertisement must "conspicuously disclose" what the typical consumer experience would be in similar circumstances as depicted; of course, the advertiser must have proof of that experience.[82] Disclaimers such as "results not typical" or even "you are likely to have a different experience" may not be sufficient, but if the advertiser has scientific evidence that the advertisement is not deceptive, then the advertiser will likely not face any enforcement action by the FTC.[83] Advertisements that do not use actual consumers must disclaim

---

[78] Id.

[79] Id. §255.1(c).

[80] Id. §255.1(d).

[81] Id. §255.2(a).

[82] Id. §255.2(b).

[83] Id. n.1.

such use with a notation such as "not an actual consumer."[84] Examples of permissible and nonpermissible consumer endorsements are found in Appendix A.

2. Expert Endorsements

Expert endorsers must have sufficient credentials to back up the expertise they are represented as having in the advertisement.[85] Also, the endorsement must be based on the expert's actual analysis of the product or service, using that expertise in the same way someone with such expertise would evaluate a product or service.[86] If the endorsement was based on a comparison with another product or service, the comparison must reflect the expert's actual conclusion with respect to that comparison and involve features of the product or service to which an ordinary consumer would have access.[87] Examples of permissible and nonpermissible expert endorsements are found in Appendix A.

3. Endorsements by Organizations

Endorsements by organizations represent the combined opinions of that organization and hence carry more weight than those of any individual. The FTC requires that any organizational endorsements must fairly represent the "collective judgment of the organization."[88] If the organization is an "expert," then the provisions of 16 CFR §§255.4 and 255.1(d) apply. For an example of this type of endorsement, see Appendix A.

---

[84] *Id.* §255.2(c).

[85] *Id.* §255.3(a).

[86] *Id.* §255.3(b).

[87] *Id.*

[88] *Id.* §255.4.

4. Disclosure of Material Connections

A connection between an endorser and an advertiser must be disclosed.[89] Examples of such connections are provided in Appendix A.

D. Contextual and Keyword Advertising

This section applies to all financial institutions and service providers regardless of regulator. Contextual advertising scans websites for keywords and then returns advertising based on those keywords. It is a form of focused advertising that relates directly to either the keywords in the user's search or to the website the user is viewing. Targeted advertisements are more likely to be clicked on and therefore to generate earnings.

Search engines also use contextual advertising to place ads on the search results page based on the search terms entered. This is sometimes referred to as keyword advertising, and there are many variations. The search engine effectively "rents" a specific keyword to a customer for a defined time period so that all searches that incorporate that keyword will return advertisements for that specific customer.

1. Trademark Infringement Issues in Contextual Advertising

Challenges arise when duly registered trademarks[90] are used for driving users to a website. If customer A "buys" trademark X as a keyword, but X is the duly registered trademark of company B, has B's trademark been infringed? If so, is A the infringer, is the search engine selling the use of the keyword the infringer, or both? Courts are divided on the answers to these questions.

---

[89] *Id.* §255.5.

[90] For a general discussion of trademark law, see Chapter 3.

Generally, a finding of trademark infringement requires the following:[91]

1. plaintiff has a valid trademark entitled to protection;
2. defendant used that mark,
3. in commerce,
4. in connection with the sale or advertising of goods or services; and
5. defendant's use of the trademark is "likely to cause confusion" regarding either a connection between the registered owner and defendant or the origin or approval of the goods or services sold by the registered trademark owner.[92]

a. 1-800 Contacts, Inc. v. WhenU.Com, Inc.

In *1-800 Contacts, Inc. v. WhenU.com, Inc.*,[93] the Second Circuit ruled that to include a trademark in an internal list of keywords to serve pop-up ads was not "use" of the trademark for trademark infringement purposes. There was no selling of the use of keywords, and the process actually served up the trademark owner's website along with the ads. The court followed the reasoning in the *U-Haul* and *Wells Fargo* cases.[94]

b. Australian Gold, Inc. v. Hatfield

In *Australian Gold, Inc. v. Hatfield*,[95] the Tenth Circuit Court of Appeals held that initial interest confusion occurs when a consumer seeks a specific trademarked product but is lured to a competitor's product via the same or similar mark as the first product's mark.[96] In *Australian Gold*, the

---

[91] 15 U.S.C. §1114(1).

[92] *Id.* §1125(a)(1)(A).

[93] 414 F.3d 400 (2d Cir. 2005); *see also* Wells Fargo & Co. v. WhenU.com, 293 F. Supp. 2d 734 (E.D. Mich. 2003); U-Haul Int'l v. WhenU.com, 279 F. Supp. 2d 723 (E.D. Va. 2003).

[94] *Wells Fargo*, 293 F. Supp. 2d 734; *U-Haul Int'l*, 279 F. Supp. 2d 723.

[95] 436 F.3d 1228 (10th Cir. 2006).

[96] *Id.*

infringers used plaintiffs' trademarks to divert traffic to their website to sell both unauthorized products of plaintiffs and products from plaintiffs' competitors. The court said that by doing this, the defendants used the goodwill of plaintiffs' trademarks in a way that lured consumers to competitors' products and, thus, violated the Lanham Act.[97]

The Tenth Circuit also confirmed a test for initial interest confusion that other courts have since adopted. To determine initial interest confusion, the court looked at the following: (1) the degree of similarity between the marks, (2) the intent of the alleged infringer in adopting the mark, (3) evidence of actual confusion, (4) similarity of products, (5) the degree of care likely to be exercised by purchasers, and (6) the strength or weakness of the marks at issue. Likelihood of confusion is a question of fact, and no single factor will determine the result of the analysis.[98] Other circuits have adopted similar tests.[99]

c. Tdata Inc. v. Aircraft Technical Publishers

The Southern District of Ohio, in the 2006 case of *Tdata Inc. v. Aircraft Technical Publishers*,[100] held that software maker Tdata infringed Aircraft Technical Publishers' (ATPs) trademarks by including them as "metatags" and "title tags" of Tdata websites. The court thought that Tdata's use of ATPs' trademarks in its metatags was not an innocent coincidence; instead, the court noted, Tdata used the trademarks "in a bad faith, bait-and-switch, create-initial-confusion sense."[101] The district court also applied a multifactor test similar to what the Tenth Circuit used in *Australian Gold* to determine whether consumers were initially confused by the use, but it

---

[97] *Id.* at 1240.

[98] *See* Sally Beauty Co. v. Beautyco, Inc., 304 F.3d 964, 972 (10th Cir. 2002).

[99] *See* Frisch's Rests. Inc. v. Elby's Big Boy of Steubenville, Inc., 670 F.2d 642, 648 (6th Cir.), *cert. denied*, 459 U.S. 916 (1982).

[100] 411 F. Supp. 2d 901 (S.D. Ohio 2006).

[101] *Id.* at 912.

also observed that initial interest confusion could be a proxy for actual confusion in the multifactor test.[102]

d. Savin Corp. v. Savin Group

The Second Circuit, however, found that using identical business names in sufficiently different contexts does not constitute infringement. In *Savin Corp. v. Savin Group*,[103] business equipment maker Savin Corp. sued engineering firm Savin Group for trademark dilution and infringement.[104] After losing in the lower court, Savin Corp. appealed, but it again failed to succeed on its claim for trademark infringement.[105] Applying an eight-factor test known as the Polaroid Factors (named for the original case applying the multifactor analysis), the Second Circuit held that Savin Group did not infringe Savin Corp.'s trademark. Although the two marks were undeniably similar, all other factors in the Polaroid Factors analysis weighed against a finding of infringement:

1. The marks were not used similarly.
2. There was virtually no evidence of actual confusion.
3. Neither company seemed likely to enter the others' industry.
4. No evidence supported that Savin Group acted in bad faith in taking up its business name.
5. The product quality of both companies was not confusingly similar.
6. Purchasers of both companies' products and services were sophisticated enough to discern the difference between the two.

---

[102] *Internet Trademark Case Summaries, Tdata Inc. v. Aircraft Technical Publishers*, FINNEGAN, http://www.finnegan.com/Tdata-Inc-v-Aircraft-Technical-Publishers-01-01-2006/.

[103] 391 F.3d 439 (2d Cir. 2004).

[104] *Id.* at 447.

[105] *Id.* at 462 (note, however, that the dilution claim, which was originally rejected in the district court, was reversed and remanded by the Second Circuit).

e. Rescuecom v. Google

Three years after its *Savin Corp.* decision, the Second Circuit heard a case that has become well known in the area of trademark infringement, *Rescuecom v. Google.*[106] Rescuecom was a national computer service franchising company that offered onsite computer services and sales; as part of its marketing program, it advertised online and used Google's ad services, which in turn used software to match ads to consumer profiles. After becoming familiar with Google's practice of allowing advertisers to purchase keywords—including trademarks—that consumers could enter as search terms, Rescuecom sued Google, alleging that its practice of selling the use of trademarks as keywords constituted trademark infringement, false designation of origin, and dilution. Observing that the trial court had misunderstood the Second Circuit's holding in another case, *1-800 Contacts, Inc. v. WhenU.com, Inc.,*[107] the Second Circuit sent the *Rescuecom* case back to the trial court for reconsideration. Before it did so, however, the court noted that in this case, Google allowed advertisers to purchase Rescuecom's specific trademark and dictate which sponsored ads would appear whenever that phrase was part of a search engine query.[108] The court made it clear that Google had used Rescuecom's trademark in commerce. The question for reconsideration by the lower court was whether that use created a likelihood of confusion. The case was later voluntarily dismissed without prejudice by the parties.

f. Buying for the Home, LLC v. Humble Abode, LLC

Another case, this time in a New Jersey federal court, illustrates the evolving (and complex) nature of trademark infringement on the Internet. In *Buying for the Home, LLC v.*

---

[106] 562 F.3d 123 (2d Cir. 2009).

[107] 414 F.3d 400 (2d Cir. 2005).

[108] *Internet Trademark Case Summaries, Rescuecom Corp. v. Google, Inc.,* FINNEGAN, http://www.finnegan.com/RescuecomCorpvGoogleInc/.

Humble Abode, LLC,[109] two competing online bedroom furniture retailers sued each another for trademark infringement (among other things). Buying for the Home ("Buying") alleged that Humble Abode ("Humble") had purchased certain keywords that caused sponsored online ads for Humble to appear next to query results when Internet users searched for Buying's website, thereby purporting to communicate falsely where the goods advertised originated. Humble, in turn, claimed that Buying had engaged in similar practices regarding sponsored content on the Web and that Buying maintained a price comparison web page that infringed Humble's trademarks.

With regard to Buying's price comparison page, the court found that the use of Humble's product names on its competitor's website constituted "nominative fair use," a type of noninfringing use of another's trademark that includes comparative advertising.[110] Regarding claims of trademark infringement arising from the purchase of sponsored content next to search results for each competitor's website, the court noted that it was too early in the case to grant a summary judgment motion in favor of one part or the other.[111] "First," the court observed, "the case presents novel issues of Internet advertising rather than flagrant violations of well-settled trademark law. Indeed, the law in this area has continued to evolve from the day this case was filed." Second, the court stated that the evidence tended to contradict a claim of bad faith or intentional infringement, at least on Buying's part, and thus the court could not at that stage find that Buying infringed Humble's trademarks, as Humble was asking it to do.[112]

---

[109] 459 F. Supp. 2d 310 (D.N.J. 2006); *see also* Interstellar Starship Servs., Ltd. v. Epix, Inc., 304 F.3d 936 (9th Cir. 2002); Brookfield Commc'ns, Inc. v. West Coast Entm't Corp., 174 F.3d 1036 (9th Cir. 1999); Hasbro Inc. v. Clue Computing, Inc., 66 F. Supp. 2d 117 (D. Mass. 1999), *aff'd*, 232 F.3d 1 (1st Cir. 2000).

[110] 459 F. Supp. 2d at 329–30.

[111] *Id.* at 332.

[112] *Id.*

g. International Trademark Association 2006 Board Resolution on Initial Interest Confusion

The cases described above illustrate the difficulty in determining whether trademark infringement has occurred in the context of keyword advertising, domain names disputes, and metatag use. Courts have struggled especially with resolving issues of whether an alleged infringer's use of a trademark in one of these online settings is "likely to cause confusion." Adding to this complexity is the fact that some courts have developed one test for determining "likelihood of confusion" and another for determining whether a consumer is initially confused as to a particular use of a trademark, even if the consumer always realizes the correct source of the goods or services before purchase (referred to as "initial interest confusion"). To clarify this area of the law, the International Trademark Association (INTA) adopted a board resolution addressing initial interest confusion.[113] In its September 2006 resolution, the INTA recommended that courts do away with the separate "initial interest confusion" test in both online and other cases, and simply consider whether consumers are likely to be confused, be it at the time of interest, time of sale, or other point in time.

2. Use of Google Adwords

Google Adwords is the system in which advertisers market products or services with the use of a "sponsored" ad appearing alongside Internet users' search results.[114] These sponsored ads are triggered by a user searching for various keywords in the search engine; advertisers bid on keywords they want to trigger the appearance of their sponsored ad.[115] While such a system is not problematic when the keyword

---

[113] *Board Resolutions, Initial Interest Confusion*, INT'L TRADEMARK ASS'N (Sept. 18, 2006), http://www.inta.org/Advocacy/Pages/InitialInterestConfusion.aspx.

[114] *What Is Google Adwords?*, VIRTUALNET MARKETING, http://www.virtualnet.co.uk/what-is-google-adwords/ (UK).

[115] Jonathan J. Darrow & Gerald R. Ferrera, *The Search Engine Advertising Market: Lucrative Space or Trademark Liability?*, 17 TEX. INTELL. PROP. L.J. 223, 228–29 (2009).

is a generic term, such as "dry cleaner," it raises questions of possible infringement when advertisers are allowed to bid on trademarked terms, which Google has allowed since 2004.[116] As two scholars have noted, "[t]his has effectively compelled trademark owners to bid against their competitors for keywords that are identical or similar to their own trademarks."[117] Not surprisingly, it has also prompted a number of lawsuits, both against Google and between competitors unhappy with the way in which the system plays out.

One of the most commonly litigated issues in lawsuits involving Adwords is whether purchasing a trademark as a keyword, which may cause a competitor's ad to appear next to search results for the trademark owner's business, involves a "use in commerce." Recall from Section II.E.1. above that to prove trademark infringement, party A must show that party B used A's trademark in commerce in connection with the sale or advertising of goods or services. Unfortunately, this legal issue remains unclear. Some of the courts in the following cases concluded that keyword purchase of trademarked words or phrases is *not* a use in commerce while others reached a different result.

a. Merck & Co. v. Mediplan Health Consulting, Inc.

In *Merck & Co. v. Mediplan Health Consulting, Inc.*,[118] Canadian online pharmacies purchased the keyword ZOCOR, the name of Merck's popular anticholesterol medication. In the first of six related lawsuits filed by Merck against the owners of the online pharmacies, the court held that the pharmacies' use of the keyword ZOCOR to trigger their own websites as sponsored links did "not involve 'placement' of the trademark 'on any goods or containers or displays or associated documents' or use 'to indicate source or sponsorship' and

---

[116] *Id.* at 229.

[117] *Id.*

[118] 425 F. Supp. 2d 402 (S.D.N.Y. 2006).

thus, [wa]s 'not use of the mark in a trademark sense.'"[119] This sort of use, noted the court, was "internal," did not communicate anything to the public, and was "analogous to an individual's private thoughts about a trademark."[120]

b. FragranceNet.com, Inc. v. FragranceX.com, Inc.

In *FragranceNet.com, Inc. v. FragranceX.com, Inc.*,[121] Internet perfume retailer FragranceNet asked the court for permission to amend its complaint to add claims that its competitor, FragranceX, had infringed FragranceNet's trademarks by purchasing keywords that contained FragranceNet's trademarks and by including FragranceNet trademarks as metatags in the FragranceX website.[122] In denying FragranceNet's request, the court held that its trademark infringement claims would not survive a motion to dismiss.[123] This was not a case where FragranceX was "passing off" its own goods as those of its competitor; instead, a sponsored ad for FragranceX appears next to the search results when a user types in FragranceNet.[124] In rejecting FragranceNet's argument, the court followed several other cases within the same circuit court of appeals that all rejected the idea that purchase of a competitor's trademark as a keyword prompting sponsored ads to appear in Internet search results was a "use in commerce" that could support a claim of trademark infringement.[125]

---

[119] *FragranceNet.com*, 493 F. Supp. 2d 545, 552–53 (E.D.N.Y. 2007) (quoting *Merck*, 425 F. Supp. 2d at 415).

[120] *Merck*, 425 F. Supp. 2d at 415 (quoting 1-800 Contacts, Inc. v. WhenU.Com, Inc., 414 F.3d 400, 409 (2d Cir. 2005)).

[121] 493 F. Supp. 2d 545 (E.D.N.Y. 2007).

[122] *Id.* at 546.

[123] *Id.* at 555.

[124] *Id.* at 550.

[125] *Id.* at 550–55.

c. Playboy Enterprises v. Netscape Communications Corp.

Sponsored advertisements do not just appear alongside query results in search engines; they also appear as banner ads within content pages themselves.[126] Banner ads, like sponsored ads, are typically triggered by keywords chosen by the advertiser.[127] One of the most well-known trademark infringement cases involving banner ads is *Playboy Enterprises v. Netscape Communications Corp.*[128] Playboy sued Netscape, alleging that its sale of keywords such as "Playboy" and "Playmate" to Playboy competitors constituted infringing use of Playboy's trademarks.[129] Significantly, the Ninth Circuit began its analysis by stating that Netscape's practice of selling keywords to trigger banner ads was a "use in commerce"—one of the elements required to find trademark infringement, and one whose application to similar online applications had been unclear prior to this. Instead, the Ninth Circuit observed, the central issue was whether consumers were likely to be confused.[130] The court held that because consumers were likely to be confused, at least initially when clicking an ad using those particular keywords, Netscape's practice was an infringing use of Playboy's trademarks.[131]

d. Google, Inc. v. American Blind & Wallpaper Factory

In *Google, Inc. v. American Blind & Wallpaper Factory,*[132] Google asked the court in the Northern District of California to declare that Google's practice of suggesting additional keywords to advertisers, which had resulted in the sale of

---

[126] Misha Gregory Macaw, Google, Inc. v. American Blind & Wallpaper Factory, Inc.: *A Justification for the Use of Trademarks as Keywords to Trigger Paid Advertising Placements in Internet Search Engine Results*, 32 RUTGERS COMPUTER & TECH. L.J. 1, 34 (2005).

[127] *Id.*

[128] 354 F.3d 1020 (9th Cir. 2004).

[129] *Id.* at 1022–23.

[130] *Id.* at 1024.

[131] *Id.* at 1034.

[132] Google, Inc. v. American Blind & Wallpaper Factory, Inc., No. 03-cv-05340 JF (RS), 2007 WL 1159950 (N.D. Cal. Apr. 18, 2007).

a number of American Blind's trademarks to its competitors as keywords, was not an infringing use.[133] The court rejected Google's claim that it could not be infringing American Blind's trademarks because Google was not "using" the trademarks in a sense that was required for trademark infringement. Instead, the court followed the Ninth Circuit's reasoning in the *Netscape* case (discussed above), saying that the relevant issue was whether consumers were likely to be confused by the use of the terms.[134] After declining to agree with Google's argument that this case was different from *Netscape* and noting that, as in *Netscape*, the question was whether a user was likely to be initially confused, the Ninth Circuit denied Google's motion to dismiss.[135]

e. Government Employee Insurance Co. (GEICO) v. Google, Inc.

After *American Blind*, the GEICO case is one of the most frequently discussed in the context of keyword-sponsored advertisements. As it did in *American Blind*, Google argued in *Government Employee Insurance Co. (GEICO) v. Google, Inc.*[136] that its keyword sales were not "uses in commerce" and that its sales were not "in connection with the sale, offering for sale, distribution, or advertising of goods and services" because Google did not use GEICO's trademarks in a way that falsely identified GEICO as the source of the sponsored ads.[137] Google analogized its case to software companies' use of trademarked keywords to generate pop-up ads, a use that courts had already said did not constitute trademark infringement.[138] The district court, however, was unconvinced. Instead, the court agreed with GEICO's argument that Google's mere

---

[133] Misha Gregory Macaw, Google, Inc. v. American Blind & Wallpaper Factory, Inc.: *A Justification for the Use of Trademarks as Keywords to Trigger Paid Advertising Placements in Internet Search Engine Results*, 32 RUTGERS COMPUTER & TECH. L.J. 1, 42 (2005).

[134] *Google v. American Blind*, 2007 WL 1159950, at *22.

[135] *Id.* at *30.

[136] 330 F. Supp. 2d 700 (E.D. Va. 2004).

[137] *Id.* at 702.

[138] *Id.* at 702–03.

offer of trademarks in the menu of available keywords for purchase could confuse advertisers because they may falsely believe that Google had GEICO's permission to use its trademarks as keywords.[139] Although GEICO and Google settled the case before an appeal had been filed, this case explains how many courts still view use of trademarked keywords as "use in commerce"—a necessary element for finding trademark infringement—even though the "use" was "invisible" to the ultimate Internet user who viewed the sponsored ad.

f. American Airlines, Inc. v. Google, Inc.

In *American Airlines, Inc. v. Google, Inc.*,[140] American Airlines sued Google for trademark infringement, claiming the Internet search giant's practice of allowing American Airlines' competitors to bid on keywords that resulted in competitors' ads appearing when Internet users search for American Airlines and similar queries took advantage of the airline's brand popularity.[141] As it had in *American Blinds*, Google argued that its practice of selling keywords, including trademarks, did not constitute a "use in commerce."[142] Because the parties settled the case in 2008, a court did not address the merits of the case; but the *American Airlines* suit demonstrates Google's basic position that its keyword sales do not infringe trademarks because the sales are not uses in commerce that are necessary to support a finding of trademark infringement. At the time this suit was settled, Google announced that it was involved in, or had recently resolved, similar cases in Germany, Israel, Italy, Austria, and Australia.[143]

---

[139] *Id.* at 704.

[140] American Airlines, Inc. v. Google, Inc., No. 4-07CV-487-A (N.D. Tex., filed Aug. 16, 2007).

[141] Erik Larsen, *American Airlines Drops Google Trademark Lawsuit (Update 1)*, BLOOMBERG (July 18, 2008, 12:17 PM EST), http://www.bloomberg.com/apps/news?pid=newsarchive &sid=aNtnl9vC6QLc.

[142] *See* Louis J. Levy & David M. Rigsby, *Use of Keyword Triggers Can Trigger Problems for "Contextual Marketing"*, MSBA BUS. L. SEC. NEWSL. (2008), http://msbabusinesslawnews letter.com/winter2008/useofkeywordtriggers.html.

[143] Larsen, *American Airlines Drops Google Trademark Lawsuit.*

g. Practical Guidance

Because of the current splits among the circuits, it is not advisable to *knowingly* use a competitor's trademark when buying keyword advertising. Doing so is likely to invite a lawsuit, even if trademark infringement is not ultimately found. Financial services companies would be wise to carefully to consider the relevant case law before using this type of online advertising.

E. Behavioral Advertising

This section applies to all financial institutions and service providers regardless of regulator. Behavioral advertising tracks and uses a web user's online activity, including Internet searches and sites visited, to present advertisements to that web user.

1. In re DoubleClick

DoubleClick placed small bits of computer code, commonly known as cookies, on to web users' computers when those users accessed DoubleClick sites.[144] The cookies tracked users' web activities so that DoubleClick could build profiles and target advertisements to each user. The plaintiffs alleged that the information stored in the cookies was unauthorized and violated the Stored Communications Act,[145] the Wiretap Statute,[146] and the Computer Fraud and Abuse Act.[147] The district court found that DoubleClick was not liable because its activities fell within the consent provisions of the Stored Communications Act and the Wiretap Statute. The court dismissed the plaintiffs' Computer Fraud and Abuse Act claims, stating that the damages caused by the cookies did not meet

---

[144] *In re* DoubleClick, 154 F. Supp. 2d 497 (S.D.N.Y. 2001).

[145] 18 U.S.C. §2701 *et seq.*

[146] *Id.* §2511 *et seq.*

[147] *Id.* §1030 *et seq.*

the statutory threshold of $5,000 for each cookie. The parties eventually settled all claims. The settlement required DoubleClick to explain its privacy policy in plain language, provide the public at large with information about how to protect their privacy, and incorporate opt-in and data cleansing procedures into their business model.

2. FTC Actions with Regard to Behavioral Advertising

a. 2010 FTC Report on Behavioral Advertising

Recognizing the potential tensions that exist between consumers' right to privacy and advertisers' interest in increasing sales through behavioral advertising, the FTC convened a series of privacy roundtables in 2010 to discuss challenges posed by new technology, in particular, behavioral advertising.[148] In a report issued in December 2010 based on these roundtables, the FTC endorsed a "Do Not Track" system whereby consumers are empowered to restrict what information advertisers may collect.[149] The most practical method for allowing consumers to opt out of being tracked, the FTC noted, would likely entail an Internet web browser setting similar to a cookie that remembered the consumer's choices about tracking and receiving targeted ads.[150]

b. Chitika, Inc.

Chitika, Inc.,[151] an online advertising network, acts as an intermediary for websites and advertisers.[152] Among other

---

[148] Rainey Reitman, *FTC's New Privacy Report Endorses "Do Not Track" Mechanism to Empower Online Consumers*, ELEC. FRONTIER FOUND. (Dec. 1, 2010), https://www.eff.org/deeplinks/2010/12/ftcs-privacy-report-calls-attention-privacy.

[149] *Id.*

[150] Press Release, Fed. Trade Comm'n, *FTC Staff Issues Privacy Report, Offers Framework for Consumers, Businesses, and Policymakers* (Dec. 1, 2010), *available at* http://www.ftc.gov/news-events/press-releases/2010/12/ftc-staff-issues-privacy-report-offers-framework-consumers.

[151] Chitika, Inc., Docket No. C-4324 (Fed. Trade Comm'n 2011).

[152] Press Release, Fed. Trade Comm'n, *FTC Puts an End to Tactics of Online Advertising Company That Deceived Consumers Who Wanted to "Opt Out" from Targeted Ads* (Mar. 14, 2011),

services it provides is behavioral advertising.[153] In response to the FTC's recommendation, Chitika instituted a system allowing Internet users to opt out of being tracked and targeted with ads. Chitika's system, however, allowed users only a ten-day opt-out period; users were required to continually go through the opt-out process after each ten-day period expired.[154]

According to the FTC, Chitika's process was deceptive and broke federal law.[155] Chitika claimed the short opt-out period was a mistake, that it should have been ten years rather than ten days.[156] Despite that, the company eventually settled with the FTC in an agreement requiring Chitika to include a link in targeted ads that consumers could use to opt out of being tracked for five or more years and to destroy data previously collected while the flawed opt-out system was in place; the linked material also alerted customers who had previously attempted to opt out that the system was defective.[157]

III. Distribution of Information and Other Communications with Customers

A. E-mail and Instant Messaging

1. FFIEC Guidance on E-Mail and Instant Messaging

a. FDIC E-mail Guidance

The prevalence of e-mail and Internet fraud prompted the FDIC to issue a Financial Institution Letter (FIL) to alert

---

available at http://www.ftc.gov/news-events/press-releases/2011/03/ftc-puts-end-tactics-online-advertising-company-deceived.

[153] *Id.*

[154] Emily Steel, *FTC Sanctions Online Firm that Tracks Users*, Wall St. J., Mar. 15, 2011, *available at* http://online.wsj.com/news/articles/SB10001424052748704893604576200833775322992.

[155] *Id.*

[156] *Id.*

[157] *Id.*

financial institutions to "fraudulent schemes targeting financial institution customers."[158] Of concern is the "frequency, intensity and creativity" of new schemes that deceive customers into revealing sensitive information such as Social Security or credit card numbers to gain access to customers' accounts or to commit identity theft.[159] These schemes could harm not only customers but also a financial institution's reputation because "customers and potential customers may attribute the activity to a perceived weakness in the institution's ability to conduct business securely and responsibly."[160] Accordingly, the FDIC advises financial institutions detecting an e-mail or Internet-related fraudulent scheme to promptly notify their regional FDIC and file a Suspicious Activity Report with local law enforcement. In addition, the financial institution may forward such information to the Special Activities Section of the FDIC.

b. Instant Messaging

The FFIEC is also concerned with publicly available instant messaging (IM) and network file-sharing applications.[161] Financial institutions face security, privacy, and legal liability risks from the authorized and unauthorized use of IM applications within those financial institutions. According to the FDIC, "[i]nstitutions should assess the risks and the business needs for IM and establish policies to allow, restrict or deny IM usage based on these risk assessments and business needs."[162] In accordance with customer information security guidelines, an institution using IM must periodically assess risk and submit status reports to its board of directors. Such reports should include the institution's position on IM, as well as any control weaknesses and how such weaknesses

---

[158] Fed. Deposit Ins. Corp., FIL-27-2004, Guidance on Safeguarding Customers Against E-mail and Internet-Related Fraudulent Schemes (Mar. 12, 2004).

[159] Id.

[160] Id.

[161] Fed. Deposit Ins. Corp., FIL-84-2004, Guidance on Instant Messaging (July 21, 2004).

[162] Id.

will be "identified and addressed during the normal course of business."[163]

B. SEC/CFTC Regulated Institutions

SEC Rules 17-a3 and 17-a4 govern securities and commodities firms' storage and retrieval of e-mail and other client communications. These are discussed in detail in Chapter 9.

IV. WEB LINKS

The use of links on the Internet has generated concern among regulators. Linking to another website could create risks for financial institutions. The sections below discuss how regulators have attempted to address these risks.

A. Guidance from the FFIEC

Linked websites allow Internet users easy access to related online resources. Links, however, can also create risks to financial institutions. Reputation risk harms the confidence its customers have in the institution, thereby weakening the institution itself. Compliance risk involves an institution's violation of statutory or regulatory law.

1. Web Linking—Reputation Risks

FFIEC-regulated financial institutions should consider the following factors when linking to a third-party website: (1) the nature of the product or service, (2) the name(s)

---

[163] *Id.*

used by the third party, and (3) the "look and feel" of the third-party website.[164]

For instance, links to websites that sell financial products may confuse the financial institution's customers. They may mistakenly believe that the financial institution sells the third-party products or that these products are insured or otherwise protected. Reputation risks may result even when the third party does not sell financial products. Customers may assume that the financial institution endorses the third-party products. If customers receive poor service or faulty products from the third-party website, they may impute those qualities to the financial institution. Finally, linking to third-party websites that use a name similar to that of the financial institution is almost certain to confuse customers, again increasing reputation risk.[165]

Another factor that increases reputational risk is the degree to which the third-party's website looks like the financial institution's website. Many factors can come into play. First, websites that use similar coloring or placement of functions within the web page could confuse customers. Second, framing or similar technologies that allow customers to view a third-party website through a "frame" from the financial institution's website, perhaps with the bank's name or logo appearing on the frame, could confuse customers. They might believe that the financial institution offers the third-party services or that these services are FDIC-insured. As noted above, this type of confusion can lead to a loss of reputation for the bank.[166] As history instructs, loss of reputation can lead to bank runs and panics.

2. Web Linking—Compliance Risk

Compliance risk occurs when a third party fails to comply with applicable regulations and this regulatory violation

---

[164] U.S. Office of the Comptroller of the Currency, OCC Bull. No. 2003-15, Weblinking: Identifying Risks and Risk Management Techniques 3 (Apr. 23, 2003).

[165] Id. at 4–5.

[166] Id. at 5.

is imputed to the financial institution. It also occurs when the relationship between bank and third party is illegal. Several factors may be involved, including the products and services offered and the relationship between the bank and the third party. For instance, the Real Estate Settlement Procedures Act prohibits certain referral payments as illegal kickbacks.[167] It is typical for websites to pay referral fees when one website drives traffic to another through linked advertisements. This type of arrangement may be prohibited and may trigger a regulatory violation by the financial institution. Further, if the third-party website itself does not comply with appropriate security or privacy measures, customers and regulators may hold the bank responsible for breaches of applicable laws and regulations.[168]

3. Web Linking—Risk Management

The FFIEC has given guidance on dealing with third-party relationships.[169] With respect to Internet links, regulators recommend a process to ensure risks are minimized, including due diligence and contractual guidelines.[170]

During the due diligence phase, banks should ask whether the third party provides the type of content or overall quality of products or services with which the bank wants to be associated. The bank should review the third party's financial statements, customer service levels, privacy policies, security and backup policies, as well as the third party's history of legal and regulatory compliance and whether any proposed linked advertisement complies with the FTC Act.[171]

---

[167] 12 U.S.C. §2607 (RESPA §8).

[168] OCC, WEBLINKING, at 5.

[169] *See generally* FED. FIN. INST. EXAMINATION COUNCIL, RISK MANAGEMENT OF OUTSOURCED TECHNOLOGY (Nov. 28, 2000).

[170] U.S. OFFICE OF THE COMPTROLLER OF THE CURRENCY, OCC BULL. NO. 2003-15, WEBLINKING: IDENTIFYING RISKS AND RISK MANAGEMENT TECHNIQUES 6 (Apr. 23, 2003).

[171] *Id.*

Agreements are strongly recommended if the financial institution is paid for allowing a link to a third-party website.[172] The contract should contain an indemnification in favor of the bank for third-party claims from (1) unsatisfied customers of the third-party service provider, (2) intellectual property infringement, and (3) breaches of confidentiality by the third-party service provider. The contract cannot require the bank to do any activity that is against the law or regulations. It should also contain a termination clause allowing the bank to end the relationship quickly and cleanly if the third party cannot provide quality service to its customers. The bank should ensure that the third-party service provider complies with applicable privacy regulations.[173] FFIEC-regulated financial institutions should also have a plan for dealing with customer complaints.

Finally, the FFIEC highly recommends that financial institutions insert an intermediate page containing a clear disclosure that the user is leaving the website of the financial institution and going to a third-party site. This page should also state that the bank is not responsible for the products and services on the third-party site and that a separate privacy policy will apply and any other disclaimer or notice of which the customer should be aware.

V. MONEY SERVICES BUSINESSES

A. Electronic Transmission of Money

The transmission of money electronically, whether online through a computer, through mobile phones, by means of a credit card, or by any other electronic means, is governed by state and federal laws and regulations. This also includes the conversion of money from one form to another.

---

[172] *Id.* at 7.

[173] *Id.*

On a federal level, the Electronic Fund Transfer Act (EFTA)[174] is the primary applicable statute. Other federal statutes and regulations may also apply, such as the PATRIOT ACT, the Bank Secrecy Act, and Regulation E.[175] Many states also have laws and regulations governing the transfer of money. These state regulators even have their own nonprofit organization, the Money Transfer Regulators Association, to help them align state regulation of money transfers.[176] These laws and regulations, both state and federal, apply to all participants in the financial transaction. Their primary aim is to protect consumers in transactions where some form of value is transmitted electronically. While not banks, money transmitters provide an important function in the economy. Providers of technology that transmit or facilitate the transmission of money, in any form, should be aware of these laws and regulations. Money transmitters also fall under the jurisdiction of the FTC with respect to "unfair and deceptive practices."

1. In re PayPal Litigation

PayPal is an online service that permits the transmission of money from one party to another. It started as a money transfer system in 1999. PayPal currently handles transfers in almost 200 countries in 28 currencies.

In 2002, a lawsuit was filed against PayPal alleging violations of the EFTA and other claims. It was subsequently certified as a class action lawsuit. Although PayPal denied wrongdoing, it agreed in late 2003 to settle, which required it to change its business practices to be EFTA compliant. Because PayPal's business has grown so large, it is now subject to international regulations.

---

[174] 15 U.S.C. §1601 *et seq.*

[175] 12 C.F.R §1005.1 *et seq.*

[176] *See* MONEY TRANSFER REGULATORS ASS'N, http://www.mtraweb.org.

VI. PRACTICAL GUIDANCE

As in *Napster* and *Tasini*, the trend with regulators is that offline laws generally apply online. The financial service regulators echo this general principle. We should expect it to continue. Careful consideration of how technologies interact with customers, especially consumers or the general public, is prudent prior to going live with any such technology. There may be concern that regulations hamper the business, but as with PayPal, they may be unavoidable.

Chapter 5

MOBILE FINANCIAL SERVICES

I. INTRODUCTION

A shopper waves his phone and pays for new clothes. A diner taps her phone and pays for dinner. These technologies are the newest ways to pay on the go. They make it easier to pay for goods and services, but because they are still in their infancy, use carries inherent risks. About 90 million Americans use mobile phones. More recently, mobile banking has made banking available regardless of location: you can conduct business anywhere a cell phone can connect. Mobile banking has also made banking available to individuals who previously did not use or have access to the banking system. Entrepreneurs have developed applications that allow individuals to transfer money to individuals or merchants. These applications can operate outside the current banking system, which also places them outside the scope of regulation. Bank regulators, however, are currently reviewing new mobile applications to determine whether regulation is needed. This author thinks it will be only a matter of time until these applications are expressly regulated since they perform traditional banking functions.

Some of the benefits of these technologies include quick payment, digital receipts, and lower overall transaction costs (including interchange fees). People are comfortable making electronic payments because of their familiarity with credit cards, but that familiarity may give a false sense of security to users of mobile payments.

In what follows, the various technologies that underlie mobile banking and mobile payments platforms are described. After a broad description of the distinction between mobile banking and payment, the regulatory risks and challenges inherent in these relatively new phenomena are laid out. Specifically, the compliance risks, uncertainty in laws and regulations, problems in overlapping regulatory oversight, and lack of data protection are explained. In light of these challenges, some best practices in mobile banking are proposed.

II. OVERVIEW OF MOBILE FINANCIAL SERVICES

A November 2012 survey conducted by the Consumer Research section of the Federal Reserve Board's Division of Consumer and Community Affairs found that Internet-enabled mobile devices are becoming ubiquitous in American daily life.[1] More than 87 percent of U.S. adults have cell phones, for example, and more than half of those are "smart" phones (i.e., Internet-enabled).[2] A significant percentage of device-owning Americans likewise use their phones and tablets to carry out mobile banking and mobile payments—48 percent of smartphone owners reported using their smartphones for mobile banking in 2012, while 24 percent reported using their smartphones to make mobile payments.[3]

The following overview of mobile banking and payments demonstrates the breadth of technological innovations that are changing, or soon will change, the way in which financial institutions operate.

---

[1] BD. OF GOVS. OF THE FED. RESERVE SYS., CONSUMERS AND MOBILE FINANCIAL SERVICES 2013, at 1, *available at* http://www.federalreserve.gov/econresdata/consumers-and-mobile-financial-services-report-201303.pdf [hereinafter FED. RESERVE SYS., 2012 SURVEY].

[2] *Id.*

[3] *Id.* at 4.

A. Mobile Banking

Mobile banking refers to the use of a mobile device, most commonly a cell phone or tablet, to carry out banking activities ranging from simple balance inquiries, to bill payment, to account transfers, and more.[4] According to the Federal Reserve, "[m]obile banking can be done either by accessing your bank's web page through the web browser on your mobile phone, via text messaging, or by using an application downloaded to your mobile phone."[5] An increasing number of financial institutions are offering mobile banking through one or more of these channels; the Federal Deposit Insurance Corporation (FDIC) reported in late 2011 that 19 of the 54 largest banks offer mobile banking services through mobile websites, web apps, and text messaging; 17 more offer services through two of these methods.[6]

A mobile website is a website configured to send and receive data to and from mobile devices. Data from the website is formatted to be easily viewed on a mobile device. Depending on the device's operating system, there may be a need for a unique version of the website that properly interfaces with the operating system and device. For complex functionality often found on bank websites, this may require extensive coding.

"Mobile app" is short for "mobile software application." An application differs from other types of software in that end users access it directly to perform a particular function or group of functions. This is different from operating systems or middleware, which operate without end users even realizing it in many cases.

Text messaging sends small amounts of data over the mobile phone network. This system can also send payment instructions.

---

[4] Jeffrey M. Kopchik, *Mobile Banking: Rewards and Risks*, Supervisory Insights (Fed. Deposit Ins. Corp. Newsl.), Winter 2011.

[5] Fed. Reserve Sys., 2012 Survey, at 7. Note that a laptop is technically a mobile device, as are notebooks and tablets. Most of the discussion in this chapter, however, centers on mobile phones.

[6] Kopchik.

B. Mobile Payments

Mobile payments send funds directly to the recipient, generally through a mobile phone using the phone's web browser, a downloaded web application, or text messaging.[7] (In contrast, mobile banking requires users to log on to a financial institution's website or to launch its web application.) The mobile payment might be charged to the consumer's credit card, deducted from his or her bank account, or included in the consumer's phone bill (referred to as "direct carrier billing" and explained in more detail below).[8] To date, consumers have not widely adopted mobile payment technology, with only about 15 percent of cell phone users in the Federal Reserve Board's survey reporting making a payment by mobile device in 2012—most commonly to pay bills and make online purchases.[9]

1. Mobile Payment Technologies

Three main technologies exist to enable mobile banking and mobile payment: near field communication chips, mobile payment apps, and barcodes and quick response codes.

a. Near Field Communication

Near field communication (NFC), the next generation of radio frequency identification technology,[10] uses near-range, high-frequency wireless communication technology to permit devices to exchange data through a simple tap or

---

[7] FED. RESERVE SYS., 2012 SURVEY, at 12.

[8] *Id.* at 12.

[9] *Id.*

[10] Jamie Carter, *What Is NFC and Why Is It in Your Phone?*, TECHRADAR (Jan. 16, 2013), http://www.techradar.com/us/news/phone-and-communications/what-is-nfc-and-why-is-it-in-your-phone-948410.

wave.[11] To enable data transfers, smartphones are increasingly manufactured with NFC chips; as of mid-2013, chips were included in numerous new Android phone models as well as phones running BlackBerry and Windows Phone operating systems.[12]

NFC is ordinarily associated with mobile wallet technology, which encompasses mobile payment apps wherein consumers can store credit and debit card information and pay for goods and services with a wave or tap of their phones in front of an NFC reader.[13] Google Wallet, which enables users to store customer loyalty card, credit card, and debit card information, is one such app.[14] Isis, another mobile wallet platform backed by AT&T, T-Mobile, and Verizon, was launched nationwide in November 2013.[15] Upon its launch, Isis identified 40 smartphone models that would work with the NFC communication; additionally, it announced that cell phone carriers would hand out free Isis-ready SIM cards (NFC chip–embedded cards that allow owners of phones without NFC technology to use Isis).[16]

b. Barcodes and Quick Response Codes

Some mobile payment apps allow users to make point-of-sale purchases by scanning barcodes or quick response (QR) codes on their phone. Square Wallet, which is known

---

[11] *What Is Near Field Communication (NFC)?*, ComputerWeekly (Jan. 2011), http://www.computerweekly.com/feature/What-is-Near-Field-Communication-NFC.

[12] Matt Hamblen, *Once Again, Apple Bypasses NFC in its New iPhones*, ComputerWorld (Sept. 11, 2013, 6:00 AM EST), http://www.computerworld.com/s/article/9242303/Once_again_Apple_bypasses_NFC_in_its_new_iPhones.

[13] Melanie Pinola, *What Is NFC and How Can I Use It?*, Lifehacker (Sept. 13, 2012, 10:00 AM), http://lifehacker.com/5943006/what-is-nfc-and-how-can-i-use-it.

[14] *Google Wallet*, Google, http://www.google.com/wallet/.

[15] Sarah Perez, *Isis, the Mobile Payments Initiative from AT&T, Verizon & T-Mobile, Launches Across the U.S.*, TechCrunch Blog (Nov. 14, 2013), http://techcrunch.com/2013/11/14/isis-the-mobile-payments-initiative-from-att-verizon-t-mobile-launches-across-the-u-s/.

[16] *Id.*

for its partnership with Starbucks, uses this technology.[17] So too does Apple's Passbook application, which allows consumers to use their iPhones as substitutes for tickets and airline boarding passes.[18] In early 2014, the *Wall Street Journal* reported that Apple was planning an expansion into mobile payment systems, which would presumably be an outgrowth of its Passbook app and would allow it to leverage its sizeable iPhone and iPad customer base and the hundreds of millions of credit cards Apple has stored through its iTunes store.[19]

c. Other Mobile Payment Apps

Despite the increasing availability of mobile wallets using NFC technology, however, the 2012 Federal Reserve survey found that both retailers and consumers were moving toward greater adoption of non-NFC-based payment platforms.[20] In fact, the survey found, mobile payment users were almost twice as likely to use a mobile app or barcode as they were to use NFC payment methods.[21] Mobile payment apps not using NFC or barcode/QR code technology are generally cloud based (credentials to customer's payment source are stored on the cloud), proximity based (merchants detect and authenticate app users within a specific range), or mobile peer-to-peer (P2P) based (payment via automatic clearing house, debt or credit card network, or intra-account transfer initiated using customer's unique identifier).[22] Newer

---

[17] *Use Square Wallet at Starbucks*, SQUARE, https://squareup.com/help/en-us/article/5039-use-square-wallet-at-starbucks.

[18] Matt Hamblen, *Once Again, Apple Bypasses NFC in its New iPhones*, COMPUTERWORLD (Sept. 11, 2013), http://www.computerworld.com/s/article/9242303/Once_again_Apple_bypasses_NFC_in_its_new_iPhones.

[19] Douglas MacMillan & Daisuke Wakabayashi, *Apple Pushes Deeper into Mobile Payments*, WALL ST. J. TECH. BLOG (Jan. 24, 2014, 7:43 PM EST), http://online.wsj.com/news/article_email/SB10001424052702303448204579341290395762338-lMyQjAxMTA0MDIwMzEyNDMyWj.

[20] FED. RESERVE SYS., 2012 SURVEY, at 6.

[21] *Id.*

[22] *Id.*

entrants to the mobile payment app sphere include Stripe,[23] Venmo,[24] and Clinckle.[25]

2. Mobile Payment Methods

a. Direct Carrier Billing

As mentioned at the beginning of this section, mobile payments may be made by charging a consumer's credit card, deducting funds from a bank account, or including the charge on the consumer's wireless bill. The first two payment methods are relatively easy to understand; the third, direct carrier billing (DCB), is a comparatively novel payment form shaping the financial services landscape and thus necessitates a more in-depth discussion.

DCB allows wireless customers to pay for goods or services—most commonly cell phone ringtones, apps, and other goods purchased using mobile payment technology—and include the associated cost on the customer's cell phone bill.[26] According to advocacy group MobilePaymentsToday. com, the number of people worldwide who have wireless phone accounts is more than the combined number of people with bank and credit card accounts.[27] Because of the high adoption rate of cell phones, DCB may be a means of reaching population segments that otherwise lack access to

---

[23] Douglas Macmillan, *Payments Startup Stripe Joins the Billion Dollar Club*, Wall St. J. Tech. Blog (Jan. 22, 2014, 7:45 PM EST), http://online.wsj.com/news/articles/SB10001 424052702304632204579337043662898228.

[24] Natalie Robehmed, *Venmo: The Future of Payments for You and Your Company*, Forbes (July 2, 2013, 12:17 PM), http://www.forbes.com/sites/natalierobehmed/2013/07/02/venmo-the-future-of-payments-for-you-and-your-company/.

[25] Dan Primack, *Clinckle Raises $25 Million to Kill Square*, Fortune, 6/27/2013; http://fortune.com/2013/06/27/clinkle-raises-25-million-to-kill-square/.

[26] Cary Stemle, *Direct Carrier Payment: The World's Most Popular Mobile Payment*, Mobile Payments Today (Oct. 15, 2013), http://www.mobilepaymentstoday.com/blog/11377/Direct-Carrier-Billing-The-world-s-most-popular-mobile-payment-Infographic.

[27] *Id.* (infographic showing 6.8 billion mobile phone accounts compared with 3.5 billion people holding bank accounts and 2.15 billion holding credit card accounts).

traditional banking services, particularly in emerging markets or among younger consumers.[28]

DCB is currently offered by the Google Play Store on mobile devices using its app with select mobile providers.[29] Facebook also supports DCB for accepting mobile payments through the Facebook app with select mobile providers.[30] One of the better-known payment processor for DCB services is BilltoMobile, a company "providing mobile phone authentication and direct billing access to other payment processors and large-scale merchants."[31] BilltoMobile has relationships with all major cell phone providers in the United States—Verizon, AT&T, Sprint, and T-Mobile— meaning customers of any of those carriers who purchase digital content from participating retailers (e.g., the Google Play Store and Facebook) may use BilltoMobile to add the charge to their next wireless bill.[32] Most cell phone providers limit the amount of digital content consumers may charge using DCB during any particular billing cycle to a relatively small amount, such as $25 or $50.[33]

III. REGULATORY RISKS AND CHALLENGES

Clearly, the choices are endless. With the myriad ways to engage in mobile banking and payments, not to mention

---

[28] *Id.*

[29] *Set Up & Pay Using Direct Carrier Billing*, GOOGLE PLAY, https://support.google.com/googleplay/answer/167794?hl=en.

[30] *Which Mobile Phone Service Providers Does Facebook Support for Carrier Billing with Facebook Payments?*, FACEBOOK, https://www.facebook.com/help/236672983110999.

[31] *About BilltoMobile*, BILLTOMOBILE, http://www.billtomobile.com/about/.

[32] Sara Perez, *Mobile Payments Company BilltoMobile Launches One-Click Checkout for the Mobile Web*, TECHCRUNCH BLOG (Jan. 18, 2012), http://techcrunch.com/2012/01/18/mobile-payments-company-billtomobile-launches-one-click-checkout-for-the-mobile-web/.

[33] *See, e.g.*, *BilltoMobile FAQs*, VERIZON, http://support.verizonwireless.com/support/faqs/FeaturesandOptionalServices/billto.html ("You can purchase up to $25 in digital content (per mobile number/bill cycle) straight from select merchants' websites. The purchase is then charged directly to your Verizon Wireless bill."); *Use Billtomobile to Charge Purchases to Your Sprint Bill*, SPRINT (last updated Nov. 16, 2013), http://support.sprint.com/ (limiting BilltoMobile purchases to $50 per number, per billing cycle).

the countless industry players with whom financial institutions might choose to partner, it is no wonder that regulation in this arena is full of uncertainty, subject to overlapping oversight, and fraught with risks. These risks are based on the lack of standards, the confusion created by overlapping regulatory oversight, privacy concerns, and similar issues.

A. Bank Entities

1. Risks Similar to Traditional Banking Activities

The FDIC noted in late 2012 that financial institutions engaging in mobile banking and payment face many of the same issues using these platforms as they do in traditional banking activities. These include possible fraud; challenges posed by managing multiple vendors in the payment process; customer credit and liquidity issues; compliance with the Bank Secrecy Act (BSA) and its anti–money laundering (AML) standards;[34] reputation management; and operations and information technology difficulties.[35] These challenges take on new dimensions in the mobile arena, however, and fall principally along two lines: (1) issues arising from adding parties to the chain of transactions involved in executing a mobile payment or banking action, and (2) issues arising from protection of data stored on, or transmitted through the use of, mobile devices.

a. Disintermediation

The first challenge, inserting entities into the mix, is referred to as the "disintermediation" problem[36] and is discussed further below in Section C.3. Financial institutions

---

[34] See Chapter 9.

[35] Robert C. Drozdowski et al., *Mobile Payments: An Evolving Landscape*, SUPERVISORY INSIGHTS (Fed. Deposit Ins. Corp. Newsl.), Winter 2012, *available at* http://www.fdic.gov/regulations/examinations/supervisory/insights/siwin12/mobile.html.

[36] *Id.*

that develop mobile banking or payment applications must work closely with app developers to ensure that the final products facilitate transactions that comply with the institutions' BSA/AML obligations.[37] Moreover, if a third party manages the app, financial institutions must also verify that the third party complies with applicable BSA/AML requirements.[38] This can be particularly difficult because many third-party app providers are entrepreneurial ventures unversed in regulatory constraints.[39]

b. Data Protection

Data protection, a challenge for all financial institutions, takes on added significance in the mobile context. As with BSA/AML compliance, financial institutions must work with third-party vendors to develop and manage mobile banking and payment systems in a way that adequately safeguards customer information.[40] Not only is this a requirement under the Gramm-Leach-Bliley Act (GLBA), whose "Safeguards Rule" mandates that companies collecting customer personal information have data protection measures in place, but also it is an important part of managing an institution's reputation. The lack—or the perceived lack—of privacy controls in mobile banking and payment platforms is discussed in more detail below. Data protection is also an essential element in any fraud prevention plan.

B. Applicable Laws and Regulations

Just as mobile banking and payment institutions share some of the same risks as traditional banks, they also share the same laws and regulations. As the FDIC noted in 2012, financial institutions offering mobile banking and payments

---

[37] Id.

[38] Id.

[39] Id.

[40] Id.

must comply with existing legal requirements.[41] Given that many laws and regulations predate mobile financial services technology, however, it is likely that institutions may not know how to achieve full compliance. In such cases, "creative solutions may be required": for example, when deciding how to satisfy disclosure requirements given a small mobile phone screen on which to display information.[42] Despite this uncertainty, the FDIC has provided some informal guidance on how federal banking laws and regulations apply in the mobile sphere:

- *Electronic Fund Transfer Act (EFTA)*.[43] The EFTA continues to apply when the payment underlying a mobile banking transaction is made from a customer's account via an EFT. Initial disclosures that must be made prior to the first EFT payment is made include, among other things, notification of the error resolution process and the terms and conditions of the EFT relationship.[44] This applies to all types of financial service companies.
- *Regulation Z*.[45] Requirements imposed by Reg. Z apply when a mobile payment is made using funds provided by a credit card or other credit account covered by Reg. Z.[46] Key disclosures normally expected under Reg. Z—including those disclosing costs, fees, dispute resolution processes, and billing systems—must also be made in the mobile setting.[47] This applies to lending activities (but not securities lending).
- *Unfair, Deceptive, or Abusive Acts or Practices (UDAP) under the FTC Act/Unfair, Deceptive or Abusive Acts or Practices*

---

[41] *Id.*

[42] *Id.*

[43] 15 U.S.C. §§1693–1693r; 12 C.F.R. §1005.

[44] Robert C. Drozdowski et al., *Mobile Payments: An Evolving Landscape*, SUPERVISORY INSIGHTS (Fed. Deposit Ins. Corp. Newsl.), Winter 2012, *available at* http://www.fdic.gov/regulations/examinations/supervisory/insights/siwin12/mobile.html.

[45] 15 U.S.C. §§1601–1616; 12 C.F.R. §1026.

[46] Drozdowski *et al.*

[47] *Id.*

(UDAAP) under the Consumer Financial Protection Act.[48] The authority to enforce the UDAP rule is held by the FTC, while similar authority to regulate against UDAAP was given to the Consumer Financial Protection Bureau (CFPB) by the Consumer Financial Protection Act of 2010.[49] Both acts, which prohibit unfair and deceptive practices in or affecting commerce (as well as abusive practices under the UDAAP rule) apply to mobile banking and payment transactions, regardless of how the underlying payment is made.[50] The FTC has developed policy statements defining what constitutes an "unfair" or "deceptive" practice,[51] while the CFPB has recently created its own deception of "unfair" and "deceptive" practices, augmented by a definition of "abusive" practices as well.[52] These apply to consumer-oriented mobile financial services.

- *GLBA.*[53] The GLBA applies any time a financial institution handles consumer personal information; in the mobile sphere, institutions must still provide privacy notices and opt-out provisions regarding information sharing. Additionally, financial entities must continue to comply with GLBA data protection requirements.[54] This applies to all financial services companies, but regulations under GLBA are promulgated and applied by different regulators.

---

[48] 15 U.S.C. § 45(a); 12 U.S.C. § 5536(a)(1)(B).

[49] Drozdowski *et al.*

[50] *Id.*

[51] Thomas G. Pareigat & Meg Sczyrba, *Don't Get Caught in the UDAP Net*, ABA BANK COMPL., May-June 2011, at 11, *available at* http://www.aba.com/Products/bankcompliance /Documents/MayJune11CoverStory.pdf.

[52] *See, e.g.*, Consumer Fin. Prot. Bureau Bull. 2013-07, *Prohibition of Unfair, Deceptive, or Abusive Acts or Practices in the Collection of Consumer Debts* (July 10, 2013), *available at* http:// www.consumerfinance.gov/f/201307_cfpb_bulletin_unfair-deceptive-abusive-practices. pdf.

[53] 15 U.S.C. §§6801–6809; 12 C.F.R. pt. 332 (FDIC privacy rule); 12 C.F.R. pt. 364, app. B (Interagency Guidelines Establishing Information Security Standards, as published in FDIC's rules).

[54] Robert C. Drozdowski *et al.*, *Mobile Payments: An Evolving Landscape*, SUPERVISORY INSIGHTS (Fed. Deposit Ins. Corp. Newsl.), Winter 2012, *available at* http://www.fdic.gov/ regulations/examinations/supervisory/insights/siwin12/mobile.html.

- *FDIC Insurance or National Credit Union Association Insurance.*[55] Consumers using mobile payment technology are protected by FDIC or NCUA insurance to the extent the underlying funds are deposited in an FDIC- or NCUA-insured account. However, such insurance does not necessarily protect a consumer's funds if a nonbank vendor in the mobile payment chain files for bankruptcy or becomes insolvent.[56] This applies to FDIC- and NCUA-regulated entities.

C. Overlapping Oversight

Perhaps one of the largest challenges financial institutions involved in mobile banking and payment activities confront today is the overlap in regulatory oversight of their actions. No fewer than five supervisory agencies may have some degree of control over financial institutions, depending on the type of transaction at issue (e.g., a purchase made via DCB or via NFC chip technology) and the underlying payment source (e.g., consumer credit or debit card, or EFT).[57] These agencies include the following:

- *Bank regulators.* The FDIC, Office of the Comptroller of the Currency, Federal Reserve Board, and NCUA all have responsibility for overseeing financial institutions.[58]
- *CFPB.* The CFPB now has exclusive rulemaking power in the consumer financial protection arena, which gives it authority over nonbank entities offering consumer financial products and the ability to regulate

---

[55] 12 C.F.R. pt. 330 (codifying FDIC insurance provisions); 12 C.F.R. pt. 745 (codifying insurance provisions covering credit union member accounts).

[56] Drozdowski *et al.*

[57] Marianne Crowe, Mary Kepler & Cynthia Merritt, The U.S. Regulatory Landscape for Mobile Payments (Apr. 24, 2012), *available at* http://www.frbatlanta.org/documents/rprf/rprf_pubs/120730_wp.pdf (summary report of meeting between Mobile Payments Industry Workgroup and federal and state regulators).

[58] Drozdowski *et al.* at n.20.

some traditional banking activities, including the
EFTA and Reg. Z.[59]

- *FTC.* The FTC, in contrast with the CFPB, has oversight authority for consumer protection, but not consumer *financial* protection. In other words, the FTC
does not have jurisdiction over depository institutions.[60] Other than that exception, and the exclusion
of insurance companies and telecommunications
companies, the FTC's jurisdiction is notably broad
and may still be applicable in the financial technology industry.[61]
- *Financial Crimes Enforcement Network.* FinCEN, an arm
of the U.S. Department of the Treasury, is charged
with fighting crime in the financial system, such as
money laundering.[62] FinCEN is the supervisory
authority responsible for compliance with the BSA.
- *Federal Communications Commission.* The FCC's supervisory authority extends to wireless service providers
and encompasses the truth-in-billing rules, which are
meant to improve customers' understanding of their
phone bills.[63] The FCC's authority likely covers DCB
as well because that payment method implicates a
customer's wireless bill.[64]

The agencies responsible for regulating financial institutions do coordinate with one another to some extent,
primarily through the Federal Financial Institutions

---

[59] *Id.*

[60] Mercedes Kelley Tunstall, *How the CFPB and the FTC Interact (Part I)*, CFPB MONITOR (Ballard Spahr Cons. Fin. Servs. Grp., Phila.), July 7, 2011, *available at* http://www.cfpb monitor.com/2011/07/07/how-the-cfpb-and-the-ftc-interact-part-i/.

[61] *About the FTC,* FED. TRADE COMM'N, http://www.ftc.gov/about-ftc ("The FTC is the only federal agency with both consumer protection and competition jurisdiction in broad sectors of the economy.").

[62] *What We Do,* FIN. CRIMES ENFORCEMENT NETWORK, http://www.fincen.gov/about_ fincen/wwd/index.html.

[63] *Truth-in-Billing Policy,* FED. COMMC'NS COMM'N, http://transition.fcc.gov/cgb/policy /truthinbill.html.

[64] Robert C. Drozdowski et al., *Mobile Payments: An Evolving Landscape,* SUPERVISORY INSIGHTS (Fed. Deposit Ins. Corp. Newsl.), Winter 2012, at n.20, *available at* http://www. fdic.gov/regulations/examinations/supervisory/insights/siwin12/mobile.html.

Examination Council (FFIEC).[65] The FFIEC, however, has not updated its guidance on compliance and data security in Internet-enabled banking since 2011.[66] Moreover, the FFIEC's guidance is not specific to mobile banking and thus fails to provide comprehensive direction for addressing risks associated with mobile applications and malware.[67]

While financial institutions may find overlapping oversight burdensome, consumers too may find it a negative. The current regulatory scheme means that the extent to which consumers are protected depends on the payment underlying their mobile transaction—whether it is credit card, debit card, EFT, or DCB.[68]

1. Lack of Agreement on How to Address Overlap in Oversight

Although there is no question that financial institutions face regulatory oversight from numerous governmental agencies, there is little agreement as to what should be done about this circumstance. On the one hand, most policymakers seem to think that the existing regulatory framework can be adapted to fit the needs of mobile banking and payment technology.[69] All agree, however, that some level of coordination among the multiple stakeholder agencies is needed.[70] As Consumers Union staff attorney Suzanne Martindale noted at an introductory hearing on mobile payments in the House of Representatives in March 2012,

---

[65] FED. FIN. INST. EXAMINATION COUNCIL, https://www.ffiec.gov/.

[66] Gail Sullivan, *Mobile Banking Continues Surge, ABA Report Finds*, CQ ROLL CALL WASH. BANKING BRIEFING, 2013 WL 75486214 (Oct. 3, 2013). The FFIEC's 2011 guidance was aimed at increasing authentication in online banking transactions. *Supplement to Authentication in an Internet Banking Environment*, FED. FIN. INSTITUTIONS EXAMINATIONS COUNCIL (2011), *available at* https://www.ffiec.gov/pdf/Auth-ITS-Final%206-22-11%20(FFIEC%20 Formated).pdf.

[67] Sullivan.

[68] Kevin Wack, *Lawmakers Begin to Explore Mobile Payments Security*, PAYMENTSSOURCE (Mar. 23, 2012, 9:40 AM EST), http://www.paymentssource.com/news/Lawmakers-Begin-To-Explore-Mobile-Payments-Security-3010096-1.html.

[69] Joe Adler, *Do Mobile Payments Need More Regulation?*, AM. BANKER (Apr. 5, 2012, 1:13 PM EST), http://www.americanbanker.com/issues/177_67/mobile-pay-1048180-1.html? zkPrintable=1&nopagination=1.

[70] *Id.*

"[t]here needs to be some cooperation between the wireless and banking regulatory frameworks, because otherwise we're going to have a mess."[71]

On the other hand, viewpoints diverge on *when* regulators should become involved in adapting the laws to the new technologies. Some legal professionals say that the mobile banking and payment industry is too young to merit revision of applicable law and that altering the regulatory landscape now would be detrimental.[72] Others believe that regulatory responsibilities should be clarified early in the development of new payment and banking technology, with participation of those in the mobile industry.[73]

2. Lack of Privacy Protection

Financial institutions must adhere to certain data protection standards when handling personal customer information under the GLBA. However, financial institutions should be aware that data privacy is not just a matter of legal compliance but a public relations issue as well. Consumers in the 2012 Federal Reserve study reported lower confidence in security of mobile financial services technology than they had in a 2011 survey, suggesting that consumers take a generally dim view toward data protection and mobile banking or payment systems.[74] Security concerns were the most often cited reason for not using mobile payment services and the second most cited reason for not using mobile banking.[75] Areas of highest concern were hacker security breaches, loss or theft of a mobile device, third-party interception of phone data, company misuse of personal information, and malware

---

[71] *Id.*

[72] *Id.*

[73] *Id.* (noting that, at a Senate Banking Committee hearing on mobile payments, a representative of the Federal Reserve Bank of Boston said that "'clarity of regulatory responsibilities' among various agencies involved 'needs to be established early on, with input from the mobile stakeholders'").

[74] FED. RESERVE SYS., 2012 SURVEY, at 6.

[75] *Id.* at 2.

or viruses.[76] Consumers noted similar concerns about mobile payments.[77]

These results demonstrate (1) possible explanations why adoption of mobile banking and payment is slower than it otherwise might be; and (2) how financial institutions can, through transparency regarding privacy and data protection practices, alleviate those concerns and encourage use of mobile platforms to their advantage. Financial institutions can further gain customer confidence by clarifying which party in the mobile banking or payment chain—whether it be an app provider, a payment processor, or a financial institution itself, for example—is responsible for resolving various types of errors and disputes. Both the EFTA and Reg. Z require customer notification for error and dispute resolution processes; however, neither regulation addresses how notification in the mobile technology sequence should work. Financial institutions should also be aware that the CFPB is currently examining "the effectiveness of disclosure practices in new mobile payment business models" to confirm that consumers have adequate information about error resolution processes with regard to each party involved.[78]

3. Nonbank Entities

Mobile payments are often facilitated with the help of a nonbank entity, such as a mobile payment processor, social network, or online payment provider.[79] These entities are subject to the laws and regulations applicable to the type of services they provide. If, for example, a DCB company provides payment processing services, it will be subject to both FTC and CFPB oversight of unfair, deceptive, or abusive

---

[76] *Id.* at 6.

[77] *Id.*

[78] *See* MARIANNE CROWE, MARY KEPLER & CYNTHIA MERRITT, THE U.S. REGULATORY LANDSCAPE FOR MOBILE PAYMENTS 7 (Apr. 24, 2012), *available at* http://www.frbatlanta.org/documents/rprf/rprf_pubs/120730_wp.pdf.

[79] *Id.*

acts or practices.[80] It may even be subject to regulation on a state-by-state basis. In its Winter 2012 *Supervisory Highlights Journal,* the FDIC raised the issue of "disintermediation" (the act of "cutting out the middleman") of financial institution involvement in mobile payments. Because information in this publication is primarily directed toward traditional financial institutions, in-depth discussion of regulation of nonbank entities is omitted. However, suffice it to say, the FDIC's 2012 commentary caused some in the legal field to remark that the FDIC is showing interest in supervising and possibly exerting authority over nonbank entities as they become increasingly significant players in the mobile payment industry.[81]

D. Mobile Banking Best Practices

The numerous challenges facing financial institutions engaged in mobile banking and payment might seem overwhelming, perhaps even more so in light of current regulatory uncertainty and possible future changes. There are still steps that bank entities can take, however, to ensure the greatest chances of success in both customer satisfaction and in legal compliance. Following are some mobile banking and payment best practices.

1. BSA/AML Compliance

Mobile payments are a novel way for criminals, terrorists, and others to launder money, by transferring income from illicit activities using mobile applications.[82] This opportunity may allow offenders to evade reporting requirements and traditional controls meant to prevent activities related

---

[80] *Id.*

[81] John Dodge, *Mobile Payment Risks,* 18 CYBERSPACE L. 1 (2013).

[82] Timothy R. McTaggart, *An Overview of Mobile Payments and Their Regulation,* BANKING L.J. (June 2010), *available at* http://www.pepperlaw.com/publications_article.aspx?ArticleKey=1813.

to money laundering and terrorist financing.[83] Because of the risk of abuse of mobile payments, financial institutions should ensure that their internal control process addresses the risk presented by mobile payments. This may be done through a combination of independent AML audits of mobile payment channels, updates of suspicious activity reporting and procedures to cover problematic mobile payments, and employee training to recognize the threat posed by mobile payments.[84] AML compliance issues are discussed in more detail in Chapter 10.

2. EFTA and Reg. Z Compliance

As discussed earlier in this chapter, a lack of perceived privacy protection over mobile banking and payment transactions may hinder adoption of these platforms. From a customer relations perspective, clarifying responsibilities between the financial institution and third-party vendors in the error resolution process is important. However, it is significant from a legal compliance standpoint as well, and the CFPB may soon mandate clear disclosure of this type.[85] It would benefit financial institutions, therefore, to proactively allocate responsibility in error resolution among themselves and third parties and incorporate notice of this allocation in customer disclosure statements.

3. GLBA Compliance

Financial institutions are already required under GLBA to deliver privacy notices and opt-out information to consumers.[86] In developing and managing mobile banking and

---

[83] *Id.*

[84] *Id.*

[85] *See* MARIANNE CROWE, MARY KEPLER & CYNTHIA MERRITT, THE U.S. REGULATORY LANDSCAPE FOR MOBILE PAYMENTS 7 (Apr. 24, 2012), *available at* http://www.frbatlanta.org/documents/rprf/rprf_pubs/120730_wp.pdf.

[86] McTaggart.

payment platforms, however, financial institutions frequently interact with third-party vendors whose obligations under GLBA are, at best, uncertain. To comply with GLBA, a financial institution should put controls in place to ensure that third parties safeguard customer financial information and limit sharing in the same manner that the financial institution itself does, in keeping with its privacy policy.[87] This would likely be carried out through contract with the third-party service provider.[88]

4. Data Security

In addition to ensuring compliance with applicable laws and regulations, financial institutions offering mobile banking and payment platforms should take care to provide the highest level of data protection possible to customers using these platforms. The FFIEC addresses methods to accomplish this in its supplemental guidance on Internet banking authentication, released in June 2011.[89] In addition to regular risk assessments, the FFIEC suggests putting in place processes to mitigate known risks as well as educating customers on potential hazards and ways to decrease the risk of data theft, loss, or misuse.[90]

E. Banking the Underbanked

Despite the regulatory problems just discussed, mobile banking and payment are reaching markets that, in the past, have avoided most traditional banking activities (e.g., owning a bank or savings account). This segment of the population

---

[87] Id.

[88] Id.

[89] Press Release, Fed. Fin. Institutions Examination Council, *FFIEC Release Supplemental Guidance on Internet Banking Authentication* (June 28, 2011), *available at* http://www.ffiec.gov/press/pr062811.htm.

[90] Id.

is commonly referred to as the "underbanked." According to the FDIC's 2012 survey on consumers and mobile financial services, the share of "unbanked" consumers—those who owned neither a checking, nor a savings, nor a money market account—is declining.[91] In the survey, unbanked consumers most commonly reported not needing or wanting a depository account; others specified a belief that they did not have enough funds to merit an account, while still others thought their infrequent use of checks made an account unnecessary.[92]

Many population sectors prone to falling into the underbanked and unbanked categories—those in younger generations, minorities, and low-income earners—nonetheless frequently own cell phones.[93] Given the rise of mobile banking and mobile payment platforms and the prevalence of cell phone ownership among the underbanked and unbanked, financial institutions have significant potential to increase access to financial services.[94] And achieving financial inclusion does not appear to take considerable effort by financial institutions: The FDIC survey found that nearly half of underbanked consumers used some type of mobile banking in the year preceding the survey.[95] Accordingly, financial institutions would do well to recognize and exploit the opportunities, rather than focusing solely on the legal difficulties, posed by these new financial services technologies.

F. Bring Your Own Device

The advent of employees using their own mobile devices for work purposes adds to security concerns, such as potential hacks, software vulnerabilities, and loss or theft

---

[91] FED. RESERVE SYS., 2012 SURVEY, at 5.

[92] Id.

[93] Id. at 4.

[94] Id.

[95] Id. at 2.

of the mobile devices themselves. Here are some of the risks involved:

- *Data leakage.* Improper use could result in business data "leaking" into a personal database such as an e-mail address book. Should a financial institution trust its data to an Internet service provider? Probably not without a lot of negotiations.
- *Privacy issues.* If not handled properly, a financial institution may be at risk for exposure of personally identifiable information (PII) through the employees' device.
- *Data loss.* Without proper backup and business continuity procedures, employees may have business data solely on a personal device that is then lost when the device is lost.
- *Other.* The employee device may not have adequate virus protection or regular software updates and therefore be vulnerable to hacking.

How would an employer ever know about any of these scenarios?

Still, the use of personal mobile devices for business purposes has advantages for both the employee and the business. Employees can have whatever device they want. The financial institution saves money by not having to buy devices for its employees. It also has the potential for making those employees available 24/7. Software programs do exist that address these issues, but they are not perfect. This may be a challenge that future entrepreneurs can address further.

IV. PRACTICAL GUIDANCE

Mobile financial services are evolving quickly within the financial services industry, and the necessary legal and regulatory structures will undoubtedly change just as quickly. However, as discussed in the prior chapter, when issuing regulations to address new technologies, regulators look first to existing laws and regulations. The offline legal framework can easily apply to mobile and other technology-heavy activities, at least until specific new laws are created.

CHAPTER 6

CLOUD COMPUTING

I. INTRODUCTION

The National Institute of Standards and Technology (NIST) defines cloud computing as "a model for enabling convenient, on-demand network access to a shared pool of configurable computing resources (e.g., networks, servers, storage, applications, and services) that can be rapidly provisioned and released with minimal management effort or cloud provider interaction."[1]

This chapter discusses cloud computing generally along with available regulatory guidance and best practices.

---

[1] NIST, Special Publication 800-145; p,6, http://csrc.nist.gov/publications/nistpubs/800-145/SP800-145.pdf.

Software issues are further addressed in Chapter 7. Data security and personally identifiable data and privacy issues are addressed further in Chapter 9.

II. CLOUD COMPUTING

Cloud computing can come in three different flavors.

1. *IaaS.* This stands for "infrastructure as a service," where the hardware and network infrastructure is provided by a third party.
2. *PaaS.* This stands for "platform as a service," where the use of hardware in combination with a specific operating system and perhaps middleware is provided, but the user-facing application is not.
3. *SaaS.* This stands for "software as a service," where the use of one specific software is made available over a network, typically the Internet. But more recently, private secure cloud offerings have been growing.

Cloud outsourcing includes traditional "service bureau" services (e.g., payroll), information technology (IT) outsourcing (e.g., processing services provided from remote data center), and technology-heavy business process outsourcing.

Cloud outsourcing is used for a number of reasons. Because cloud computing allows customers to access computing power at a fraction of the cost of actually buying the equipment, financial savings is often one goal. Other motivations include cost identification, savings, or predictability; access to infrastructure or software at a lower cost; and management focus on core competencies

A major cloud outsourcing, similar to outsourcing in general (discussed in Chapter 8), has several significant characteristics, including significant resource commitment and a fixed contract term, often with complex contract terms. The market for cloud computing services is still in flux.

A. Risks of Cloud Computing

Some risks are inherent in the cloud computing model. For instance, information security breaches may not be immediately noticed by the service provider. Data may be held or processed in jurisdictions without adequate data protection, leading to noncompliance with privacy and data protection laws or, worse, a data hack or breach of some sort. Often, service providers have a "one size fits all" offering, which gives them too much discretion in the contract. Also, service providers may want to use data for their own purposes, without express permission from the cloud customer.

Other risks stem from the fact that accountability and responsibility for the services may be with a chain of unknown subcontractors of the cloud provider. Also, the customer loses some degree of control over his data and data processing. The infrastructure may be shared with unknown parties, leading to possible data security issues. In general, the cloud customer may not have the ability to adequately monitor the service provider or his own data.

Of course, the customer should carefully review the terms and conditions of the cloud provider contract, which may contain some onerous terms. Here are some sample provisions taken from the basic Amazon Web Services terms:

> You are responsible for properly configuring and using the Service Offerings and taking your own steps to maintain appropriate security, protection and backup of Your Content, which may include the use of encryption technology to protect Your Content from unauthorized access and routine archiving Your Content.[2]

Similar conditions appear in the Apple iCloud terms:

> Apple reserves the right to modify or terminate the Service (or any part thereof), either temporarily or permanently. Apple may post on our website and/or will send an email to the primary

---

[2] AWS Customer Agreement, http://aws.amazon.com/agreement/, last retrieved, 07/02/14.

address associated with your Account to provide notice of any material changes to the Service. It is your responsibility to check your iCloud email address and/or primary email address registered with Apple for any such notices. You agree that Apple shall not be liable to you or any third party for any modification or cessation of the Service.[3]

Clearly, no business should permit terms like those above in a cloud computing contract. Initially this led to a slow acceptance of cloud computing, but more recently, secure cloud providers have entered the market. These providers offer security, visibility into the service providers' business continuity and disaster recovery plans, and sometimes even real service level agreements (SLAs).

B. FFIEC-Regulated Institutions

According to the Federal Financial Institutions Examination Council's *IT Examination Handbook,* including the *Outsourcing Technology Services Booklet,* financial institutions need to consider risk and risk management when making any decision to outsource. They should perform adequate due diligence on the service provider, including confirming that the service provider is able to comply with the same regulatory challenges that financial institutions face. The financial institution should have the ability to audit the outsourced cloud service. There should be some way to effectively monitor the security of the data kept in the cloud. Also, the financial institution should make sure the service provider has the resources and plans to ensure its own continuity of business.

Because of the risks inherent in outsourcing to a third party, cloud computing business models have evolved away from the basic cloud provisions cited above to more robust and secure "private cloud" offerings. These often provide more SLAs and other assurances that the service and the

---

[3]iCLOUD TERMS AND CONDITIONS, https://www.apple.com/legal/internet-services/icloud/en/terms.html, last retrieved 07/02/14.

service provider is in business for the long haul. These newer models are not unlike "old school" network outsourcing.

C. European Commission

The European Commission has issued a communication called "Unleashing the Potential of Cloud Computing in Europe" with the hope of creating consistent cloud-computing standards and contracts in Europe.[1] The communication attempts to (1) develop fairer and clearer terms for SLAs through model terms, (2) advance consistent data protection and security standards, (3) create consistent interoperability standards, (4) provide data portability standards, and (5) reduce the environmental impact of large data centers through consumption and emission standards.

D. Recent Cases Addressing Cloud Computing

There are not that many court cases involving cloud computing, but here are some of the more interesting ones.

- *Forward Foods LLC v. Next Proteins, Inc.*, 2008 BL 238516 (N.Y. Sup. Ct. 2008). Use of cloud may increase number of "contacts" for personal jurisdiction.
- *Cartoon Network v. CSC Holdings, Inc.*, 536 F.3d 121 (2d Cir. 2008), *cert. denied*, 129 U.S. 2890 (2009). Cloud-based remote storage digital video recorder system did not directly infringe on content providers' copyrights.
- *Google v. United States*, 95 Fed. Cl. 661 (2011). Google challenged the Department of the Interior's decision to use Microsoft's cloud services for messaging system and requested an open and competitive bid process.

---

[1] Dated 9/27/12, *See also* Cloud Standards Coordination, Final Report, Nov. 2013, VERSION 1.0.

E. Negotiating the Cloud Computing Agreement

As with any large or complex outsourcing, there are many issues that should be addressed when negotiating the terms with the service provider.

- Will the service provider provide any upfront investment?
- Is the service provider guaranteeing any pricing or cost reductions?
- How long is the term of the agreement? Is there a "termination for convenience" clause?
- Are there SLAs with credits?
- Has there been adequate planning and due diligence?

F. Other Resources

The Cloud Security Alliance[5] (CSA) is a nonprofit industry group with a mission to promote the use of best practices for providing security assurance within cloud computing. It comprises industry practitioners, corporations, associations, and other key stakeholders. It provides the Security, Trust, and Assurance Registry, which documents the security controls provided by various cloud computing offerings. The CSA also provides education with an emphasis on cloud security issues and even a Certificate of Cloud Security Knowledge.

The International Working Group on Data Protection in Telecommunications[6] (IWGDPT) was founded in 1983 to promote privacy in telecommunications. It has published the following recommendations for the use of cloud computing.

---

[5] cloudsecurityalliance.org.

[6] http://www.datenschutz-berlin.de/content/europa-international/international-working-group-on-data-protection-in-telecommunications-iwgdpt.

— Cloud computing data protection standards should not be lower than conventional data processing.
— Companies should assess privacy impact and risks before embarking on cloud computing projects.
— Service providers should offer greater transparency, security, accountability, and trust in cloud computing solutions and more balanced contracts.
— There should be further efforts in research, third-party certification, standardization, privacy by design technologies, and other related schemes to increase trust in cloud computing.
— Legislators should reassess adequacy of existing laws with respect to cross-border transfers of data and privacy safeguards.
— Privacy and data protection authorities should continue to provide information to parties involved in cloud computing and legislators regarding privacy and data protection.[7]

The IWGDPT also offers advice on best practices for using cloud computing. First, there should be adequate audit trails to show user locations and allow transaction monitoring. Copying and deletion of any audit trails should be recorded so that unauthorized activities can be detected.

The service provider should have in place technical measures to prevent illegal transfers and automatic logging of all uses of personal data. Encryption keys should not be used by more than one customer at a time. Unused or obsolete personal data should be properly and adequately deleted.

The service provider should provide transparency regarding data location and storage and regarding subcontractors and their service contracts. They should follow best practices and allow third parties to assess the adequacy of their service through benchmarking and other means. The providers' standard terms and conditions should respect privacy and have appropriate safeguards.

The IWGDPT also has advice for cloud customers:

---

[7] *Id.*

— Ensure location transparency in contracts.
— Restrict data transfers by provider and ensure that [you have] the ability to inspect transfers.
— Ensure the contract with the service provider only allows it to process data pursuant to [your] instructions.
— The contract should include right to hire a third party to monitor processing of personal data in contract.
— Perform risk assessment before engagement of a service provider.
— Regularly review risk assessments so long as personal data is being processed.
— Before engagement, ensure there is a real exit option.
— Determine whether there should be a copy of data outside of provider's control.
— Ensure [you] will receive prompt notification in case of data breach and that [you] can fulfill any ensuing legal obligations.
— Ensure contract allows data subjects to exercise rights of access, rectification, erasure, or blocking of data.

G. Practical Guidance

Cloud outsourcing contracts present some unique negotiation considerations. An effective cloud outsourcing contract requires a clear definition of the parties' expectations, including clear service description and pricing. Accountability features such as practical SLAs with credits and termination rights give the cloud customer flexibility to deal with future business and technology changes. Most important, the contract should adequately protect all customer data, relevant to the circumstances, and allow for timely transfer of all data back to the customer at the end of the contract.

CHAPTER 7

TECHNOLOGY LICENSING

I. Introduction

This chapter addresses intellectual property (IP) licensing issues inherent in technology licensing. These can involve software licensing, but a growing market involves software as a service (SaaS). SaaS allows customers to use the software without buying a license. SaaS may be structured as a subscription agreement or a term license agreement, typically beginning with a one-year term and annual renewals thereafter.

IP ownership clauses can and should be drafted to meet the specific situation at hand. It is important to not let terminology or pride of authorship control the situation. Careful review and understanding of each party's concerns and business needs will assist the drafting of these important clauses.

A software or other technology license may cover several types of IP. Clearly copyright is one type, but trade secrets, patents, and even trademarks may be inherent in the software license agreement. The licensor owns the technology while the licensee-customer buys the license or right to use the technology. This chapter applies across the financial services industry, except for Section III, which applies only to Federal Deposit Insurance Corp. (FDIC) regulated institutions.

II. Licensing Variables

Different variables come into play in a software or other technology license. "Technology license" here means any rights to use a specific technology, whether it is software that runs on the licensee's hardware or software that runs on the licensor's hardware but is accessed by the licensee through a network connection (most commonly via the Internet). This configuration is more commonly referred to as a SaaS license. In this model, the license and right to use software and hardware are intertwined. Other licenses may involve databases or even data itself. Common variables found in all types of licensing include the following.

A. Exclusive vs. Nonexclusive

An exclusive license allows only one party to use the software or technology. This type of license has to be drafted carefully, for even if the licensor retains a narrow bundle of rights, it can be found to have infringed the exclusive license to a work it created.[1] It is not always clear whether a license is exclusive.[2] For this reason, most technology licenses are drafted as nonexclusive licenses. This allows the licensor to market and sell the technology to multiple customers and allows the licensee to have enough rights to make use of the technology in its business.

B. Internal Use

Another variable is the ability to use technology internally in the licensee's business or externally in other contexts. Technology licensors generally frown on external use because it may reduce the licensor's ability to sell to other customers. If those external parties can use the software without buying a license, then sales of the software would be reduced. Common exceptions to this include affiliated companies, customers of the licensee, and third-party service providers or outsourcers.

Use by affiliated companies is often negotiated when the licensee is a large company that has many affiliates. Often, these companies run software from centralized technology centers where all of their affiliates have access to the data center. Use of the company's technology is often shared among its affiliates. For instance, a company may have several subsidiaries or divisions, each of which is focused on a particular market segment. However, all would need access to accounting software, HR software, or other technology

---

[1] *See* Kepner-Tregoe Inc v. Victor H Vroom, 186 F.3d 283 (2d Cir. 1999) (licensor found liable for breach of contract and copyright infringement when he exceeded usage rights retained in materials he coauthored that were otherwise exclusively licensed to licensee).

[2] Courts generally agree that it is the actual language in the agreement, not merely the use of the term "exclusive," that determines the meaning of a license. *See generally* HyperQuest, Inc. v. N'Site Solutions, Inc., 632 F.3d 377 (7th Cir. 2011); *In re* Isbell Records, Inc., 586 F.3d 334, 337–38 (5th Cir. 2009); SCO Grp., Inc. v. Novell, Inc., 578 F.3d 1201, 1209–10 (10th Cir. 2009); Kennedy v. National Juvenile Detention Ass'n, 187 F.3d 690, 694 (7th Cir. 1999).

common to all of the respective businesses. Leveraging its size allows the large company to get maximum benefit from its use of technology. Selling to large companies allows the technology vendors to make large sales. It can be a win-win situation for both sides.

Use by the licensee's customers is not granted as frequently, but in some circumstances it may make sense. Allowing a licensee's customer to access and use accounting software would definitely cut into the software licensor's market. This type of "service bureau use" typically is forbidden. However, in some circumstances it may be allowed. For instance, for some types of software, use by the licensee's customers is inherent (examples include ATM software, use of websites for the transferring of money or making payments, or even project management software). In those cases, the parties should make clear in the license agreement that use by the licensee's own customers is permitted. The parties may wish to distinguish whether the grant of use applies to existing customers only or whether it includes future customers. Also, the parties must determine whether such customer use rights will extend to all of the functionality of the technology or just certain portions of it. In financial services, technology is often licensed in to "license out," meaning the technology will be incorporated into some other customer-facing software and/or service. Use by customers is often a critical part of any negotiations.

Normally use of technology by third parties is not considered internal use. It is clearly external to the licensee and therefore not permitted. The only exceptions to this are when the third party uses the technology to benefit the licensee. Consultants, data processors, auditors, joint ventures, joint venture partners, outsourcers, and other third-party service providers may need to use the technology to provide services to the licensee, or the licensee may decide that it does not want to take on the expense of owning hardware needed to make use of the technology. In these cases, some limited use by third parties is often permitted; however, the licensee is often asked to indemnify for any breach by such third party's breach of the license agreement.

C. Resale Limitations

If the licensee is also intended to be a reseller, then other terms may be needed. The parties should describe when and on what conditions the technology can be sublicensed. Factors to take into consideration include license terms for downstream users and pricing, as well as the other licensing terms described here. The parties should make clear how payments for the license are made, whether they are made directly to the licensor or made via the reseller.

D. Rights Retained by Licensor

The licensor typically retains certain rights in its technology. In fact, it is best practice to include a broad retention of all rights not otherwise expressly licensed in the agreement. Licensors typically retain the following rights:

- to maintain and modify the technology (which requires access to source code and would also provide licensors an added revenue stream);
- to copy the technology (because copies would take away potential revenue from the licensor); and
- to transfer the technology (because licensors do not want their technology to fall into the hands of competitors; an exception is resale arrangements).

The licensee generally keeps any original source code secret. The code may contain trade secrets and, at the same time, receive copyright protection. Source code is generally not disclosed to anyone, with the possible exceptions of open source software and pursuant to a source code escrow (see Chapter 11, at Section III).

E. License Term

Technology licenses are either perpetual or for a defined period of time. Perpetual means that the licensee has the right to use the software in perpetuity, absent breach by the licensee. A license that is also "irrevocable" cannot be terminated for breach. The licensor will have a claim for damages but cannot prevent the licensee from continuing to use the software.[3] Some licenses are for a prescribed period of time, such as a subscription service.

F. Nonproduction Uses

Nonproduction uses of technology are normally considered part of any license agreement, but it is wise to explicitly state them when drafting the agreement so there is no misunderstanding later. These uses include the right to make copies for backup purposes, disaster recovery (cold and/or hot failover), and testing.

G. Privacy of Data

If the software or SaaS provider processes any personally identifiable data, it should be made clear in the agreement what the provider's responsibilities are with regard to that data. It should also be clear what responsibility the service provider has regarding any security breaches. The service provider should promptly notify the financial institution in the event of any data breach and provide sufficient information so that the financial institution can determine its obligations under privacy and data breach laws and regulations. Finally, the service provider should pay the costs of notification under various state data breach laws and possibly indemnify the financial institution for third-party claims resulting from those breaches. Note that in the recent Target data breach case, it was a service provider that caused the breach. Nonetheless, Target is the party being sued for the breach. Privacy and other data issues are addressed in Chapter 9.

---

[3] *See* Nano-Proprietary Inc. v. Canon Inc., 537 F.3d 394 (5th Cir. 2008).

H. Effect of License Termination or Expiration

Only rarely will a license extend beyond its termination or expiration period. Some instances make an extension desirable (e.g., data that cannot be used without the technology), but the use should be restricted to a short, reasonable period (e.g., to allow the data to be converted into a useable format). Otherwise the licensee may be held hostage for more fees to migrate off the technology. The agreement should also specify what happens to data after termination of the agreement. Is the vendor prohibited from using that data? Is the vendor required to destroy and certify destruction of the data? These important issues should be addressed.

I. Practical Guidance

Technology licensing agreements often present unique problems as well as opportunities. Any license agreement should be drafted carefully to minimize misunderstandings or disputes later on. Clear drafting can also help maximize the value of IP, by addressing ownership issues up front. This advice applies no matter the type of agreement or business model involved, whether a pure software license, SaaS, or other agreement.

III. FDIC Guidance on Due Diligence in Selection of Software

A. Commercial Software

The FDIC has issued specific guidance[1] regarding the performance of proper due diligence in the selection of

---

[1] Fed. Deposit Ins. Corp., FIL-121-2004, Guidance on Developing an Effective Computer Software Evaluation Program to Assure Quality and Regulatory Compliance (Nov. 16, 2004).

computer software and service providers. Highlighting the importance of ensuring that software and service providers comply with applicable laws including the Bank Secrecy Act and the USA PATRIOT Act, the FDIC noted that it had "identified various Bank Secrecy Act and Anti-Money Laundering (BSA/AML) software products used by financial institutions that do not comply with applicable laws and regulations."[5] "[M]anagement will be held responsible for ensuring COTS [commercial off-the-shelf] and vendor-supplied-in-house computer systems solutions comply with all applicable laws and regulations and should use due diligence in assessing the quality of the COTS software packages and vendor-supplied in-house computer systems used by their financial institution."[6]

There are two ways to assure product quality:

1. validating the process by which the product has been developed; and
2. evaluating the quality and functionality of the final product.

New software products should be evaluated based on a risk/benefits analysis, including an analysis of compliance risk, technical risk, legal risk, and security risk.[7] In addition, management should evaluate product quality prior to purchase, performing the following minimum steps:

- Identify the specific function of the product.
- Identify areas where the product does not meet selection criteria and/or where action plans may be necessary.
- Determine the risks associated with each of the criteria not met by the product.
- Document how the financial institution will mitigate or alleviate those risks.

---

[5] *Id.*

[6] *Id.*

[7] *Id.*

- Obtain a list of current users and contact users.
- Implement selected system(s) in a test mode and fully test the system to ensure all requirements are met.
- Determine product security and the potential impact to the operation if that security is breached.
- Evaluate the support for the products, including the vendor's stability, product strategy, support record, and update policy.[8]

Finally, management should include a clause in its licensing agreements for core processing and/or mission-critical applications to require vendors to maintain the software in compliance with all applicable federal and state regulations.[9]

B. Free and Open Source Software

The Federal Financial Institutions Examination Council (FFIEC) also issued guidance[10] regarding the risks and risk management practices applicable to the use of free and open source software (FOSS). Regulators noted that although "[t]he use of FOSS by financial institutions does not pose risks that are fundamentally different from those presented by the use of proprietary or self-developed software[,] . . . FOSS adoption and usage necessitates some distinctive risk management practices with which institutions must be familiar."[11]

Regulators identified several key risk management areas, including the following.

Code customization. The ability to customize FOSS source code presents risks similar to self-developed code and, therefore, those risks should be handled similarly.

---

[8] *Id.*

[9] *Id.*

[10] FED. FIN. INST. EXAMINATION COUNCIL, FIL-114-2004, GUIDANCE ON RISK MANAGEMENT OF FREE AND OPEN SOURCE SOFTWARE (Oct. 21, 2004).

[11] *Id.*

IT architecture. FOSS may have issues with interoperability and compatibility as the software may not be formally certified.

Product maturity. Management must consider the maturity of the software in assessing risks, looking at issues such as:

- How long has the software been supported or in use?
- How is the development community organized, and how well does it function?
- How active is the development community?
- How much published material is devoted to the software?
- How many commercial vendors support the software?
- What is the security track record of the software?

Forking. The splitting of a development path in one or several directions—forking—can often lead to concerns as to the direction of the software. "Institutions should mitigate this risk by ensuring that adequate support is available for the current FOSS software either in-house, through vendors, or other outside sources."[12]

Systems integration and support. There are several types of operational risks that occur in the context of FOSS, including code integrity, sufficiency of documentation, contingency planning, and support.[13]

Total cost of ownership/legal risks. Legal risks associated with FOSS include licensing, infringement, indemnification, and warranties. The guidance recommends that "prior to selecting a FOSS solution, institutions should consult with counsel knowledgeable in the areas of copyright and patent law."[14] In light of substantial FFIEC activity in this area, as well as evolving technology and business models, financial institutions can expect to meet new and expanding regulatory standards.

---

[12] *Id.*

[13] *Id.*

[14] *Id.*

IV. Sarbanes-Oxley Section 404

Section 404 of the Sarbanes-Oxley Act[15] requires publicly traded companies to have ample controls over the reporting of required '33 Act financial reports. Information technology (IT) controls can have an impact on the financial reporting process. Both the Public Company Accounting Oversight Board and the Securities and Exchange Commission have issued guidance on Section 404 that says that the risk assessment required should address IT controls only to the extent needed to address the financial risks. Section 404 has been interpreted to address risks from transaction processing. General IT controls ensure that software performs as expected and creates reliable financial reports. Any errors or problems in financial reporting should be promptly rectified. Publicly traded financial institutions should periodically review IT controls with respect to financial reporting to ensure Section 404 compliance. In addition, those companies should negotiate appropriate representations from the supplier of any financial software that helps generate these reports. This is especially true when the software is delivered in the SaaS model.

V. Practical Guidance

One should take care when licensing in-bound technology to first understand how the organization intends to use the technology. It is worth spending some time thinking through how the software will be used. If it is only intended to be used internally, then uses should be discussed and teased out of the internal users. If the technology is to be bundled with a company's own proprietary products or services, those rights should be spelled out in the contract. It is impossible to properly draft a technology license without first understanding the technology and its uses.

---

[15] Pub. L. No. 107-204, 116 Stat. 745 (2002).

Note that open source software can sometimes be governed by more than one license. It may be worth reviewing all potential licenses before choosing one. Note also that open source software does not come with any IP indemnification protection. Finally, the recent Heartbleed[16] episode illustrates the need for concern when it comes to open source software.

---

[16] *See* Brian X. Chen, *Q. and A. on Heartbleed: A Flaw Missed by the Masses*, N.Y. Times, Apr. 9, 2014; Farhod Manjoo, *Users' Stark Reminder: As Web Grows, It Grows Less Secure*, N.Y. Times, Apr. 9, 2014; Molly Wood, *Flaw Calls for Altering Passwords, Experts Say*, N.Y. Times, Apr. 9, 2014.

CHAPTER 8

USE OF THIRD-PARTY SERVICE PROVIDERS: SOURCING AND OUTSOURCING

I. INTRODUCTION

Outsourcing is "[t]he assumption by a third party of responsibility for one or more of a company's business or technology functions, typically under a long-term contract and often in a transaction involving the company's transfer of assets and employees to the outsourcer."[1] Sourcing is very similar: hiring a third party to provide a product or service rather than using in-house resources. For discussion purposes in this book, the same general rules and advice that apply to outsourcing also apply to sourcing.

Banks and other financial services companies frequently outsource services required in their businesses. Typically these services are not part of the institution's core business but support its core business or general operations. Outsourced services may include payroll, data/call center operations and management, help desk functions, administrative support, facilities management, and discrete functions such as software development or maintenance.

The Federal Financial Institutions Examination Council (FFIEC) has issued a handbook with guidance on the use of third-party technology service providers.[2] This manual not only sets forth best practices for FFIEC-regulated financial institutions, but it also contains valuable information for any company using third-party service providers in its business. That information is summarized in this chapter along with additional recommendations from the author's experience.

Some overarching principles apply when hiring third-party service providers. First, the regulated financial institution is responsible for the acts and omissions of the service provider from a regulatory standpoint. In other words, the service provider must not violate any applicable regulations. Second, inexperienced service providers are often reluctant to agree to such restrictions in a contract. But third, any service provider pursuing business in the financial services

---

[1] Gartner Group; http://www.texasbarcle.com/Materials/Events/929/27071.htm.

[2] FED. FIN. INST. EXAMINATION COUNCIL, SUPERVISION OF TECHNOLOGY SERVICE PROVIDERS (Oct. 2012).

industry must become familiar with regulations applicable to their activities.

This chapter generally applies across the financial services industry except for Section IV., which applies only to FFIEC-regulated institutions.

II. Reasons to Outsource

The following are some of the reasons companies use when determining whether to outsource, or even to source resources.

A. Cost Identification, Savings, or Predictability

Savings are frequently a major driver of outsourcing transactions. The important question is can a third-party service provider provide the same or better level of service at a lower cost? If done correctly, outsourcing to save money is easy to understand and measure. It can also be an easy "win" to show senior management. Often, the customer does not know the true costs of providing the services prior to the outsourcing. The contract should reflect the process for accurately measuring and reporting these costs. Care should be taken, however, to adequately and thoroughly measure internal and external costs before and after the outsourcing. This is the only way to accurately determine whether the outsourcing met the goal of cost savings.

B. Access to Skills

Outsourcing to gain access to a particular skill set is another common goal. Often a company will need certain skills that it cannot acquire internally or that it needs for only a limited period of time. Third-party service providers may have more resources and, hence, economies of scale, or they may simply have more experience in providing a particular type of service. In those instances, it would make sense for a company to hire a third party with those skills.

C. Noncore Functions or Business Processes

Outsourcing noncore business functions or processes allows management to focus on the company's core competencies. A typical example is payroll. In theory, this frees up company resources for more profitable core functions.

D. Accountability for Functional Performance

The use of a third-party service provider that can provide unique functionality is often another reason to outsource. This allows the financial institution to focus on an area of its business, often in a more objective and strategic manner. However, as with any set of business goals, focusing on too many goals can result in none of the goals being met. It is better to stick with one or two goals, as they are easier to manage.

III. Key Characteristics of Outsourcing

Outsourcing transactions typically share certain characteristics. These include

- a major commitment of resources by the service provider;
- a long-term contract, typically five years or more;
- complex contractual terms and conditions;
- a poorly defined market for the services with poorly defined pricing (i.e., not a commodity service); and
- significant expense for the outsourcing financial institution.

A. Avoid Win-Lose Negotiating

Outsourcing contracts bind customer and service provider together—for a long, usually multiyear period. Taking a "scorched earth" approach during the initial contract negotiation can lead to unrealistic expectations for the customer and overly onerous terms for the service provider. Such an approach may set the relationship up for failure from the very start. Although both parties will come to the table with "must haves," a reasonable, flexible approach to negotiating is key.

Make the description of services the starting point for contract negotiations. "Scope" issues are often grounds for dispute. The customer may believe that the service provider failed to perform adequately, while the service provider may believe that the service or task complained about is not contained in the description of services. The proper definition of "baseline services" is critical.

B. Request for Proposal Process

A request for proposal (RFP) is a very useful tool in the outsourcing process, especially when

- more than one supplier is offering similar solutions;
- the customer seeks to determine the "best value" of suppliers' solutions;
- the project requires different skills, expertise, and technical capabilities from suppliers; or
- the problem requires suppliers to combine and subcontract products and services.

If there is a need that could be resolved through the purchase of an outside vendor's equipment and/or services:

- Develop and implement a plan for understanding the problem.

- Identify appropriate potential suppliers and solutions.
- Gain visibility for internal acceptance of the identified need and potential solutions.
- Establish the project budget.
- Develop a project schedule and organize project personnel.
- Create real requirements and ensure that they are clearly stated and measurable.
- Develop rigorous evaluation criteria, thus ensuring an objective evaluation.

The RFP process is not useful when

- too little time is allocated for the RFP process;
- the requirements are overly restrictive and limit suppliers to a single predetermined solution;
- the requirements unfairly limit the range of suppliers that may participate;
- the requirements are unclear;
- the project deadlines are too short to allow for reasonable project development by suppliers;
- the project team has not been fully educated about available technologies; or
- an adequate budget has not been established or verified and is not sufficient for the project.

RFPs provide flexibility and give both customer and service providers more freedom to propose and evaluate services and pricing models without being locked in. This process requires a sufficient dedicated staff to prepare, review, and evaluate the RFP and responses. The team must allow enough time for the entire RFP process. Often a consultant is useful in preparing the RFP. Finally, it is always important to seek and incorporate input from within the organization regarding RFP requirements.

The RFP process can streamline decision making for purchasing decisions no matter how complex. The more time and effort put into the RFP process, the better the results.

C. Final Contract Negotiations

Negotiating an outsourcing contract is the process of ironing out the details of the customer/supplier relationship. The parties should allow sufficient time for negotiations and have adequate data available to negotiate intelligently. Since the financial institution is getting into a long-term relationship with the service provider and the service provider is providing a service that realistically cannot be easily terminated, it is best to practice win-win negotiating rather than a "scorched earth" approach. Nonetheless, the financial institution must understand its deal killers and be prepared to fight for them.

The function of the contract is to allocate and define the risks and rewards for the parties. The negotiation process is used to establish clear mutual expectations in services, scope, quality, responsibility, and pricing. A paradox in this situation is that well-negotiated contracts end up in a drawer and are rarely looked at again. Poorly negotiated contracts get frequent scrutiny.

IV. FFIEC REGULATORY GUIDANCE—THIRD-PARTY SERVICE PROVIDERS

The FFIEC has clearly stated that the use of a third party does not relieve a regulated financial institution of its obligation to comply with applicable laws and regulations.[3] With respect to risk management, the regulated institution may outsource the function to a service provider, but the responsibility for compliance cannot be outsourced. Regulators expect the regulated financial institution to create and maintain risk management processes that are appropriate with risk faced by the regulated financial institution. It is

---

[3] U.S. Office of the Comptroller of the Currency, OCC 2013-29, Risk Management Guidance 1 (Oct. 30, 2013) [hereinafter OCC 2013-29, Risk Management Guidance].

important to note that while this guidance is issued by the FFIEC, it also represents best practices across the financial services industry.

These processes must be even more stringent and thorough when the service provider performs "critical activities." Critical activities include payments, clearing and settlement functions, custodial accounts, significant technology, or other services that (1) increase major risk to the regulated financial institution if the service provider fails to provide those services; (2) could have a major impact on customers; (3) would otherwise require a major investment in internal resources to implement and manage the risks associated with using the service provider; and (4) could significantly impact the operation of the regulated financial institution if the service provider relationship is terminated and the service provider has to be replaced or the services performed in-house.[4]

The third-party risk management process should include the following:[5]

1. Planning
2. Due diligence and selection
3. Contract negotiation
4. Ongoing monitoring
5. Termination
6. Oversight/accountability
7. Documentation/reporting
8. Review

The regulatory guidance describes a Risk Management Life Cycle consisting of the following phases.

A. Planning

Planning is critical when engaging a third-party service provider. The FFIEC requires senior management to

---

[4] *Id.* at 2.
[5] *Id.*

develop an overall plan for engaging and managing the use of third-party service providers. This plan should anticipate the potential risks involved in the service provider's activities or services, reputation, legal compliance issues, and similar considerations. During the planning phase, management should also consider how to meet strategic goals (e.g., cost reduction, specialized expertise, unique technology, or additional manpower or other resources). Finally, management should plan how to align the use of a third-party service provider with the financial institution's long-term goals and strategies.

Others factors to consider at the planning stage include the complexity of the potential engagement. Will the services be provided onsite, offsite, or perhaps even overseas? How much will the provision of the services impact internal resource usage? What other resources will be needed to maximize use of what the service provider has to offer?

Management must consider whether any potential financial gains exceed the direct cost of using the service provider as well as any indirect costs to manage the relationship and terminating legacy providers. Additional questions that should be answered include these:

- How will using this third-party service provider impact any other strategic plans of the financial institution, such as Mergers and Acquisitions or other structural changes, investments in new technology, or growth plans?
- If historically the activities have been performed in-house, how will any transition to an external service provider be addressed?
- Are there any data and information security requirements that must be met for the service provider to connect to the financial institution's systems?
- How does the service provider fit in with the financial institution's disaster recovery and contingency plans?
- Does the service provider have its own disaster recovery and contingency plans?

- Are those plans sufficient, and do they comply with any applicable regulations or industry standards?
- Will the service provider impact the financial institution's financial reporting (e.g., flow into any regulatory required data reporting such as Federal Reserve or Securities and Exchange Commission (SEC) required reports)?
- Are the activities themselves subject to any laws or regulations (e.g., check processing, anti–money laundering)?
- Is the use of the third-party service provider consistent with other policies of the financial institution?
- What oversight mechanisms are in place or need to be put in place to manage the service provider, including for contract compliance?
- How will the case for outsourcing "critical services" be made to the financial institution's senior management?

B. Due Diligence and Selection of Third-Party Service Provider

The U.S. Office of the Comptroller of the Currency (OCC)—and, in fact, all regulated financial institutions—are required to perform due diligence on service providers prior to entering into a contractual relationship with those service providers. Due diligence is crucial as it informs the contract negotiations, which in turn determine whether the regulated financial institution can work with the supplier.

The FFIEC has set forth an extensive format for the due diligence process and selection of third-party service providers. This process has the following 16 components, described below, with added questions for each that may be useful when assessing a particular supplier.[6] The answers to

---

[6] *Id.* at 4–7.

these questions may raise more questions or suggest a different course of action. In any event, the FFIEC suggests that senior management of the regulated financial institution review the results of the due diligence process to determine whether the regulated financial institution's expectations will be met. If expectations will not be met, the FFIEC suggests that either the third-party supplier make changes to meet those expectations or the regulated financial institution find some other means to do so (e.g., find another supplier, perform the services in-house, or even discontinue the activity).[7]

1. Strategies and Goals

The regulated financial institution should review the supplier's strategies and goals to make sure they agree with those of the regulated financial institution. Important questions to ask include:

- Does the supplier have any partnerships or other business relationships that are significant to the provision of services?
- What would happen if those relationships turned sour?
- What are the supplier's certifications, quality ratings, and history of employment practices?
- Are these characteristics all in harmony with what the regulated financial institution expects to achieve in establishing a relationship with the supplier?

2. Legal and Regulatory Compliance

The regulated financial institution should consider the third-party service provider's ability to comply with applicable laws. Does the supplier have the necessary experience,

---

[7] *Id.* at 7.

resources, processes, and controls to assist the regulated financial institution in compliance with appropriate regulations and regulatory bodies?

3. Financial Condition

The financial condition of any third-party service provider is extremely relevant. Generally, the more mission critical the services or technology provided, the more in-depth the financial review should be. Important questions to ask include:

- Does a review of the supplier's audited financial statements or publicly available SEC filings reveal any significant concerns as to the supplier's ability to provide services?
- Are there any unfunded liabilities, litigation or other issues that would reasonably raise an alarm?

4. Business Experience and Reputation

The regulated financial institution should review the business experience and reputation of the supplier. Important questions to ask include.

- Does the supplier have a history of lawsuits, especially with its customers?
- Are there any customer complaints about the supplier registered with the Better Business Bureau, state attorney generals' offices, or other similar relevant organizations?
- How long has the supplier been in business?
- Do the supplier's marketing materials comply with the regulated financial institution's expectations? Do they overstate the supplier's capabilities?
- Does the supplier intend to list the regulated financial institution as a customer?

5. Fee Structure and Incentives

The regulated financial institution should review pricing and all fees and expenses offered by the service provider. Important questions to ask include:

- Is the pricing in line with other similar service offerings that the regulated financial institution is aware of?
- Is the pricing structured in such a way that the regulated financial institution does not bear undue risk if the service provider fails to perform?

6. Qualifications, Backgrounds, and Reputations of Company Principals

Regulated financial institutions are required to perform background checks on service provider personnel who perform services onsite. The FFIEC suggests that the regulated financial institution should consider whether the service provider performs background checks on its own personnel, even if not onsite. This should include subcontractors who may have access to confidential data and information, as well as essential IT systems. Important questions to ask include:

- What policies and procedures are in place for background checks on the supplier's employees?
- What steps are taken to remove employees who do not pass background checks?

7. Risk Management

An evaluation of the supplier's risk management programs is a crucial part of due diligence. Depending on the type of system involved, it may even be appropriate to analyze the internal controls of the supplier. Appropriate questions to ask include:

- Are there any existing service organization control reports such as an SSAE 16? If so, do they contain enough information to understand any risk associated with the supplier?
- Do any such reports raise even more questions about the supplier?
- Will the supplier's systems integrate with the regulated financial institution's systems so that Sarbanes-Oxley compliance is required?
- Are any certifications for international or domestic internal controls required (e.g., NIST, the American Institute of Certified Public Accountants (AICPA), or the International Standards Organization (ISO))?

8. Information Security

An assessment should be made of the third-party service provider's IT security program. Important questions to ask include:

- Does the supplier have enough experience managing its IT systems so that it can mitigate any security threats?
- Is the infrastructure secure?
- Are there any vulnerability or penetration testing reports available?
- What are the supplier's policies and procedures for correcting any deficiencies?

9. Management of Information Systems

The regulated financial institution should be able to understand what business processes and technology the supplier uses. If technology is a significant part of the services to be provided by the supplier, the regulated financial institution should review the operations of the supplier to make sure there are no gaps between what the supplier will deliver and what the regulated financial institution expects. The

FFIEC believes that having a grasp of the supplier's performance metrics will ensure that the regulated financial institution understands what it is getting.

10. Resilience

Regulated financial institutions should consider the supplier's ability to respond to force majeure events. Important questions to ask include:

- What are the supplier's disaster recovery and business continuity plans?
- What are the time frames under those plans to restore services?
- How is data cared for and recovered before, during, and after an event?
- What redundancies are in place, especially telecommunications and server technologies?
- How does the supplier become aware of existing and new cybersecurity threats?
- Are there any business continuity or disaster recovery test reports available?
- How has the supplier performed during those tests?

11. Incident-Reporting and Management Programs

In assessing a third-party service provider's incident-reporting and management programs, important questions to ask include:

- How does the supplier respond to outages and other incidents?
- What processes does the supplier use to identify, document, and report such incidents?
- What processes are in place for investigation and escalation of incidents?

- Do these processes meet the regulated financial institution's needs, including regulatory requirements?

12. Physical Security

The regulated financial institution should understand how its data and other information will be kept secure. Important questions to ask include:

- What security measures are in place at supplier's data centers?
- What security is in place at other facilities from which services are provided?
- How often are these reviewed and updated?
- Are there redundant power supplies to support these security features?
- Is there any ongoing monitoring of these security measures to ensure that any failures are corrected immediately?
- What is the supplier's history with respect to security?
- How often are security failures reviewed and updated?

13. Human Resources Management

The ability of a service provider to perform often comes down to its people. Appropriate questions to ask include:

- How does the service provider train its employees to provide services?
- What mixture of new employees and experienced senior employees will be used to provide the services?
- How does the service provider plan for succession of its employees?
- How are key employees handled?
- How are employees informed and updated on new technologies, cyberthreats, and other matters that may impact the delivery of services?

14. Reliance on Subcontractors and Other Third Parties

It is important to understand what and how subcontractors are used by the supplier. Important questions to ask include:

- What portion of the services will be provided by subcontractors?
- What components of the technology come from subcontractors?
- How does the supplier evaluate and manage risks associated with the use of subcontractors?
- How does the supplier ensure a coherent level of service regardless of any subcontractors' location?
- Is due diligence on the supplier's subcontractors needed?
- Is any third-party software or open source software used to provide the services?

15. Insurance Coverage

All third-party service providers should have adequate insurance coverage to backstop their various obligations under the contract. Important questions to ask include:

- Does the supplier have insurance coverage for dishonest and negligent acts?
- Does the supplier have hazard insurance covering physical damage?
- Is loss of data covered?
- Are intellectual property (IP) rights covered?
- Is the regulated financial institution listed as a "named insured"?
- What coverage amounts are appropriate given the services to be provided by the supplier?
- Are there any other coverage types that would be appropriate?

16. Conflicting Contractual Arrangements with Other Parties

This can usually be uncovered during the contracting process, but it is useful to get these questions on the table as early as possible. Important questions to ask include:

- Are there any contracts that would legally prevent the supplier from providing the services as expected by the regulated financial institution?
- If there are any subcontractors or suppliers to the third-party service provider, do those arrangements permit the provision of services?
- Does the third-party service provider have the necessary IP rights to provide the services?
- Is any third-party software or open source software used to provide the services?[8]

C. Contract Negotiation

Contract negotiation is often a tedious process, yet it is the last chance to catch mistakes and ensure that the service provider is the right fit for the organization. How the service provider acts during the contracting process is often an indication of how easy or difficult it will be to work with it as a supplier.

The FFIEC recommends that any third-party contract for "critical services" receive board approval before signature.[9] Specifically, it recommends that financial institutions address the following issues when negotiating a contract for "critical services" and when periodically reviewing existing contracts.

---

[8] This is a very important question, so yes, it is intentionally in here twice.

[9] OCC 2013-29, Risk Management Guidance, at 7.

1. Nature and Scope of Arrangement

The contract should specify the services to be delivered as well as "the frequency, content, and format of the service," and include any related services such as software maintenance, software support, and end user training. The contract should specify which activities each party will conduct and whether the service provider will supply any services onsite. Finally, the contract should spell out limits on any use of the regulated financial institution's information, employees, facilities, hardware, and software.

2. Performance Measures or Benchmarks

Performance measures help define the expectations for the service provider and the regulated financial institution. They may be written to govern almost anything, but are typically used to motivate the service provider to perform. They should be clearly focused on the goals of the regulated financial institution so as not to incentivize undesired performance (e.g., encouraging speed, but not accuracy). Industry standard benchmarks should be utilized where available.

3. Responsibilities for Providing, Receiving, and Retaining Information

The third-party service provider should be contractually obligated to provide relevant information and reports and maintain accurate records. These should allow management to monitor the service provider's performance. The regulated financial institution should stipulate in the contract which reports will be made available by the service provider and the content and frequency of those reports.

The FFIEC further suggests that the contract sets forth

1. ways to address breaches of the agreement, including termination;

2. prompt notification by the supplier of financial difficulties, force majeure events, and other significant events such as loss of data, service interruptions, compliance or regulatory lapses, and law enforcement actions;[10]

3. the regulated financial institution's limits and procedures for notifications of contract breaches and service disruptions;

4. notification to the regulated financial institution before any significant changes to the services due to acquisitions, subcontracting, key personnel changes, or new policies or procedures or technology;

5. notification of changes to the service provider's business that may affect the services, such as acquisitions, divestitures, and other corporate restructurings;[11]

6. limitations of the service provider's ability to allow third parties access to the regulated financial institution's data and systems used to provide the services; and

7. any obligation by the regulated financial institution to notify the service provider of any significant changes that may affect performance of the contract.

4. Audit Rights and Remediation

The regulated financial institution should have the ability to audit the service provider for compliance with all aspects of the contract. The contract should specify how any failures to comply will be remedied. The contract should include the type and frequency of reporting, especially any Statements on Standards for Attestation Engagements (SSAE) reports. The audit process should include a review of the supplier's information security and its business continuity and disaster recovery programs.

---

[10] It would be a good idea to add significant litigation to this list.

[11] Note that it would be unlikely that any large public company could agree to give this type of notice prior to a transaction; however, prompt notice afterward is not unreasonable.

5. Responsibility for Compliance with Applicable Laws and Regulations

The regulated financial institution should ensure that the contract addresses compliance with applicable laws, rules, and regulations. Service providers are often reluctant to promise this as they are not typically regulated entities; however, if the services they provide are regulated, or they hold data that is regulated, they should be held to the regulatory standard. For example, credit card processers should give assurances the services they provide comply with Payment Card Institute (PCI) rules,[12] and entities that hold personally identifiable information (PII) must agree to comply with the Gramm-Leach-Bliley Act.[13]

6. Costs and Compensation

One of the most important elements in the contract—fees and charges due under the contract—should be explained in detail so they can be easily understood. Out of all the provisions in a contract, this one will be referred to over and over. Also, because the parties that draft and negotiate a contract are usually not the ones who implement and manage the contract afterward, having sufficient and clear detail on pricing will lead to fewer conflicts. Contracts may be on a fixed-fee basis, a time and materials basis, a cost plus basis, or some other basis, even a combination of two or more of these. Business models tend to change over time. The FFIEC recommends that pricing be clear and not include up-front fees that may be burdensome to the regulated financial institution. Other factors to consider include payment for audit expenses, travel expenses, and legal costs. These can add to the cost and should be

---

[12] *See* Chapter 9.

[13] *See* Chapter 9.

addressed so the regulated financial institution has a clear picture of what it is paying. The contract should also address when and under what circumstances the supplier can raise prices.

7. Ownership and Licenses

The parties should be clear about the rights and licenses each has. The regulated financial institution needs a license to use the services and any output from the services, while the service provider needs the right to use its customer's data, but only to provide the services. Often service providers will ask for a license to use the regulated financial institution's name and/or logo in its marketing and on its website. The regulated financial institution should take plenty of time to consider whether to allow this as such use could be seen as a quasi-endorsement. Also, trademark law requires a trademark owner to police uses of its trademark.

8. Confidentiality and Integrity

The service provider should not be able to use any information learned during the engagement, except as needed to provide the services or otherwise comply with contractual requirements. Any permitted subcontractors should be bound by these requirements as well. The service provider should also agree to promptly disclose any security breaches, including any that trigger data breach notification requirements. Notices should contain information about any effects on the regulated financial institution and any corrective action undertaken by the service provider. Consider whether a data breach would allow the regulated financial institution to require additional security measures by the service provider or even to terminate the contract. Also, the regulated financial institution should consider having a joint security exercise with the service provider.

9 Business Resumption and Contingency Plans

The contract should require the service provider to have adequate disaster recovery and failover so that there is no decline in service if a force majeure or other similar event occurs. The service provider should be responsible for backing up data and otherwise protecting its equipment and systems. The regulated financial institution should also have the ability to transfer the services to a third party, without penalty, in the event the service provider cannot promptly recover from a disaster. The FFIEC recommends that the regulated financial institution require the service provider to provide it with the procedures for disaster recovery. In practice, some service providers may balk at this as those plans are usually considered a trade secret. Still, a reasonable confidentiality provision should allay this concern.

10. Indemnifications

The service provider should indemnify the regulated financial institution against claims by third parties, especially claims for IP infringement and any other claims appropriate to the transaction. The regulated financial institution should be cautious in giving any indemnification to the service provider.

11. Insurance

The regulated financial institution should require the service provider to have appropriate insurance. Adequate insurance will provide a backstop for the service provider's contractual obligations, such as warranties and indemnifications. At a minimum, the supplier should have insurance coverage for dishonest and negligent acts, and hazard insurance covering physical damage, especially to computer hardware and other equipment. If the service provider will be onsite at the regulated financial institution's location, then personal injury insurance is required. The regulated financial institution should consider whether loss of data and/or IP rights coverage should be required. A comprehensive umbrella policy is a must.

In addition, the regulated financial institution should be listed as a "named insured/loss payee" on an insurance certificate, which should be delivered to the regulated financial institution at or soon after contract signature. Insurance companies will not pay on a claim by the regulated financial institution if this is not in place.

Coverage amounts should be geared toward the value of the contract and the nature of the services provided by the supplier. Other coverage types may be appropriate.

12. *Dispute Resolution*

The contract should have some type of dispute resolution process. This will allow the parties to resolve some disputes rather than litigating. The FFIEC does not specify what type of dispute resolution should be used. I recommend using an internal escalation procedure requiring the parties to at least talk to one another before filing any lawsuit (with an exception for injunctive relief). Some believe that arbitration is a better alternative to litigation. However, I believe since court outcomes are generally more uncertain, the parties may be willing to settle rather than to fully litigate. Arbitration has a reputation as being cheaper, faster, and easier than the courts, but that is not always the case. In addition, the contract should specify that the supplier continue to provide services pending the resolution of any dispute, or at least until the regulated financial institution can transfer to another supplier or perform the services in-house.

13. *Limitations of Liability*

Any limitations of liability should be proportional to the potential losses under the contract and the value of the contract. Some claims should be excluded from any limitation of liability, such as IP indemnifications, gross negligence, and breaches of confidentiality. Note that limitations of liability may not be enforceable or restricted in some jurisdictions. The FFIEC further recommends that the regulated financial institution consider whether it will face an "undue risk of litigation"[14] if the suppler infringes a third party's IP right. This is something that should be addressed during due diligence as well.

14. Default and Termination

Terminating a contract for default is never a desired outcome. It is always an available remedy, but not always a realistic option. There may be difficulties with alternatives, i.e., transferring to a new vendor or bringing the service in-house, all on short notice. There seems to be some duplication of this issue in the OCC guidance, but I will address it all here in one place. The contract should be clear as to what comprises default. It should stipulate what remedies are available and spell out the consequences of termination for both parties.

Typical events of default include material breach of the contract, insolvency, or bankruptcy of the vendor;[15] some predefined level of service failures; and, rarely, change in control. The OCC has recommended a termination event if required by the regulators.[16] From the regulated financial institution's perspective, termination for default should be limited to failure to pay undisputed amounts otherwise due under the agreement. Remedies for default by the vendor should allow for suspension of the contract or partial termination, so that the vendor has the opportunity to cure any

---

[14] OCC 2013-29, RISK MANAGEMENT GUIDANCE, at 10.

[15] While this is often written into contracts, its enforceability is dubious. *See* Chapter 11.

[16] OCC 2013-29, RISK MANAGEMENT GUIDANCE, at 10.

default (if curable), all at the regulated financial institution's option. There should be adequate notice periods as well.

The effects of termination should be addressed as well. The vendor should provide the regulated financial institution with a copy of its data within a reasonable time after termination for any reason. Costs should be allocated as of the termination date. Depending on the reason for termination, consider whether the vendor should continue to provide some level of service after termination to allow for an orderly transition to another vendor.

Finally, the regulated financial institution should have the right to terminate the contract, without cause, with reasonable notice to the vendor.

15. Customer Complaints

If the service provider is providing services directly to the regulated financial institution's customers, then the issue of which organization handles customers' complaints becomes paramount. If the supplier is responsible, then there should be specific service-level agreements (SLAs) with adequate reporting to the regulated financial institution. At a minimum, these SLAs should address the timeliness of responses by the supplier, as well as time frames for responses; correction, if possible; and full reporting back to the regulated financial institution. There should be enough information so that the regulated financial institution can make sense of the complaints, analyze them, and take corrective action.

16. Subcontracting

If the regulated financial institution determines that the supplier may subcontract one or more activities, certain safeguards should be put in place. Any subcontractors should comply with all other terms of the contract as if they were the supplier, especially if confidential information or

PII is involved. The regulated financial institution should also require routine reporting on any subcontracted activities and an indemnification from the supplier for any acts or omissions of the subcontractors. A failure of any permitted subcontractor should be excluded from any definition of a force majeure event. Finally, the contract should allow the regulated financial institution to terminate the contract without penalty if any of the provisions regarding subcontracting are materially breached.

17. Foreign-Based Third Parties

The FFIEC recommends that for non-U.S.-based suppliers, the contract specify a governing law and jurisdictional venue. However, such a clause would be appropriate in any contract with a supplier, even a domestic supplier. As with any contract, enforceability is the glue that keeps the contract in place, and knowing ahead of time which court and law applies will help alleviate risk.

18. Supervision

All contracts for OCC-regulated institutions are subject to regulatory oversight pursuant to 12 U.S.C. §§1867(c) and 1464(d)(7). Similar rules apply to other FFIEC-regulated institutions. Under these provisions, the OCC/FFIEC has the authority to review and regulate the activities performed by the supplier as if those activities were performed by the regulated financial institution itself at its own locations.

19. Additional Requirements

FFIEC-regulated financial institutions are further required to conduct ongoing monitoring (including any bank employees that supervise service provider employees), have contractual provisions that adequately address the risks of termination of the contract by either party, and have adequate documentation and reporting requirements that include reporting to senior management and, in some instances, the board of directors of the financial institution. Also, the outsourcing arrangement must be subject to independent review and review by the applicable regulator, if requested.

V. PRACTICAL GUIDANCE

With any significant outsourcing, termination is not always an easy remedy for the customer. It may be disruptive to migrate to another service provider, and any migration would have to be seamless. SLAs offer an intermediate remedy that perform several functions.

First, they are not really a separate agreement from the main outsourcing contract but are usually in their own exhibit or attachment to the main contract. Second, they provide an early warning system for problems with the service provider. Third, they are composed of key metrics or SLAs that are relevant for the services involved and the customer. For instance, in a data processing outsourcing, the speed of transactions and availability of the systems may be pegged to numeric values that are realistic for the service provider and acceptable to the customer. For a business process outsourcing, such as payroll, metrics around financial accuracy, record-keeping, and reporting would be relevant.

These metrics are usually reported monthly, and if the service provider fails to meet a metric, typically a credit is given to the customer. Other complications include using a basket of metrics to measure performance (e.g., if three metrics are missed in a particular month, then a credit is given). The metrics can also be weighted so that some metrics are worth more than others. In addition, it is not uncommon for customers to have the right to partially or completely terminate the agreement if SLAs are missed several months in a row or several months in a year. Designed properly, SLAs provide an early warning system to the customer of problems with the service provider. They allow both parties an opportunity to recognize that things may not be working as planned. The parties can then either work toward a solution or terminate. The customer will then have time to line up another service provider before actual notice of termination is given.

Chapter 9

INFORMATION GOVERNANCE

I. Introduction

Data is important in any organization. Much of the data used in the financial services industry contains sensitive information about customers, their behaviors, and their personal finances. This type of data can be used to commit crimes but also to detect them.

This chapter addresses regulations and guidance governing the use of data, including requirements to protect data and business records. This chapter applies generally across the financial services industry, with the following exceptions: Section II.B. applies only to the credit card industry; Section III. applies only to Federal Deposit Insurance Corp. (FDIC) regulated entities; Section IV.A. applies only to Federal Financial Institutions Examination Council (FFIEC) regulated entities; and Section IV.B. applies only to Securities and Exchange Commission (SEC), Commodity Futures Trading Commission (CFTC), and Financial Industry Regulatory Authority (FINRA) regulated entities.

A. Types of Data

Not all data is created equal. This chapter discusses four types of data. First is personally identifiable information (PII), which includes names, addresses, phone numbers, Social Security numbers, physical addresses, and e-mail addresses. The main law protecting PII is the Gramm-Leach-Bliley Act (GLBA).[1]

---

[1] Pub. L. No. 106-102, 113 Stat. 1338 (1999).

Next, companies in the financial services industry often have access to and hold material nonpublic information (MNPI) of third parties, including publicly traded companies. These third parties are not individuals whose information is protected. Securities underwriters and brokerages often have information about third parties, but lending banks also typically require disclosure of relevant financial information as part of the lending process. This information is often MNPI if the disclosing party or third party is a publicly traded company.

A third category of protected data includes information that company is contractually obligated to keep confidential through nondisclosure agreements or other contractually protected data.

The final category is data that contains a company's own trade secrets (discussed generally in Chapter 3, "Intellectual Property Issues").

II. DATA SAFEGUARDS

A. Privacy

So much has been written about data privacy, it is somewhat redundant to mention it here.[2] However, it is an important part of financial services technology and deserves at least a minimal discussion of regulatory and other issues. The major privacy legislation is GLBA, which applies to all financial institutions. It governs the use, storage, and protection of PII. GLBA defines a financial institution as a company that "is engaging in financial activities as described in section 1843 (k) of title 12."[3] This broad definition applies to many nonbank institutions. In a rare moment of regulatory

---

[2] An excellent resource is KRISTEN J. MATHEWS, PROSKAUER ON PRIVACY: A GUIDE TO PRIVACY AND DATA SECURITY LAW IN THE INFORMATION AGE (2013–2016).

[3] 15 U.S. Code §6809.

cooperation, the FFIEC, SEC, CFTC, and Federal Trade Commission (FTC) issued a joint regulation on privacy, called the Financial Privacy Rule. It requires financial institutions to provide consumers with a privacy notice at least annually. The privacy notice should explain what information is collected about the consumer and about how that information is shared, used, and protected. This privacy notice should also inform the consumer of his or her right to opt out of any sharing of the consumer's PII with unaffiliated parties. Changes in the privacy policy must be communicated to consumers in a reasonable amount of time so the consumer can again opt out, if desired. Any unaffiliated parties that receive PII must be held to the same terms as the financial institution under its agreement with the consumer.

A much larger concern for financial institutions is not so much the safeguarding of data, but the consequences of a breach of data security that exposes PII. Those are discussed below in Section V.

B. Credit Card Data Security

In May 2005, a credit card processer, CardSystems Solutions (CSS), disclosed that its systems had been hacked and that information on 40 million credit card accounts had been accessed. This was the largest such data breach at that time. What made matters worse was that the data was unencrypted, and CSS had been contractually obligated to delete the data. This was truly a perfect storm of data breach liability. CSS was subsequently bought by Pay By Touch,[4] a payment company using biometric payment systems. Various lawsuits and regulatory actions ensued, ensnaring Visa, MasterCard, and American Express among others. Below are some of these cases.

---

[4] Pay By Touch went out of business in March 2008.

1. FTC v. CardSystems Solutions

In late 2005, the parties reached a settlement that required regular reporting, assessment, and compliance requirements.[5]

2. Merrick v. Savvis

Merrick sued Savvis for falsely certifying that CSS was compliant with appropriate data security standards.[6] Merrick was an "acquiring bank," meaning that it had relationships with thousands of merchants for which it acted as a sort of clearing agent for the merchants, transmitting payments between the merchants and the card-issuing (i.e., cardholders') banks. In 2004, Merrick hired CSS to perform certain credit card data processing and other related services; however, under the agreement, CSS could not perform the work until it was certified as being compliant with Visa and MasterCard rules for data security.[7] Savvis performed the certification, and after the breach was disclosed, Merrick sued Savvis for negligence and negligent representation. The case survived a motion for dismissal and was settled for an undisclosed amount in 2010.

3. Payment Card Industry Data Standards

The Payment Card Industry (PCI) Security Standards Council was founded in 2006 by the major credit card brands.[8] It has issued data standards and requirements for those in the credit card industry and actively works to

---

[5] In the Matter of CardSystems Solutions, Inc. & Solidus Networks, Inc. d/b/a Pay By Touch Solutions, FTC File No. 0523148, September 5, 2006.

[6] Merrick Bank Corp. v. Savvis Inc., Savvis Communications Corp., Case No. 2:08-CV-2233-PHX-CKJ (D. Ariz.) (06/08/2010).

[7] One such requirement was that data be encrypted.

[8] American Express, Discover Financial Services, JCB International, MasterCard Worldwide, and Visa Inc.

promote the use of these standards.[9] The first, the PCI Data Security Standard (PCI-DSS), sets requirements for protecting credit card data. It applies primarily to merchants who accept credit card payments and to processors of credit card payments and information. Note that processors are usually third-party service providers to the financial institution; therefore, it is important that the financial institution perform adequate due diligence and receive appropriate assurances that the processor is compliant with this standard. (See Chapter 8, "Use of Third-Party Service Providers: Sourcing and Outsourcing.")

Two other standards issued by PCI are the Payment Application Data Security Standard (PA-DSS) and the Personal Identification Number Transaction Security Requirements or PIN or PTS. PA-DSS is used by software developers to create applications that process credit card information. PTS applies to manufactures of point-of-sale devices. Basic due diligence requires that these standards be complied with where appropriate (e.g., when buying ATMs, a financial institution should check whether PTS and PA-DSS are met by the supplier of the ATMs).

While PCI data standards are not the law, several states have passed PCI-like statutes.[10] Still, failure to comply with PCI standards could give rise to claims of negligence as in the CardSystems cases above.

a. PCI-DSS

The PCI-DSS has six primary goals:

1. to create and maintain information technology (IT) networks for the transmission and processing of credit card data that are not easily vulnerable to attack;
2. to safeguard the data on those networks;

---

[9] *See* PCI SECURITY STANDARDS COUNCIL, https://www.pcisecuritystandards.org/index.php.

[10] *See* MINN. STAT. 365E.64 (governs the storage of credit card data); NEV. REV. STAT. ch. 603A (requires compliance with PCI-DSS); WASH. REV. CODE §19.255.020 (codifies most PCI-DSS requirements).

3. to manage any weaknesses in those networks;
4. to restrict access to data through both physical and virtual means;
5. to routinely examine and scan the network for vulnerabilities; and
6. to have an IT security policy that incorporates all of the above.

Compliance with PCI-DSS requires the following:

1. Keep cardholder data behind a firewall.
2. Change any vendor supplied parameters for security measures to ones specific to the organization.
3. Safeguard credit card data that has been collected and/or stored.
4. Encrypt credit card data when transmitted over unsecured networks.
5. Employ commercially reliable anti-malware measures.
6. Design secure applications and systems and maintain them in a secure manner.
7. Limit virtual access to credit card data to those with actual business needs for such access.
8. Require each person with such access to have a unique user name and password
9. Limit physical access to credit card data to those with actual business needs for such access.
10. Have appropriate measures for tracking and scrutinizing all access to credit card data.
11. Examine and assess all networks and security systems on a regular basis to ensure compliance.
12. Have an IT security policy in place that incorporates all of the foregoing.

Of course, these requirements are only the minimum requirements. It would be pointless to have a policy if it was never communicated throughout relevant parts of the organization to individual personnel responsible for working with secure credit card data. Financial institutions should also develop systems for routinely checking, testing, and applying software patches. Other commonsense approaches to these requirements should be taken.

Note also that each individual brand has its own variation of these requirements. For specifics on each brands' requirements, consult the following:

> American Express: www.americanexpress.com/datasecurity
> Discover Financial Services: www.discovernetwork.com/ fraudsecurity/disc.html
> JCB International: www.jcbglobal.com/english/pci/index. html
> MasterCard Worldwide: www.mastercard.com/sdp
> Visa Inc.: www.visa.com/cisp

b. PA-DSS Requirements

PA-DSS applies to software developers, integrators, and service providers for commercially available payment software.[11] It requires that any payment software allow secure remote access, including via wireless access, and allow software updates to be applied remotely. It also requires data encryption and firewalled access. Providers of payment software must also facilitate training programs for customers, resellers, and integrators. Further details are available on the PCI website.[12] For financial institutions, the PCI website contains lists of PCI-certified compliant payment software vendors and service providers.

c. PTS Requirements

PTS requires virtual and physical security, encryption, and other standards for maintaining the integrity of credit card data, both while stored on the device and when transmitted via IT networks. While PTS requirements apply to manufacturers of hardware used to process credit card data,

---

[11] Custom-developed payment software must comply with PCI-DSS.

[12] PCI SECURITY STANDARDS COUNCIL, https://www.pcisecuritystandards.org/index.php.

an awareness of these standards is necessary if engaged in credit card processing services. A financial institution could not escape liability if it used non-PTS-compliant hardware. The PCI-SSC website has a list of PTS-compliant hardware.

4. PCI Criticisms/Enforcement

While in most places PCI-DSS are not law, they can be enforced through contractual and other legal means. All companies that accept or process credit card data must encrypt transmission of credit card data, have periodic network scans, control virtual and physical access to credit card data, and meet the other requirements of the various data standards. Failure to comply can result in fines of up to $500,000 per incident if credit card data is exposed. This may also result in private lawsuits and FTC actions.

PCI standards incorporate sound security practices but are not without some shortcomings. Only the largest processors, those with more than 6 million transactions annually, must have expensive PCI-compliance audits. For all other, compliance is self-certifying. This has the potential for permitting gaps in compliance.

For financial institutions acting as "acquiring banks," it may be difficult to determine whether specific merchants are compliant as they lack the experience or ability to ensure compliance with PCI data standards.

III. FDIC GUIDANCE ON THE PROTECTION OF CUSTOMER DATA

A. Computer Viruses

The FDIC issued a Financial Institution Letter (FIL) covering computer viruses.[13] It advised managers to understand

---

[13] FED. DEPOSIT INS. CORP., FIL-62-2004, COMPUTER VIRUS PROTECTION (June 7, 2004).

the risks of computer viruses and to take appropriate actions to protect the financial institution's information systems. The FDIC stated:

> Customer information security guidelines require periodic risk assessments and status reports be provided to the Board of Directors. The effectiveness of the institution's computer virus protection program should be addressed in these periodic assessments and reports. Any control weaknesses should be identified and addressed during the normal course of business.[14]

B. Disposal of Consumer Information

On February 2, 2005, the FDIC issued another FIL regarding guidelines for proper disposal of consumer information under the Fair and Accurate Credit Transactions Act of 2003 (FACT Act).[15] Consumer information includes "any record about an individual, whether in paper, electronic, or other form that is a consumer report or is derived from a consumer report and that is maintained or otherwise possessed by or on behalf of the institution for a business purpose"; it does not include any record or compilation of such records that does not identify the individual.[16] The FDIC noted that the federal bank and thrift regulatory agencies had recently jointly issued final guidelines to implement Section 216 of the FACT Act, which is designed to protect consumers by protecting against identity theft and other types of fraud.[17] In its final rules implementing Section 216, the FDIC requires each financial institution to develop and maintain, as part of its information security program, appropriate controls designed to ensure that it properly disposes of "consumer information" derived from a consumer report in a manner consistent with the financial institution's existing obligation

---

[14] *Id.*

[15] FED. DEPOSIT INS. CORP., FIL-7-2005, FAIR AND ACCURATE CREDIT TRANSACTIONS ACT OF 2003—GUIDELINES REQUIRING THE PROPER DISPOSAL OF CONSUMER INFORMATION (Feb. 2, 2005).

[16] *Id.*

[17] *Id.*

under the guidelines to properly dispose of customer information. The guidelines direct financial institutions to assess the risks to their consumer information as well as customer information by evaluating security measures to control these risks. Therefore, financial institutions must design their information security programs to dispose properly of customer information and consumer information.[18] Since July 1, 2005, banks have been required to satisfy these guidelines regarding proper disposal of consumer information. In addition, financial institutions must contractually obligate service providers, or "any person or entity that maintains, processes or otherwise is permitted access to customer information or consumer information through its provision of services directly to the bank," to implement appropriate measures to comply with the guidelines regarding the proper disposal of consumer information.[19]

IV. RECORD-KEEPING REQUIREMENTS

A. FFIEC-Regulated Financial Institutions

The FFIEC has established record-keeping requirements for various records, which may be stored in electronic form. No matter how they are stored, the records must be easily accessible in a reasonable time period. The records listed in Appendix B, "Record Retention," must be retained for at least five years.[20]

B. SEC/CFTC/NASD Record-Keeping Requirements

Broker-dealers and SEC members are required to create and maintain certain records.[21] If electronic media are

---

[18] *Id.*

[19] *Id.*

[20] 31 C.F.R. §103.

[21] 17 C.F.R. §240.17A-4.

used to store records, they must be maintained in a "non-rewritable, non-erasable format."[22] These regulated entities must provide its primary regulator with confirmation that the electronic media meet these requirements.[23] The entity must also have appropriate audit trails and systems to accurately preserve the source of the records.[24] Electronic records must be downloadable from electronic media to any other acceptable media.[25]

Regulated entities are required to preserve the following exhaustive list of records:

(1) All records required to be made pursuant to § 240.17a-3(a)(4), (a)(6), (a)(7), (a)(8), (a)(9), (a)(10), (a)(16), (a)(18), (a)(19), (a)(20), and analogous records created pursuant to § 240.17a-3(f).

(2) All check books, bank statements, cancelled checks and cash reconciliations.

(3) All bills receivable or payable (or copies thereof), paid or unpaid, relating to the business of such member, broker or dealer, as such.

(4) Originals of all communications received and copies of all communications sent (and any approvals thereof) by the member, broker or dealer (including inter-office memoranda and communications) relating to its business as such, including all communications which are subject to rules of a self-regulatory organization of which the member, broker or dealer is a member regarding communications with the public. As used in this paragraph (b)(4), the term communications includes sales scripts.

(5) All trial balances, computations of aggregate indebtedness and net capital (and working papers in connection therewith), financial statements, branch office reconciliations, and internal audit working papers, relating to the business of such member, broker or dealer, as such.

(6) All guarantees of accounts and all powers of attorney and other evidence of the granting of any discretionary

---

[22] *Id.* §240.17A-4(f).

[23] *Id.* §240.17A-4(f)(2)(i).

[24] *Id.* §240.17A-4(f)(3)(v).

[25] *Id.* §240.17A-4(f)(3)(viii).

authority given in respect of any account, and copies of resolutions empowering an agent to act on behalf of a corporation.

(7) All written agreements (or copies thereof) entered into by such member, broker or dealer relating to its business as such, including agreements with respect to any account.

(8) Records which contain the following information in support of amounts included in the report prepared as of the audit date on Form X-17A-5 (§ 249.617 of this chapter) Part II or Part IIA or Part IIB and in annual audited financial statements required by § 240.17a-5(d) and § 240.17a-12(b):

(i) Money balance position, long or short, including description, quantity, price and valuation of each security including contractual commitments in customers' accounts, in cash and fully secured accounts, partly secured accounts, unsecured accounts, and in securities accounts payable to customers;

(ii) Money balance and position, long or short, including description, quantity, price and valuation of each security including contractual commitments in non-customers' accounts, in cash and fully secured accounts, partly secured and unsecured accounts, and in securities accounts payable to non-customers;

(iii) Position, long or short, including description, quantity, price and valuation of each security including contractual commitments included in the Computation of Net Capital as commitments, securities owned, securities owned not readily marketable, and other investments owned not readily marketable;

(iv) Amount of secured demand note, description of collateral securing such secured demand note including quantity, price and valuation of each security and cash balance securing such secured demand note;

(v) Description of futures commodity contracts, contract value on trade date, market value, gain or loss, and liquidating equity or deficit in customers' and non-customers' accounts;

(vi) Description of futures commodity contracts, contract value on trade date, market value, gain or loss and liquidating equity or deficit in trading and investment accounts;

(vii) Description, money balance, quantity, price and valuation of each spot commodity position or commitments in customers' and non-customers' accounts;

(viii) Description, money balance, quantity, price and valuation of each spot commodity position or commitments in trading and investment accounts;

(ix) Number of shares, description of security, exercise price, cost and market value of put and call options including short out of the money options having no market or exercise value, showing listed and unlisted put and call options separately;

(x) Quantity, price, and valuation of each security underlying the haircut for undue concentration made in the Computation for Net Capital;

(xi) Description, quantity, price and valuation of each security and commodity position or contractual commitment, long or short, in each joint account in which the broker or dealer has an interest, including each participant's interest and margin deposit;

(xii) Description, settlement date, contract amount, quantity, market price, and valuation for each aged failed to deliver requiring a charge in the Computation of Net Capital pursuant to § 240.15c3-1;

(xiii) Detail relating to information for possession or control requirements under § 240.15c3-3 and reported on the schedule in Part II or IIA of Form X-17A-5 (§ 249.617 of this chapter);

(xiv) Detail of all items, not otherwise substantiated, which are charged or credited in the Computation of Net Capital pursuant to § 240.15c3-1, such as cash margin deficiencies, deductions related to securities values and undue concentration, aged securities differences and insurance claims receivable; and

(xv) Other schedules which are specifically prescribed by the Commission as necessary to support information reported as required by § 240.17a-5 and § 240.17a-12.

(9) The records required to be made pursuant to § 240.15c3-3(d)(4) and (o).

(10) The records required to be made pursuant to § 240.15c3-4 and the results of the periodic reviews conducted pursuant to § 240.15c3-4(d).

(11) All notices relating to an internal broker-dealer system provided to the customers of the broker or dealer that sponsors such internal broker-dealer system, as defined in paragraph (a)(16)(ii)(A) of § 240.17a-3. Notices, whether written or communicated through the internal broker-dealer trading system or other automated means, shall be preserved under this

paragraph (b)(11) if they are provided to all customers with access to an internal broker-dealer system, or to one or more classes of customers. Examples of notices to be preserved under this paragraph (b)(11) include, but are not limited to, notices addressing hours of system operations, system malfunctions, changes to system procedures, maintenance of hardware and software, and instructions pertaining to access to the internal broker-dealer system.

(12) The records required to be made pursuant to § 240.15c3-1e(c)(4)(vi)(D) and (E).[26]

1. Copies of Customer Records

FINRA Rule 4511 requires member firms to keep all records without a prescribed retention period for six years after the account is closed, effectively the default period.[27] FINRA Rule 4512 requires regulated firms to retain customer account information, including the name of the account holder or holders and their signature(s).[28] This rule also requires firms to keep account information that is updated for at least six years after the update was done or at least six years after the account is closed. Firms may also be subject to further requirements under the Securities Exchange Act.[29]

2. Customer Complaints

FINRA Rule 4513 requires regulated firms to keep customer complaints for at least four years. These complaints must be kept at the office that generated those complaints.[30]

---

[26] *Id.* §240.17a-4(b).

[27] FIN. INDUS. REGULATORY AUTH., Regulatory Notice 11-19, SEC APPROVES CONSOLIDATED FINRA RULES GOVERNING BOOKS AND RECORDS 2 (Apr. 2011).

[28] *Id.*

[29] *Id.* at 3.

[30] *Id.*

3. Negotiated Instruments

FINRA Rule 4514 requires regulated firms to keep copies of negotiated instruments drawn on a customer's account and the customer's authorizations for those instruments for three years from the date the authorization expires.[31]

4. Changes in Account Names

FINRA Rule 4515 requires that changes in account names, designations, and circumstances around such changes must be documented *prior* to the execution of a trade. Investment advisors are allowed to allocate their orders for customers on whose behalf the orders are submitted, but the allocation must be done by noon of the next trading day *after* the trade was executed.[32]

5. Order Audit Trail System Requirements

The Order Audit Trail System (OATS) is a system of order, quote, and trade information for all National Market System stocks and over-the-counter equity securities with FINRA-mandated audit trails. OATS is owned and maintained by the National Association of Securities Dealers (NASD). This system is used to reconstruct orders and monitor member firms. FINRA-regulated firms are required to capture and report data to OATS regarding order execution.[33] This applies even when another firm clears transactions for the regulated financial institution.

A FINRA-regulated entity may hire another firm to transmit its OATS data, but, at a minimum, the agreement with the transmitting firm should require the transmitting entity to

---

[31] *Id.* at 4.

[32] *Id.*

[33] Fin. Indus. Regulatory Auth., Rules 7410–7470.

1. be reasonably knowledgeable with OATS Rules and Reporting Technical Specifications;
2. have completed or expect to complete testing, as described in the OATS Technical Specifications;
3. agree to make reports to OATS in compliance with OATS Rules and Technical Specifications, as amended;
4. agree that any data prepared on behalf of the customer firm and maintained by the transmitting firm is the property of the customer firm and will be turned over promptly on the customer firm's request;
5. agree to permit audit of any records, at any reasonable time, by FINRA and to promptly furnish to FINRA or its designee true, correct, complete copies of any part of these records;
6. have processes and procedures reasonably designed to ensure compliance with OATS requirements;
7. notify the customer firm immediately on the occurrence of any event that would adversely affect the transmitting firm's ability to perform OATS reporting; and
8. provide for the disposition of the customer firm's data in the event that the transmitting firm is unable or unwilling to provide for data storage. In no event should any data be deleted without an appropriate copy being maintained.

6. Supervision of Communications

FINRA-regulated firms are required to review incoming, outgoing, and internal electronic communications. But it's not as simple as it sounds. Firms must identify the types of communications to be reviewed and the person responsible for the reviews. Different types of communications may need to be reviewed by different persons at different levels within the organization. External communications and internal communications, including e-mail, message boards, electronic faxes, and so on, are all subject to review,[34] Regulated firms must name the individuals who will perform the reviews. The persons doing the reviews should have adequate experience and training.[35] Of course, the person conducting the reviews cannot review his or her own communications.[36] Firms must also determine the method and frequency of review. The method for review must be effective and take into account any special conditions, such as encrypted communications.[37] The review can be based on keywords, random reviews, or some combination. No matter how the review is done, the firm should periodically check for defects in the system. Software or other electronic means may be used to conduct the reviews; however, care must be taken to understand the limitations of such means.

Firms should consider the size of the business, the type of business, the scope of activities engaged in, the type of customers, geographic location, the disciplinary records of the persons involved, and the volume of communications when determining the frequency of conducting reviews.[38] Finally, firms must document that the supervision was properly and timely performed. This documentation can be electronic or hard copy.[39]

7. FINRA v. Barclays

Recently, FINRA settled charges against Barclays for failing to properly keep electronic records.[40] FINRA alleged that Barclays violated Securities Exchange Act Rule 17a-4, NASD Rules 3110 and 2110, and FINRA Rules 4511 and 2010, by failing to preserve electronic records in a "Write-Once,

---

[34] Fin. Indus. Regulatory Auth., Regulatory Notice 07-59, Supervision of Electronic Communications 8–9 (Dec. 2007).

[35] Id. at 10.

[36] Id. at 11.

[37] Id.

[38] Id. at 14.

[39] Id.

[40] Fin. Indus. Regulatory Auth., Letter of Acceptance, Waiver and Consent No. 2011026679201. Mar., 2014

Read-Many" (WORM) format. Barclays was also charged with failing to keep certain e-mails (including attachments) and instant messages. Barclays averaged approximately 500,000 e-mails per day, but for many of those e-mails with attachments, the attachments were removed when the e-mails were stored. Barclays was found to have failed to timely establish and maintain the required monitoring system, including policies and procedures. The firm was censured and fined $3.75 million.[41]

V. Breaches of Data Security

More than 40 states have laws that address data breaches and theft of data. Aside from that, the threat of private lawsuits can be much worse than any legal or regulatory violation. The recent data breach at Target illustrates this point quite well. Although a merchant and not a financial institution, Target is subject to PCI data compliance. In addition, since the hacker initially gained entrance to Target's network using stolen credentials from one of its third-party service providers, the need for vendor management cannot be overstated. (See Chapter 8, "Use of Third-Party Service Providers: Sourcing and Outsourcing.")

According to Bloomberg Businessweek,[42] the following scenario began about six months prior to the actual breach: Hackers either stole or socially engineered login IDs and passwords from one of Target's heating and cooling vendors. Using this information, they accessed and surveilled Target's network, possibly for many weeks. Eventually, they installed malicious software ("malware") on all cashier stations at more than 1,700 U.S. Target stores. Target meanwhile had installed sophisticated security software from a company

---

[41] *Id.*

[42] Michael Riley, Ben Elgin, Dune Lawrence & Carol Matlack, *Missed Alarms and 40 Million Stolen Credit Card Numbers: How Target Blew It*, BLOOMBERG BUSINESSWEEK, Mar. 13, 2014, http://www.businessweek.com/articles/2014-03-13/target-missed-alarms-in-epic-hack-of-credit-card-data.

called FireEye FireEye software has the ability to detect and destroy unfamiliar code within its customer's systems. On November 30, 2013, in the heat of the Christmas shopping season, the malware, which had begun collecting every credit card number swiped at Target and other information, also began to transmit it to servers located in Moscow. At this point, the FireEye software detected the malware, but it did not delete the malware. Target had failed to configure that functionality. It is not clear whether that improper configuration was intentional or not. Still, the FireEye software had worked and alerted Target to the malware. For some reason, Target did not act quickly enough to stop the damage, a failure that has led to more than 90 lawsuits.[43] Target is sure to be embroiled in litigation for years to come.

A. Practical Guidance—Data Breaches

There are no federal data breach notification laws; they exist only at the state level. Each state has rules regarding when, how, and to whom notification of data breaches must be reported. Some like Louisiana, require notification of the state government as well as the individuals involved. Some, like Massachusetts, carry hefty fines for each violation. Most, however, exempt the company from notification requirements if the data accessed was encrypted. A simple solution, therefore, is to have all sensitive data encrypted. This eliminates most disclosure requirements and limits potential exposure for data breaches. Appendix C, "Data Breaches," contains a simple decision tree that can be used in the event of a data breach or, better yet, to plan against a data breach.

B. Big Data

The term "big data" refers to the collection and analysis of large amounts of data. This data can be collected from

---

[43] *Id.*

many different sources. These sources include publicly available databases, such as the phone book. They can also be purchased from legally available sources, such as mailing lists. The data itself may include PII and "de-identified" data as well. Once this large amount of data is accumulated, it can then be analyzed. Seemingly unconnected data can be analyzed to uncover potential customer behavior and spot market trends. It can also be used to connect PII to other seemingly unrelated bits of data. It is thought that 80 percent of the people in the United States can be identified by name and address merely by using free publicly available databases. Of course, financial institutions collect vast amounts of internal data. This comes from various publicly accessible websites and even its own internal transactions. Big data analytics is being applied to this internal data to help financial institutions better understand their markets and customers. As financial institutions collect more and more data, the analysis of big data will only grow.

Chapter 10

ELECTRONIC CRIMES

I. INTRODUCTION

Criminals have existed in every age and civilization. Today's electronic age is no different; however, in some ways our online lifestyle has made it easier for criminals. Banks are susceptible to some of this activity as they are the lifeblood to any economic activity, whether legitimate or not.

This chapter discusses various antifraud measures applicable to financial institutions. The first deals with online authentication and tackles the problem of how to know whether it is actually the financial institution's customer who is attempting to transact business online. Next, it discusses anti–money laundering (AML) measures and associated record-keeping and reporting requirements. Finally, it discusses identity theft and ways that financial institutions are required to combat it.

II. ONLINE AUTHENTICATION

Federal Financial Institutions Examination Council (FFIEC) regulated entities must evaluate their information technology (IT) security programs to make sure that they appropriately measure risks, contain adequate mitigation for those risks, and manage customer awareness of those risk mitigation efforts. They must also manage the programs to compensate for changes in the IT security environment, such as changes in technology, customer information, and IT security threats.[1]

Paramount to any IT security is the verification of a customer's identity before allowing a transaction to take place. The most common method of verification is to have a customer provide some "factor" as identification. These include "something a person knows" (e.g., password or PIN), "something a person has" (e.g., some type of physical device like

---

[1] *See* FED. FIN. INST. EXAMINATION COUNCIL, AUTHENTICATION IN AN INTERNET BANKING ENVIRONMENT (Oct. 12, 2005).

an ATM card, an RFID chip, or even a cookie on the user's computer), or "something a person is" (e.g., a biometric identifier like a fingerprint or voice pattern).[2]

The FFIEC has determined that single-factor identification is inadequate to ensure the protection of customer information or prevent an unauthorized transfer of funds.[3] The regulators require that a layered system of multifactor authentication be used with both consumer and non-consumer customers.[4] At a minimum, this system should include the ability to detect and react to threats and potential threats related to unauthorized logins and unauthorized transfers of monies. In addition, for business accounts, regulated financial institutions should add security for system administrators to prevent unauthorized changes to the ability to access account information and further configure account settings.[5]

III. Anti–Money Laundering and Record-Keeping

Money laundering makes crimes like terrorism and drug trafficking possible. By facilitating the introduction of money gained from illegal activities into the mainstream economy, this activity also threatens the legitimate aims of monetary policy. The penalties for money laundering include up to 20 years in prison and fines up to $500,000. Current AML laws developed in a patchwork manner over time. A brief summary of relevant AML laws follows. Note that these apply across the financial services industry.

Bank Secrecy Act (BSA) (1970). The BSA established record-keeping and reporting requirements and required regulated financial institutions to (1) report cash transactions over $10,000 on a Currency Transaction Report (CTR);

---

[2] *Id.* at 7.

[3] *Id.* p. 6.

[4] *See* Fed. Fin. Inst. Examination Council, Supplement to Authentication in an Internet Banking Environment (June 22, 2011).

[5] *Id.* at 5.

(2) confirm the identify of any persons conducting such transactions; and (3) maintain an appropriate audit trail for such transactions.

Money Laundering Control Act of 1986. The Money Laundering Control Act established money laundering as a federal crime and prohibited structuring large cash transactions to evade CTR filings rules. It also directed regulated financial institutions to establish and maintain procedures to monitor compliance with the reporting and record-keeping requirements of the BSA.

Anti-Drug Abuse Act of 1988. This act defined "financial institution" to include businesses such as car dealers and certain real estate closing business in order to require them to file CTRs and mandated the confirmation of purchasers of financial instruments over $3,000.

Annunzio-Wylie Anti-Money Laundering Act (1992). This act required the filing of Suspicious Activity Reports (SARs) and required record keeping for wire transfers.

Money Laundering Suppression Act (1994). This act required bank regulators to develop AML examination procedures. It also required money services businesses (MSB) to be registered and to maintain a list of authorized agents, and made operating an unregistered MSB a federal crime. Further, it recommended that all states adopt similar laws for MSBs.

Money Laundering and Financial Crimes Strategy Act (1998). This act required AML training for bank examiners, authorized financial regulators to develop a national AML strategy, and authorized law enforcement task forces to coordinate federal, state, and local law enforcement AML efforts.

International Money Laundering Abatement and Financial Anti-Terrorism Act of 2001 (Title III of the USA PATRIOT Act). This act required regulated financial institutions to have adequate due diligence procedures to detect the financing of terrorism, and to share information with the U.S. government and with other regulated financial institutions; increased AML requirements for regulated financial institutions; and facilitated records access and required banks to respond to regulatory requests for information within 120 hours (five days) of such request.

Intelligence Reform and Terrorism Prevention Act of 2004. This act required the reporting of certain cross-border funds transfers.

A. SEC Rule 17a-3(a)(17) and Anti–Money Laundering

Because of the fractured nature of financial services regulation, the current AML rules differ from preexisting Securities and Exchange Commission (SEC) rules. Appendix D contains a Financial Industry Regulatory Authority (FINRA) publication that sets forth FINRA's analysis of the differences and gaps between these rules.

B. FFIEC Anti–Money Laundering Regulations

The FFIEC has issued a 400+ page manual on AML that addresses what regulators should look for and what FFIEC-regulated institutions should do in response to suspected money laundering.[6] Regulated financial institutions are required to conduct a risk assessment with respect to AML and to have a compliance program to ensure compliance with the applicable regulations. Regulators believe that certain financial products and services, including electronic banking and electronic payment services, may carry with them a higher degree of anonymity and thus pose a higher risk of involvement with money laundering. Banks are responsible for having an AML detection program. There are several software tools available to help with AML monitoring, some of which are quite useful. However, the financial institution is responsible for compliance regardless of the effectiveness of these tools.

---

[6] FED. FIN. INST. EXAMINATION COUNCIL, BANK SECRECY ACT/ANTI-MONEY LAUNDERING EXAMINATION HANDBOOK (2010).

Appendix F contains an AML checklist provided by the FFIEC, and Appendix F contains FFIEC suggested red flags for AML activity. These should both be incorporated into any AML detection program.

IV. Identity Theft Red Flag Rules

A. FFIEC/FTC Red Flag Rules

The Fair and Accurate Credit Transactions Act of 2003 (FACTA)[7] was enacted partially to address the issue of identity theft. The Red Flag Program Clarification Act of 2010[8] further clarified some parts of FACTA. The Federal Trade Commission (FTC) issued regulations applicable to FFIEC-regulated financial institutions on February 9, 2009, but they did not go into effect until January 1, 2011.[9] The regulations apply to FFIEC-regulated financial institutions, creditors, and any other entity that holds a consumer "transaction account."[10] A "creditor" is an entity that extends or renews credit or arranges for other entities to extend or renew credit.[11] Regulated entities are required to have an identity theft red flag program. This issue is so important that the regulators require that the initial red flag program be approved by the board of directors of the financial institution.[12] This program must

1. identify relevant identity theft red flags;
2. detect identity theft red flags;
3. prevent and mitigate identity theft red flags; and

---

[7] 15 U.S.C. §1681 *et seq.*

[8] Pub. L. No. 111-319, 124 Stat. 3457 (2010).

[9] 16 C.F.R. pt. 681 *et seq.*

[10] *Id.* pt. 681.1(b).

[11] *Id.*

[12] *Id.* pt. 681.1(e)(1).

4. regularly assess and update its identity theft red flag program.[13]

Regulated financial institutions may implement a red flag program that is appropriate to the institution as long as it has these characteristics.

Several types of red flags may indicate some type of identity theft activity, including (1) notifications from a credit reporting agency; (2) suspicious documentation; (3) suspicious information used to identify the account holder, such as an address that differs from that on file; (4) the unusual use of a covered account; or (5) notices from consumers, law enforcement, or others regarding possible identity theft in connection with a covered accounts. Credit card issuers must notify cardholders whenever there is a change in address for the account.[14]

Regulated institutions should attempt to detect red flags when opening new accounts and when working with existing accounts. For new accounts, the financial institution should try to verify the name, address, and other information provided from other sources. For existing accounts, the institution should be careful to confirm the identity of the person attempting to access or make use of an account, through authentication (if online) or through appropriate identification techniques (if in person). If the institution is using software to detect identity theft red flags, it is still responsible for having an effective program. Care should be taken during negotiations with the software vendor to ensure that the software will enable the financial institution to comply with the requirements outlined herein.

Financial institutions should monitoring accounts for red flags and respond when appropriate by contacting the account holder, changing passwords or other means of authentication when a red flag is triggered. More extreme measures may include closing and then reopening the account, refusing to open a new account, and notifying the

---

[13] *Id.* pt. 681.1(d)(2)(iv).

[14] *Id.* pt. 681.2.

appropriate law enforcement agency. Of course, the financial institution may decide to do nothing.

Finally, the financial institution must have continuous oversight, and routinely update and maintain the red flag program. This includes monitoring the performance of any third-party service providers relevant to the program. Appropriate training of those personnel administering the program is required.[15] The program should also be discussed annually with the board of directors even if no incidents have occurred, but more often if there have been incidents of identity theft.

B. SEC/CFTC Red Flag Rules

Identity theft is a problem that has expanded in the electronic age. The ease with which information is available has increased criminals' opportunity to commit various crimes, including perpetrating identity theft. Not only does identity theft defraud an individual, it also defrauds the financial institution. It can pose risk on customers and impact the safety and soundness of the financial institution. For these reasons, Congress and regulators have established rules designed to detect and reduce incidences of identity theft. By scanning data for common clues of identity theft or "red flags" and then investigating those, institutions protect not only themselves but their customers as well.

In 2007, pursuant to the Fair Credit Reporting Act (FCRA),[16] the U.S. Office of the Comptroller of the Currency, the Federal Reserve Board, Federal Deposit Insurance Corporation, Office of Thrift Supervision, National Credit Union Association, and Federal Trade Commission issued joint rules regarding red flags covering regulated financial institutions.[17] At that time, those rules applied to SEC- and CFTC-regulated entities as well. However, in 2010, the

---

[15] *Id.* pt. 681.1(e)(3).

[16] 15 U.S.C. §1681 *et seq.*

[17] OCC Bulletin 2007-45.

Dodd-Frank Act[18] amended the FCRA and required the SEC and CFTC to issue and enforce their own separate regulations regarding identity theft red flags.

Effective May 20, 2013, the CFTC and SEC jointly issued their own final red flag rules regarding identity theft. These rules apply to SEC- and CFTC-regulated entities and include broker-dealers, investment advisors, investment companies, and futures commission merchants. The rules are essentially the same as those issued by the FTC and FFIEC; however, some important distinctions exist.

The SEC and CFTC provided clarifications applicable to their respective jurisdictions. The clarifications primarily address these questions: Who is required to have a red flag program? What should be the objectives of each program? What elements are necessary for a program? And finally, how should a program be administered?

1. Who Is Required to Have a Red Flag Program?

Under FACTA, "financial institutions" and "creditors" that offer "covered accounts" are required to have red flag programs.[19]

a. Financial Institution Defined

The SEC and CFTC define "financial institution" as defined in the FCRA, as amended by Dodd-Frank.[20] Basically, any institution that holds a "transaction account" of a consumer or an individual is deemed to be a financial institution.[21] Of course, this applies only to entities that are otherwise subject to SEC or CFTC regulation.

---

[18] Pub. L. No. 111-203, 124 Stat. 1376 (2010).

[19] 15 U.S.C. §1681m(e)(1)(A) and (B).

[20] Id. §1682(a)(t).

[21] SEC. & EXCH. COMM'N & COMMODITY FUTURES TRADING COMM'N, Release Nos. 34-68359, IA-3582, IC-30456, IDENTITY THEFT RED FLAG RULES, at 15 (Apr. 10, 2013) [hereinafter RED FLAG RULES].

Under the SEC rules, entities that meet the FCRA definitions of "financial institution" and "creditor" and that are required to register under the (a) Exchange Act, (b) Investment Advisers Act, or (c) Investment Company Act, and are regulated as either a business development company or an employees' securities company, are deemed to fall under the red flag requirements. However, certain entities that would otherwise be regulated are specifically exempt.[22]

Both the SEC and CFTC make clear that even when an entity is not currently subject to the red flag rules, it should periodically review its operations to ensure that the status has not changed. Note also that Section 615(e)(1)(C) of the FCRA requires the SEC and CFTC to issue rules governing customer address changes. These rules are similar to those prescribed under the FFIEC red flag rules discussed in Section IV.A. above; however, both the SEC and CFTC have clearly stated that there is little or no chance of any entities under either jurisdiction to issue credit cards.[23] As long as this remains true, there is no concern. Other credit card issuers, however, would be subject to red flag regulations as discussed in Section IV.A. above.

Under the CFTC rules, "financial institution" has the same meaning as in Section 603(t) of the FCRA.[24] In addition, the CFTC specifically mentions the following as types of entities that are covered financial institutions, if they hold transaction accounts of consumers: futures commissions merchants, retail foreign exchange dealers, commodity trading advisors, commodity pool operators, introducing brokers, swap dealers, and major swap participants.[25] In

---

[22] See Sec. & Exch. Comm'n, Release No. 3222, Exemptions for Advisors and SEC Rule 203m (June 22, 2011).

[23] Red Flag Rules at 41.

[24] "[A]ny other person that, directly or indirectly, holds a transaction account (as defined in Section 19(b) of the Federal Reserve Act) belonging to a consumer." 15 U.S.C. §1681a(t). "Transaction account" is defined in §19(b) of the Federal Reserve Act and includes the right to make payments or transfers to third parties. See 12 U.S.C. §461(b)(1)(C).

[25] Red Flag Rules at 10.

addition, the CFTC "creditor" is any of the foregoing entities that arranges, participates in, or extends credit.[26]

b. Accounts Defined

According to the SEC, the following are examples of
accounts that are covered by the regulations: a broker-dealer
that offers custodial accounts, a registered investment company that allows individual investors to somehow make payments to third parties, and some investment advisors.

Advisory accounts, where the advisor has the lawful ability to withdraw funds from the account and use those funds to
make payments to third parties as instructed by the investor,
are covered by these red flags rules. This is true even when
the actual account is held at another institution as custodi-
an.[27] Similar accounts that only allow the advisor to withdraw
funds to pay for its own fees, and not to pay third parties,
are not covered as there is no ability to make payments to
third parties.[28] This also includes registered investment advisors to "private funds" as defined in 15 U.S.C. §80b-2(a)(29).
For purposes of these red flag rules, an advisor is deemed to
hold a covered transaction account if it can lawfully direct
the investor's proceeds from any redemption to another person, if instructed by the investor.

c. Creditor and Credit Defined

For both the SEC and CFTC, "creditor" is defined in the
Equal Credit Opportunity Act as "any person who regularly
extends, renews, or continues credit; any person who regularly arranges for the extension, renewal or continuation of
credit; or any assignee of an original creditor who participates in the decision to extend, renew or continue credit."[29]

---

[26] 17 C.F.R. pt. 162.1(b).
[27] RED FLAG RULES at 18.
[28] Id.
[29] 15 U.S.C. §1691a(e).

"Credit" is defined as "the right granted by a creditor to a debtor to defer payment of debt or to incur debts and defer its payment or to purchase property or services and defer payment therefor."[30] Excluded from this definition are creditors that advance funds for certain incidental expenses.[31]

In addition, the CFTC included a specific list of entities that are deemed to be creditors for the purpose of these rules.[32] These include futures commission merchants, commodity trading advisors, retail foreign exchange dealer, commodity pool operators, introducing brokers, swap dealers, or major swap participants that extend credit as set forth above.

The SEC added broker-dealers offering margin accounts, securities lending services, and short selling services to its definition of a creditor.[33] Private fund advisors would not necessarily be creditors under the rules solely because their private funds routinely borrow funds from third parties while waiting for investor contributions; "creditors" do not include indirect creditors.[34]

d. Covered Accounts Defined

Financial institutions are not subject to the red flag rules unless they have "covered accounts." Covered accounts are defined as either (1) accounts offered for primarily personal or household purposes, or (2) any other consumer account that may reasonably be at risk for identity theft. The CFTC definition includes margin accounts.[35] The SEC definition includes brokerage accounts with broker-dealers or mutual fund accounts that permits payments to third parties.[36]

"Accounts" are defined as a "continuing relationship established by a person with a financial institution or

---

[30] Id. §1681a(r)(5).

[31] Id. §1681m(e)(4)(B).

[32] RED FLAG RULES at 20.

[33] 17 C.F.R. §248.201(b)(5).

[34] RED FLAG RULES at 23.

[35] 17 C.F.R. §162.30(b)(3)(i).

[36] Id. §248.201(b)(3)(i); this also includes accounts held by an agent of a mutual fund.

creditor to obtain a product or service for personal, family, household or business purpose."[37] The CFTC definition includes the purchase of property or services via a deferred payment.[38] The SEC definition includes brokerage accounts, mutual fund accounts, and investment advisory accounts.[39]

Each regulated entity is required to periodically investigate and decide whether the accounts it offers meet the definitions and conditions of the regulations. This investigation should include (1) account opening methodology, (2) account access methodology, and (3) any previous identity theft incidents.[40] A regulated entity may determine that the red flag rules are not applicable because the entity does not offer accounts for household or personal uses, or that they apply only to a limited number of accounts because the entity has only a limited number of such accounts. In either case, the entity is still required to periodically determine whether and to what extent the red flag rules apply and whether it is required to have a red flag program in place, even if it is limited in scope.[41]

e. Red Flag Programs

Both the SEC and CFTC have issued guidance on red flag programs. This guidance includes the objectives of any such program, the required elements of the program, and the proper way to administer the program.

2. Objectives of Red Flag Programs

Red flag programs are required to (1) detect, (2) prevent, and (3) mitigate identity theft. Each institution, if it

---

[37] RED FLAG RULES at 24.

[38] 17 C.F.R. §162.30(b)(1).

[39] *Id.* §248.201(b)(1).

[40] *Id.* §§162.30(c) (CFTC regs.), 248.201(c) (SEC regs.).

[41] *Id.* §§162.30(c) (CFTC regs.), 248.201(c) (SEC regs.).

has determined that the regulations apply, must have a program that is appropriate to the financial institution or creditor itself. For instance, a typical large financial institution that has accounts for both individual and commercial customers must have a program to address identity theft with respect to the consumer accounts, but not the commercial accounts. A smaller institution that perhaps has only commercial accounts may not need a program, but it would still be required to periodically assess whether it is covered by these regulations.

3. Elements of Red Flag Programs

The red flag regulations require that each program contain reasonable policies and procedures (1) to determine what red flags may signal identity theft; (2) to detect identify theft red flags; (3) to respond promptly and adequately to any red flags that are detected; and (4) to periodically update each program based on current risks, both to customers and to the safety and soundness of the financial institution.[42] There is no need to have a completely separate set of policies and procedures if the requirements of the red flag regulations are met. The identity theft program can be incorporated into an existing antifraud or other regulatory compliance program.[43]

In addition, regulated entities should consider relevant portions of the FCRA[44] and the USA PATRIOT Act[45] when developing and administering a red flag program. Regulated entities subject to 31 U.S.C. §5318(g) may need to file a SAR. In addition, 15 U.S.C. §1681c-1(h) may prohibit the extension of credit when fraud is detected, and 15 U.S.C. §1681s-2 governs the reporting of information to a credit

---

[42] *Id.* §§162.30(d)(2) (CFTC regs.), 248.201(d)(2) (SEC regs.).

[43] RED FLAG RULES at 35.

[44] 15 U.S.C. §1681 *et seq.*

[45] Pub. L. No. 107-56, 115 Stat. 272 (2001).

reporting agency if the information is inaccurate or incomplete; it further prohibits the reporting of information that is reasonably believed to be inaccurate. Finally, 15 U.S.C. §1681m prohibits the sale, transfer, or collection of debts resulting from identity theft.

a. Identification of Red Flags

As part of their guidance, the SEC and CFTC have provided risk factors for identifying red flags, possible sources of red flags, and categories of red flags. The regulators believe that a flexible approach allows regulated entities to adapt to new ways that identity thieves develop to steal personal identities and therefore mitigate the risks of identity theft.[46]

　　i. Risk Factors. In determining what red flags may signal identity theft, the regulators have provided a list of factors that regulated entities should consider: (1) the types of accounts the entity offers or maintains; (2) the entity's account opening methodology; (3) account accessing methodology; and (4) past identity theft experience.[47] Thus, red flags that are common for one type of account may not be so for another type of account. Adequate diligence at account opening allows the entity to stop identity theft before any real harm is done. Particular attention should be paid at this stage of the client relationship. Finally, by incorporating prior identity theft experience, the regulated entity is using highly relevant information in identification of red flags for its market.

　　ii. Sources of Red Flags. The regulators have provided examples of sources that regulated entities should

---

[46] RED FLAG RULES at 30.

[47] *Id.*

consider to procure their own identity theft red flags, but the list is not exhaustive. These sources include past incidents of identity theft at the regulated entity, identity theft methods identified by the regulated entity that address changes in identity theft risk, and regulatory guidance applicable to identity theft and/or fraud prevention.[48]

iii. Categories of Red Flags. In addition, the SEC and CFTC have provided five categories of red flags that regulated entities must consider incorporating into any red flag program:

1. Notifications from consumer reporting agencies, including fraud detection notifications
2. Suspicious documents, including any that appear to be forged or modified
3. Suspicious information, such as new addresses
4. Suspicious activity with a covered account
5. Actual notices about possible identity theft, whether from a customer, law enforcement, or other source[49]

Examples of red flags from each of these categories is found in Appendix G. Again, note the flexibility this affords the financial institution, but also note that the onus of red flag detection is placed primarily on the institution. It is not possible to comply with these regulations without some thought and effort specifically addressing the individual institution.

b. Detection of Red Flags

The regulators do not provide any specific way of detecting identity theft but do provide various examples of

---

[48] *Id.* at 89.

[49] *Id.* at 36.

how to do it. These include obtaining appropriate information about and verifying the identity of a person opening an account and, with respect to existing accounts, verifying the validity of address changes, monitoring transactions, and authenticating customers.[50]

c. Responses to Red Flags

While the regulators have provided a list of responses that mitigate identity theft, regulated financial institutions and creditors are not limited by these responses and are encouraged to develop their own appropriate responses. Possible responses provided by the SEC and CFTC include but are not limited to the following: (1) monitoring covered accounts; (2) verifying changes with the customer; (3) changing or locking security devices with respect to a covered account, such as passwords or other security codes; (4) reopening the account with a new number; (5) refusing to open a new account; (6) closing an existing account; and (7) notifying law enforcement.

d. Updating a Red Flag Program

As noted above, regulated entities are required to periodically update their red flag programs. When updating a program, the following should be taken into account: (1) past experience of the regulated entity with identity theft; (2) changes in the practices of identity thieves; (3) changes in available methods for prevention, detection, and mitigation of identity theft; (4) changes in the types of accounts offered by the regulated entity; and (5) changes in the structure or business of the regulated entity, such as mergers and acquisitions or the use of third-party service providers.[51]

---

[50] *Id.* at 90.
[51] *Id.* at 38.

4. Administration of Red Flag Programs

The regulators have prescribed four requirements for the administration of red flags programs.[52] First, the initial program must be approved by with the board of directors of the financial institution or creditor, by a committee of that board, or, if the entity has no board, then by its senior management. This should include specific responsibility for implementation of any program, reviewing reports on identity theft activity at the financial institution or creditor, and approval of any material changes to the program.

Second, these same individuals must be involved in the administration of the program, including its development and implementation. This ensures continuity for the program. Any personnel that work directly on the red flag program should report directly to the board or senior management as applicable, at least annually. Any changes to the program or suggestions for future changes should be included in this reporting. In addition, such reporting should also address the effectiveness of the program, applicable arrangements with third-party service providers, and any significant identity theft occurrences along with the entity's response to those occurrences.[53] Board or applicable senior management members should keep in mind that the financial institution or creditor is responsible for the overall effectiveness of its program and make sure that its program addresses the size, complexity, and nature of its business.

Third, the entity must provide sufficient training about the programs to its employees.

Fourth, in the event that any third-party service providers are used to implement the program, the entity is required to adequately supervise and oversee any such service providers. These include any third parties that facilitate the opening of accounts, provide software, and manage other technology to verify customer identity, detect red flags, or facilitate payments. The service provider may have its own

---

[52] *Id.* at 32–34.

[53] *Id.* at 39.

procedures to detect, prevent, and mitigate identity theft; however, those procedures must meet the requirements of the red flag rules. Regulated entities that use such service providers should still require the service providers to address the identity theft issue as set forth in the regulations and report to the regulated entity their activities in this regard. The contractual arrangements with service providers should require adequate reporting to the regulated entity by the service provider so that the regulated entity can determine its compliance with the red flag rules.[54]

---

[54] *Id.* at 39–40.

BANKRUPTCY

I. INTRODUCTION

The 2008 financial crises had the financial services industry on the edge of collapse. The then-existing regulatory structure was inadequate to address the situation. Postcrisis, new laws and regulations were put into place to address and mitigate the risks of system-wide failure.

Bankruptcy is another area of the law that intersects with technology, often in new and novel ways. Knowledge of the law and its pitfalls for various parties would be useful when drafting agreements over the use of intellectual property (IP), especially where one is licensing software or other IP that may be critical to a business.

This chapter addresses issues involving insolvency and dispositions of financial service companies, as well as technology issues that arise in a bankruptcy situation. This chapter applies generally across the financial services industry.

II. Bankrupt Licensor of Technology

An early case in this arena, *Lubrizol Enterprises, Inc. v. Richmond Metal Finishers, Inc.*,[1] set off an awareness of the insufficiency of then-existing law to address issues brought out in bankruptcy. The court in that case struck down an existing (software) license, cutting off the ability of the licensee to use the software. The possible consequences of such a situation are easy to imagine. Software and technology underlies so many business processes that the sudden inability to use a specific software program could easily cripple any business. This case caused an uproar and led to legislation to reform bankruptcy law. A big part of that legislation was designed to protect licensees from debtor-licensors. The legislature recognized the need to protect licensees from termination of software and other IP licenses.

A significant part of that legislation is Section 365(n) of the Bankruptcy Code, which provides:

> (n)(1) If the trustee rejects an executory contract under which the debtor is a licensor of a right to intellectual property, the licensee under such contract may elect—
> > (A) to treat such contract as terminated by such rejection if such rejection by the trustee amounts to such a breach as would entitle the licensee to treat such contract

---

[1] 756 F.2d 1043 (4th Cir. 1985), *cert. denied*, 475 U.S. 1058 (1986).

as terminated by virtue of its own terms, applicable non-bankruptcy law, or an agreement made by the licensee with another entity; or

(B) to retain its rights (including a right to enforce any exclusivity provision of such contract, but excluding any other right under applicable nonbankruptcy law to specific performance of such contract) under such contract and under any agreement supplementary to such contract, to such intellectual property (including any embodiment of such intellectual property to the extent protected by applicable nonbankruptcy law), as such rights existed immediately before the case commenced, for—

(i) the duration of such contract; and

(ii) any period for which such contract may be extended by the licensee as of right under applicable nonbankruptcy law.

(2) If the licensee elects to retain its rights, as described in paragraph (1)(B) of this subsection, under such contract—

(A) the trustee shall allow the licensee to exercise such rights;

(B) the licensee shall make all royalty payments due under such contract for the duration of such contract and for any period described in paragraph (1)(B) of this subsection for which the licensee extends such contract; and

(C) the licensee shall be deemed to waive—

(i) any right of setoff it may have with respect to such contract under this title or applicable nonbankruptcy law; and

(ii) any claim allowable under section 503(b) of this title arising from the performance of such contract.

(3) If the licensee elects to retain its rights, as described in paragraph (1)(B) of this subsection, then on the written request of the licensee the trustee shall—

(A) to the extent provided in such contract, or any agreement supplementary to such contract, provide to the licensee any intellectual property (including such embodiment) held by the trustee; and

(B) not interfere with the rights of the licensee as provided in such contract, or any agreement supplementary to such contract, to such intellectual property (including such embodiment) including any right to obtain such intellectual property (or such embodiment) from another entity.

(4) Unless and until the trustee rejects such contract, on the written request of the licensee the trustee shall—

> (A) to the extent provided in such contract or any agreement supplementary to such contract—
>> (i) perform such contract; or
>> (ii) provide to the licensee such intellectual property (including any embodiment of such intellectual property to the extent protected by applicable non-bankruptcy law) held by the trustee; and
>
> (B) not interfere with the rights of the licensee as provided in such contract, or any agreement supplementary to such contract, to such intellectual property (including such embodiment), including any right to obtain such intellectual property (or such embodiment) from another entity.

A. Determining Whether a Contract Is Executory

Aside from trademarks, Section 365(n) does provide some protections for licensees from bankrupt licensors. However, that protection is largely centered on whether the contract/IP license is an "executory contract" under the Bankruptcy Code. While the Bankruptcy Code itself does not define an executory contract, case law does provide some guidance on the issue. In fact, there are two lines of cases that provide that answer, those using the Countryman test and those using the functional test.

1. Countryman Test

Under the Countryman test, in an executory contract the obligations of the debtor and the nondebtor party are, as of the bankruptcy filing, unfulfilled so that the failure of either party to perform those obligations would be a material breach such that the performance of the other party would be excused.[2]

---

[2] Vern Countryman, *Executory Contracts in Bankruptcy: Part I*, 57 MINN. L. REV. 439, 460 (1974).

This test has been adopted by the Third,[3] Fourth,[4] Seventh,[5] Eighth,[6] and Ninth Circuits.[7]

2. Functional Test

This test focuses on whether the debtor's estate will benefit from the assumption or rejection of the contract, regardless of whether a party has outstanding obligations. If the assumption or rejection of a contract would benefit the debtor's estate, it may be found executory.[8] The Sixth Circuit requires courts to use both tests.[9]

The Bankruptcy Code does not provide guidance on at what point the determination of whether a contract is executory is to be made. Generally, the executory nature of a contract is made as of the date the bankruptcy petition was filed.[10] However, even other cases suggest that sometimes the resolution of whether a contract is executory should be made only when a motion to assume or reject is actually made.[11]

---

[3] See Enterprise Energy Corp. v. United States (In re Columbia Gas Sys.), 50 F.3d 233 (3d Cir. 1995).

[4] See RCI Tech. Corp. v. Sunterra Corp. (In re Sunterra Corp.), 361 F.3d 257 (4th Cir. 2004).

[5] See In re Streets & Beard Farm P'ship, 882 F.2d 233 (7th Cir. 1989).

[6] See Cameron v. Pfaff Plumbing & Heating, Inc., 966 F.2d 414 (8th Cir. 1992).

[7] See In re Pacific Express, Inc., 780 F.2d 1482 (9th Cir. 1986).

[8] Shoppers World Cmty. Ctr., L.P. v. Bradlees Stores (In re Bradlees Stores, Inc.), 2001 U.S. Dist. LEXIS 14755 (S.D.N.Y. Sept. 20, 2001) (quoting Sipes v. Atlantic Gulf Communities Corp. (In re General Dev. Corp.), 84 F.3d 1364, 1374 (11th Cir. 1996)); see also In re Jolly, 574 F.2d 349, 351 (6th Cir. 1978).

[9] See In re Cardinal Indus., 146 B.R. 720, 729 (Bankr. S.D. Ohio 1992) (Courts "must consider the applicability of both the functional approach and the Countryman definition.").

[10] See Enterprise Energy Corp. v. United States (In re Columbia Gas Sys.), 50 F.3d 233 (3d Cir. 1995); In re Pomona Valley Med. Grp., Inc., 476 F.3d 665 (9th Cir. 2007); In re General DataComm Indus., Inc., 407 F.3d 616 (3d Cir. 2005); In re Sunterra Corp., 361 F.3d 257 (4th Cir. 2004); Stewart Title Guar. Co. v. Old Republic Nat'l Title Ins. Co., 83 F.3d 735 (5th Cir. 1996); In re Newcomb, 744 F.2d 621 (8th Cir. 1984).

[11] See In re B & K Hydraulic Co., 106 B.R. 131, 136 (Bankr. E.D. Mich. 1989) ("When termination of the contract requires an affirmative act of the non-debtor party, the contract remains executory because such an act is stayed under 11 U.S.C. § 362(a). When termination occurs without any action by the non-debtor party, the contract is no longer executory

3 Election to Retain a Contract Under Section 365(n)

Depending on the circuit, it may take some analysis to determine whether a contract is an executor contract and, therefore, whether a nondebtor licensee[12] can retain use of the software or other technology as contracted for. Types of relevant contracts include computer equipment purchase contracts, technology services contracts, software license agreements, and outsourcing agreements. The consequences of a potential debtor-licensor situation should be taken into consideration when negotiating all of these types of agreements. In bankruptcy, each contract is subject to one of three options: (1) rejection by the trustee-debtor, (2) assumption by the trustee-debtor, or (3) assumption and assignment by the trustee-debtor. The contract must either be assumed or rejected in its entirety.

Under chapter 7 of the Bankruptcy Code, if the trustee-debtor does not explicitly reject the contract within 60 days of the order of relief (or any additional time granted by the court), then the contract is deemed rejected.[13]

Under chapter 9, 11, 12, or 13, the trustee-debtor may either assume or reject a contract any time before confirmation of a plan by the court; however, if requested by a party to the contract, the court may order that the contract be assumed or rejected within a specified period of time.[14]

With respect to leases of computer hardware, the trustee-debtor must timely perform all of the obligations of the debtor-licensor "first arising from or after 60 days after the order for relief under Chapter 11," until the lease is

---

and no longer subject to assumption or rejection."); *In re* Pesce Baking Co., 43 B.R. 949, 957 (Bankr. N.D. Ohio 1984) ("The critical date for determining the executory nature of a contract is the date on which the bankruptcy court considers the debtor's application. [Citation omitted.] Although a collective bargaining agreement may be executory on the date the debtor's bankruptcy petition is filed, once the agreement expires of its own terms, the debtor's application to reject it becomes moot."); *In re* Riodizio, Inc., 204 B.R. 417, 421 (Bankr. S.D.N.Y. 1997) (Whether a contract is executory is normally determined as of the petition date, but certain postpetition events may effect that determination. The court may make a determination as of the date the motion to assume or reject is made or heard.).

[12] Debtor-licensees are discussed below.

[13] 11 U.S.C. §365(d)(1).

[14] *Id.* §365(d)(2).

assumed or rejected (notwithstanding Section 503(b)(1)), unless the court orders otherwise.[15] This does not affect the trustee's obligations under Section 365 (b) or (f), and acceptance of any performance of such obligations does not constitute a waiver of the debtor-licensor's rights.[16]

Excluded from such obligations are breaches of any provisions relating to (1) the insolvency or financial condition of the debtor prior to commencement of the case; (2) the commencement of a case under the Bankruptcy Code; (3) the appointment of or taking possession by a receiver; or (4) the satisfaction of any penalty provision relating to a failure by the debtor to perform nonmonetary obligations under the contract.[17] Note that while these types of clauses are common in many contracts, not just technology contracts, they are typically unenforceable. However, it is common for clients to insist on having them in an agreement. Care must be taken to address the goals of the contract, with an understanding these clauses would likely not be enforced in court.

B. Nonexecutory Contracts

Some courts have found exclusive perpetual licenses, where licensors have no continuing obligations, to be sales contracts, not executory contracts.[18] Consequently, the debtor-licensor could reject the contract, and the licensee would not have the protections of Section 365(n).

C. Licensee Obligations Under Section 365(n)

The Bankruptcy Code imposes certain obligations on licensees who wish to take advantage of the benefits of

---

[15] *Id.* §365(d)(5).

[16] *Id.*

[17] *Id.* §365(b)(2).

[18] See *In re* Learning Publ'ns Inc. 94 B.R. 763 (Bankr. M.D. Fla. 1988); *In re* Qintex, 950 F.2d 1492 (9th Cir. 1991); *In re* Patient Educ. Media, Inc., 210 B.R. 237 (Bankr. S.D.N.Y. 1997).

Section 365(n). First, the licensee must continue to pay any royalty payments under the license agreement. Courts have interpreted this to include payments based on the use of the intangible IP,[19] although the right to receive royalty payments is not transferred merely by a sale of the IP.[20]

A licensee seeking to retain its rights under Section 365(n) must forgo any right to setoffs under the contract.[21] Debtors will argue that this applies to any type of recoupment. Therefore, the license drafter should be clear that any payments are not setoffs.[22]

D. Cross-Border Bankruptcies

Chapter 15 of the Bankruptcy Code addresses cross-border bankruptcies. Where a company has locations in countries other than its home country but files for bankruptcy in its home country, chapter 15 allows the law of that home country to govern cases in the other nonhome countries. Only one reported case discusses Section 365(n) in the context of a cross-border bankruptcy.

Qimonda AG was a technology manufacturer headquartered in Munich, Germany. In January 2009, it commenced a proceeding under Germany's insolvency laws. It then commenced a chapter 15 proceeding in the U.S. Bankruptcy Court for the Eastern District of Virginia. The purpose of that proceeding was to marshal and administer Qimonda's U.S. assets. The German administrator attempted to terminate certain licenses for Qimonda's U.S. patents. The patent licensees asserted their rights under Section 365(n). The German administrator then made a motion to effectively enforce German law, which allowed him to "non-perform" the licenses rather than reject them under Section 365(n). While the Bankruptcy Court initially granted the motion,

---

[19] *In re* Prize Frize, 150 B.R. 456, 459 (9th Cir. BAP 1993).

[20] *In re* CellNet Data Sys. Inc., 327 F.3d 242 (3d Cir. 2003).

[21] 11 U.S.C. §365(n)(2)(C)(i).

[22] See *In re* Big Idea Prods., Inc., 372 B.R. 388 (Bankr. N.D. Ill. 2003).

the licensees appealed and the U.S. Court for the Eastern District of Virginia remanded the case back to the bankruptcy court to determine (1) by limiting the applicability of Section 365(n), were the interests of the foreign debtor and the U.S. patent licensees appropriately balanced while still protecting the licensees, and (2) would limiting the application of Section 365(n) violate public policy.[23] The bankruptcy court found that the German insolvency administrator, by electing to "non-perform" the U.S. patent licenses, effectively terminated the licensee's rights to use the patents. The court found that without Section 365(n), the licensees would be unable to use those patents and, hence, would "put at risk" research and manufacturing based on those patents.[24]

E. Limitations of Section 365(n)

When a debtor-licensor-trustee assumes an agreement, it waives the ability to set aside fraudulent transfers, preferential transfers, and certain unperfected transfers.[25] However, if an agreement is rejected and the licensee uses Section 365(n) to retain its rights, the debtor-licensor-trustee probably retains these powers. It is not clear whether Section 365(n) avoids the ability to set aside these transfers. In addition, a licensee should understand that a sale of the IP may eliminate its rights under Section 365(n).[26]

1. Trademarks

Another important limitation of Section 365(n) is that the term "intellectual property" as defined in the Bankruptcy

---

[23] In re Qimonda AG Bankruptcy Litig., 433 B.R.. 547, (E.D. Va. 2010) at 571.

[24] Id.

[25] Alvarado v. Walsh (In re LCO Enters.), 137 B.R. 955 (B.A.P. 9th Cir. 1992), aff'd, 12 F.3d 938 (9th Cir. 1993).

[26] Precision Indus., Inc. v. Qualitech Steel SBQ, LLC (In re Qualitech Steel Corp.), 327 F.3d 537 (7th Cir. 2003).

Code does not include trademarks.[27] Therefore, a pure trademark license is not subject to Section 365(n) and any rejection of that agreement would terminate the licensee's right to use the trademark.[28] Most software and technology agreements do, however, contain an element of trademark usage. Trademarks are inherent in the use of many software and technology packages. Courts have held that when a trademark is linked to the other IP otherwise protected under Section 365(n), the trademark is also protected.[29] However, in a situation where the licensee had earlier rejected the trademark license, it could not benefit from Section 365(n).[30]

While it may be less relevant with ordinary use by a licensee for internal use only, if the contract in question entails any type of development, distribution, channel partner, or other similar agreement, it would be helpful to include a provision granting a security interest in the trademarks and then to follow up with appropriate UCC-1 and PTO filings to perfect the security so that it will survive any bankruptcy. It may also be helpful to include a provision that states that any trademarks are essential to the licensee's other usage rights of the protected IP, and if the licensee is prevented from using the relevant trademarks as set forth in the agreement, it would materially adversely impact such rights.

III. SOURCE CODE ESCROWS

One strategy for guarding against the risk of a bankruptcy or any loss of services from a technology provider is the use of a source code escrow. Source code is the human-readable code that is created by programmers. Source code contains the structures and elements of a software program.

---

[27] 11 U.S.C. §101(35A).

[28] *See In re* HQ Global Holdings Inc., 290 B.R. 507 (Bankr. D. Del. 2003); *In re* Centura Software Corp., 281 B.R. 660 (Bankr. N.D. Cal. 2002).

[29] *In re* Matusalem, 158 B.R. 514 (Bankr. N.D. Cal. 2002).

[30] *In re* Centura Software Corp., 281 B.R. 660 (Bankr. N.D. Cal. 2002).

It includes the instructions for processing and other functions that make the software useful. Because source code can be understood by other programmers, it can be readily copied.[31] Most companies treat source code as a trade secret.[32] Licensees of software do not normally receive a copy of the source code.

Before it can be used, source code is converted, or compiled, into a machine-readable form known as object code. Object code is composed of zeros and ones and is not comprehensible to humans. Therefore, object code is distributed to licensees to run on their computers. Typically, the licensor provides maintenance and support services with the software to correct errors or bugs. Without these services, most software would become unusable.

A licensee may decide that the software it is licensing is crucial to its business and that it wants to ensure the availability of the software. Other risk factors include whether the licensor is a small or start-up company, the proximity of the licensor, or the financial stability of the licensor. A source code escrow is one tool used by licensees to mitigate these risks. As good vendor management is required of financial institutions, source code escrows have become common. One leading source code escrow provider, Iron Mountain, now even offers an escrow service for software as a service (SaaS) software.

With a source code escrow, similar to other types of escrows, one party, here the licensor, places its source code, including any relevant documentation and instructions for compiling the source code, into an escrow arrangement with an escrow agent. The licensee, escrow agent, and licensor sign a three-party escrow agreement that provides that the escrow agent holds the source code until a certain event, called a release condition, occurs. Typical release conditions include the licensor's bankruptcy, insolvency, or business closing; acquisition, merger, or sale; failure to maintain and support the software; or breach of the license agreement.

---

[31] It is likely that source code is copyrightable and, hence, protected by copyright law.

[32] See Chapter 3 herein regarding trade secrets.

An important note is that the license grant in any software agreement typically does not include source code. If a source code escrow is contemplated, there must be an explicit source code license in the license agreement. Note that bankruptcy law does not allow a "springing" license; therefore, a valid source code license should be included in the license agreement and not in the escrow agreement.

Source code escrow vendors typically offer different levels of services. A basic service takes the source code and holds it until notified of a release. Upgraded services include actually testing and compiling the code to ensure that it is usable in the event a release condition occurs. It is advisable to use a more advanced service if the licensee considers the software to be mission critical or important to its core business.

Source code escrows are useful when the licensee determines that it wants the ability to maintain the software in the event the licensor goes out of business or otherwise fails to provide maintenance services. They involve a three-party agreement between the licensor, licensee, and escrow agent. Under this escrow agreement, the licensor deposits the source code and related materials. On the occurrence of a release condition specified in the agreement, the escrow agent will release the source code to the licensee. Typical release events include failure by the licensor to comply with its maintenance obligations and failure of the licensor to conduct its business completely. Another common release event is the filing of a bankruptcy petition by the licensor, but it is questionable whether that would be enforceable.

After release under the escrow agreement, the licensee is allowed to modify, maintain, and copy the software, including the source code, to keep using the software. However, the licensee does not have unrestricted use of the software and cannot commercialize it, even if the licensor has gone out of business.

Source code escrows, however, have limited practical use. Several factors may contribute to the inability to make use of the source code. First, if a licensor is having financial difficulties, it may not put updates and bug fixes into the escrow. Therefore, the escrow may not contain the complete code and it may not work, even after release. Second, source code, while readable by programmers, can be hard to understand. Someone unfamiliar with the way the source code is structured may only make any problems worse.

IV. TERMINATION CLAUSES

Most software or technology service contracts have a clause that provides for termination because of (1) insolvency of a debtor, (2) commencement of a bankruptcy action, or (3) appointment of a trustee or receiver. Note, however, that if the contract is an executory contract, such ipso facto clauses are unenforceable.[33]

---

[33] *See In re* Cardinal Indus., Inc., 116 B.R. 964 (Bankr. E.D. Ohio 1990).

CHAPTER 12

GLOBAL ISSUES

I. Introduction

This chapter discusses global issues that do not apply to any one of the major segments of the financial services industry. In fact, this chapter could apply to all of them. It is an area that will grow as financial services technology grows.

II. BITCOIN

The field of financial services technology can be quite fascinating as there are always new segments developing. Where does something like Bitcoin fit in? Is it simply technology? Is it money? Bitcoin in its simplest terms is a system for making payments from one party to another without the use of a financial intermediary, such as a bank. Although Bitcoin is currently unregulated, law enforcement has restricted its use.

In more technical terms, Bitcoin is an open source digital currency. It is created or "mined" by computer users who record transactions in a registry that is open to the public. These users may receive fees and bitcoins in exchange for their efforts. Other ways to accumulate bitcoins are through sales of goods or services online. Bitcoins can also be bought with traditional government-issued currencies. Bitcoin uses cryptography to control the creation, use, and transfer of value.

Bitcoin uses a database called a block chain that records all transactions and serves as a public record. The block chain records Bitcoin addresses, not individual names. However, some Bitcoin transactions do track the personal information of bitcoin owners. Through the use of cryptography, the Bitcoin software generates a public and a private key. In a Bitcoin transaction, ownership of the bitcoins is transferred to the new owner's address. This address is derived from the public key. The private key protects the owner of the bitcoins as Bitcoin transactions can be completed only by using the private key.

The concept of Bitcoins was introduced in a paper published in 2008 by Satoshi Nakamoto, which is believed to be a pseudonym. The true identity of Nakamoto is the subject of some debate. It has been theorized that the Bitcoin creator is really a team of people or some other group effort, rather than an individual.[1] For purposes of this book,

---

[1] *See* Adam Penenberg, *The Bitcoin Crypto-currency Mystery Reopened*, FAST COMPANY (Oct. 11, 2011), http://www.fastcompany.com/1785445/bitcoin-crypto-currency-mystery

it doesn't really matter. What is important is the impact this type of technology can have.

A. Is Bitcoin Money?

Money is typically defined as having three characteristics: (1) a medium of exchange, (2) a store of value, and (3) a unit of account. Bitcoin can be used to purchase goods and services, so it functions as a medium of exchange, however, only in a very small way. At time of writing, it is estimate that there are about 15,000 items that can be purchased with bitcoins.[2] The fact that Bitcoin can be used to buy real goods and services distinguishes it from virtual currencies, which can be used only within certain boundaries, such as video game money or loyalty points.[3] Bitcoins may also be converted into other "real" currencies, such as dollars or euros. Therefore, it is more like a digital currency.

What about the other characteristics? Are bitcoins a store of value? Seemingly, yes. Holders of bitcoins certainly can hold them and use them at a later time. There is risk that the value will fluctuate either up or down during that time. Dollars and euros fluctuate in value also, but not normally to the extent seen with bitcoins.

Where Bitcoin seems weakest is as a unit of account. It isn't used to price goods or services, and you can't go through your day using only bitcoins to pay for the things you need.[4] Still, this may change as Bitcoin becomes more widely accepted.

Some authorities have deemed Bitcoin as a commodity rather than money. The Bank of England has declared it to

---

-reopened; Alec Liu, *Who Is Satoshi Nakamoto, the Creator of Bitcoin?*, MOTHERBOARD BLOG (May 22, 2013, 10:45 AM EST), http://motherboard.vice.com/blog/who-is-satoshi-nakamoto-the-creator-of-bitcoin; *Who Is Satoshi Nakamoto?*, BITCOIN EXAMINER BLOG (July 7, 2014), http://bitcoinexaminer.org/who-is-satoshi-nakamoto/; Leah McGrath Goodman, *The Face Behind Bitcoin*, NEWSWEEK, Mar. 6, 2014.

[2] *Is Bitcoin a Digital Currency or a Commodity?*, EXAMINER.COM.

[3] *Is Bitcoin a Digital Currency or a Virtual One?*, COINDESK.COM.

[4] *Id.*

be a commodity[5] Goldman Sachs has deemed it useful, but not money.[6]

So are bitcoins money? Probably not yet, but that may change.

B. Law Enforcement and Bitcoin

Although some people believe Bitcoin is not money, law enforcement apparently has a different take. In January 2014, Robert Faiella, a/k/a BTCKing, and Charlie Shrem from BitInstant.com were arrested and charged with violations of the Bank Secrecy Act (BSA).[7] The Department of Justice alleged the pair provided bitcoins to users of the website Silk Road, which offered illegal drugs for sale, among other things.[8] In February 2014, Michell Abner Espinoza and Pascal Reid were arrested in Florida and charged with violating that state's laws regarding licensed money transmitters for selling bitcoins online and in person.[9] If Bitcoin isn't money, how can one be guilty of money laundering or violating money transfer laws? It will be interesting to see how these cases play out.

Concerned about potential use by terrorists and other illegal activities, Israeli authorities have warned against the use of bitcoins.[10] However, some countries do not believe that bitcoins should be banned just because some people use them for illegal purposes.[11] After all, dollars and euros can be used to buy illegal drugs. That certainly doesn't make them inherently bad.

Still, the Financial Crimes Enforcement Network (FinCEN) has acknowledged that an entity that uses value as a substitute

---

[5] *Bank of England: Digital Currencies Are Similar to Commodities,* COINDESK.COM.

[6] *Goldman Sachs: Bitcoin Isn't a Currency But Underlying Tech Holds Promise,* COINDESK. COM.

[7] 31 U.S.C. §5311 *et seq.*

[8] *US Makes Bitcoin Exchange Arrests After Silk Road Closure,* www.bbc.co.uk.

[9] *Two Florida Men Charged with Money Laundering for Selling Bitcoins,* rt.com.

[10] *Government Issues Warning Against Bitcoin,* TIMES OF ISRAEL, Feb. 19, 2014.

[11] *Dutch Official Downplays Law Enforcement Need for Bitcoin Ban,* COINDESK.COM.

for currency should be regulated as a money services business under the BSA.[12] This includes non-U.S. residents engaging in these activities. It is not clear how U.S. law could have such global reach. In addition, the Commodity Futures Trading Commission has stated that it intends to regulate Bitcoin. Thus, while bitcoins may or may not be money, they are still subject to regulation.

It is too early to tell how the issues concerning virtual money will be settled, but they illustrate the complex legal and regulatory challenges around financial services technology.

III. GLOBAL COOPERATION AND STANDARDS

Several international organizations are worth mentioning when considering global financial services. While not all regulatory in nature, they do regulate their own areas of expertise that are essential to financial services around the globe.

A. Society for Worldwide Interbank Financial Telecommunication

The Society for Worldwide Interbank Financial Telecommunication (SWIFT) was created in 1973, under Belgian law, to provide a secure network for financial institutions to send and receive information in a secure manner. SWIFT currently connects more than 9,000 financial institutions worldwide. SWIFT sends not money but payment orders. These are then settled through the use of correspondent accounts that financial institutions maintain with one another.

The SWIFT message format is now the industry standard in payment messaging and is used by many payment systems.

---

[12] *See* 31 C.F.R. 1010, 31 C.F.R. Parts 1021–1022.

SWIFT also maintains several ISO standards,[13] including ISO 9362:1994, for bank messages; ISO 10383:2003, for securities and similar financial instruments; and ISO 20022-1:2004 and 2022-2:2007, a universal financial industry messaging format. These formats facilitate finance and commerce throughout the world. SWIFT also provides a set of software tools that permit financial institutions to use its network.

In 2006, it was disclosed that the U.S. Central Intelligence Agency had accessed the SWIFT network.[14] According to the U.S. government, this was done to track payments to and from persons suspected of being terrorists. Belgian authorities charged that this use violated Belgian and European law. Subsequently, an agreement was made between the United States and the European Union to permit some access, although this access is somewhat controversial. More recent reports indicated that the National Security Agency also accessed the SWIFT network, presumably to investigate terrorism-related payments.

B. Financial Stability Board

Created in 2009, the Financial Stability Board (FSB) is composed of G-20 nations[15] and provides oversight to financial institutions in its member states. The FSB is tasked with overseeing capital, liquidity, and risk management; increasing transparency and value; addressing the uses of credit ratings; increasing responsiveness to risks; and creating mechanisms to address stress in the financial system. The FSB has issued guidance on everything from shadow banking to systemically important financial institutions (SIFIs)

---

[13] ISO stands for International Organization for Standardization, which develops and publishes international standards used in industry and commerce.

[14] Eric Lichtblau & James Risen, *Bank Data Is Sifted by U.S. in Secret to Block Terror*, N.Y. TIMES, June 23, 2006.

[15] These are Argentina, Australia, Brazil, Canada, China, France, Germany, Hong Kong, India, Indonesia, Italy, Japan, Mexico, The Netherlands, Russia, Saudi Arabia, Singapore, South Africa, South Korea, Spain, Switzerland, Turkey, the United Kingdom, and the United States.

to securities lending and retail banking. Up until now, this guidance has not directly impacted the use of technology in financial services, but it has impacted services driven by technology such as payments and clearing, commercial paper, and credit card processing. One key resource provided by the FSB is a Compendium of Standards. This lists global standards concerning financial service regulation. This is the body to which national regulators may look when setting future policy. Therefore, it would be prudent to keep an eye on developments at the FSB.

C. International Association of Insurance Supervisors

The International Association of Insurance Supervisors (IAIS) performs a number of important functions. It collects and reports information on the global insurance market, including risk analyses; studies the impact of insurance and reinsurance on financial stability; sets standards for insurance regulation; provides information and support to help implement its recommendations worldwide; and helps identify globally systemically important insurers and any risks posed by them. Since insurance regulators in more than 190 countries look to the IAIS for recommendations on domestic insurance regulation, it would be prudent to follow and understand this organization to prepare for possible changes in national regulations.

D. Global Intellectual Property Laws

No global law governs intellectual property (IP); however, the World Intellectual Property Organization (WIPO) administers 26 IP treaties. Most developed and developing countries have signed most of these treaties, which serve as a basis for global IP law. They are classified into three groups: IP protection treaties, treaties comprising the global protection system, and classification treaties.

1. IP Protection Treaties

These treaties define internationally agreed standards of IP.

- Beijing Treaty on Audiovisual Performances—governs copyright protection for audiovisual performances.
- Berne Convention—governs copyright protection generally.
- Brussels Convention—governs the distribution of live or recorded audiovisual material via satellite.
- Madrid Agreement (Indications of Source)—governs trademark rights.
- Marrakesh VIP Treaty—created carve-outs to copyright law to increase the availability of versions of books and other copyrighted works for persons with print disabilities.
- Nairobi Treaty—governs the protection of the Olympic symbol.
- Paris Convention—governs patent and trademark protection.
- Patent Law Treaty—governs the harmonization of patent applications.
- Phonograms Convention—protects copyrights on sound recordings.
- Rome Convention—protects certain electronic copyrighted materials.
- Singapore Treaty on the Law of Trademarks—governs the harmonization of trademark registrations and licensing.
- Trademark Law Treaty—governs the harmonization of trademark registrations.
- Washington Treaty—protects integrated circuits.
- WIPO Copyright Treaty—governs copyright protection for software, databases, and other technology.
- WIPO Performances and Phonograms Treaty—provides standardized protection for performers and producers of phonograms.

2. Global Protection System Treaties

These treaties allow one registration to provide IP protection globally in all the countries that are signatories to the treaty.

- Budapest Treaty—governs patent protection for microorganisms.
- Hague Agreement—governs the registration of an industrial design in more than one country with one application, in one language, and one fee.
- Lisbon Agreement—governs the use of appellations of origin for goods.
- Madrid Agreement (Marks)—governs trademark registrations globally.
- Madrid Protocol—governs trademark registrations globally.
- Patent Cooperation Treaty—governs patent applications, searching and examination.

3. Classification Treaties

These treaties organize information about inventions, trademarks, and other IP.

- Locarno Agreement—adopts universal classification system for industrial designs.
- Nice Agreement—governs the classification for goods and services for trademark registrations.
- Strasbourg Agreement—adopts a universal classification systems for patents.
- Vienna Agreement—establishes an international classification system for figurative marks.

4. Other WIPO Activities

WIPO also administers and maintains WIPOnet, a global network connecting the IP offices of WIPO member countries, allowing increased communications. WIPO also maintains an Arbitration and Mediation Center that resolves Internet domain name disputes. To date, it has handled more than 25,000 domain name cases. Finally, WIPO operates Technology and Innovation Support Centers to help companies in developing countries to better use technology.

IV. CONCLUSION

This book has covered a lot of ground, hopefully in a useful way. Areas such as online and mobile financial services are changing every day. Cloud computing still has tremendous growth potential. Financial service companies are hit continuously with an explosion of information and data. This book divides these companies into four categories to make them easier to discuss, but the real world is messier than that. Other issues, like the Heartbleed[16] bug, may be a hidden trap waiting to be sprung.

All of this creates challenges and opportunities. Evolving regulatory environments struggle to keep up with technological changes. As financial services continue to expand globally, the role of international nongovernmental organizations further complicates the situation. In addition, entrepreneurs and their backers are working to solve problems and challenges in the financial services industry. Given this mix of players, the only certainty is that things will change.

---

[16] *See* Chapter 7, Section V.

ONLINE ENDORSEMENTS

FTC Examples Regarding Advertising Endorsements

§255.0 Purpose and Definitions.

Example 1: A film critic's review of a movie is excerpted in an advertisement. When so used, the review meets the definition of an endorsement because it is viewed by readers as a statement of the critic's own opinions and not those of the film producer, distributor, or exhibitor. Any alteration in or quotation from the text of the review that does not fairly reflect its substance would be a violation of the standards set by this part because it would distort the endorser's opinion. [*See* 16 C.F.R. §255.1(b).]

Example 2: A TV commercial depicts two women in a supermarket buying a laundry detergent. The women are not identified outside the context of the advertisement. One comments to the other how clean her brand makes her family's clothes, and the other then comments that she will try it

---

Source: 16 C.F.R. pt. 255 ("Guides Concerning Use of Endorsements and Testimonials in Advertising").

because she has not been fully satisfied with her own brand. This obvious fictional dramatization of a real life situation would not be an endorsement.

Example 3: In an advertisement for a pain remedy, an announcer who is not familiar to consumers except as a spokesman for the advertising drug company praises the drug's ability to deliver fast and lasting pain relief. He purports to speak, not on the basis of his own opinions, but rather in the place of and on behalf of the drug company. The announcer's statements would not be considered an endorsement.

Example 4: A manufacturer of automobile tires hires a well-known professional automobile racing driver to deliver its advertising message in television commercials. In these commercials, the driver speaks of the smooth ride, strength, and long life of the tires. Even though the message is not expressly declared to be the personal opinion of the driver, it may nevertheless constitute an endorsement of the tires. Many consumers will recognize this individual as being primarily a racing driver and not merely a spokesperson or announcer for the advertiser. Accordingly, they may well believe the driver would not speak for an automotive product unless he actually believed in what he was saying and had personal knowledge sufficient to form that belief. Hence, they would think that the advertising message reflects the driver's personal views. This attribution of the underlying views to the driver brings the advertisement within the definition of an endorsement for purposes of this part.

Example 5: A television advertisement for a particular brand of golf balls shows a prominent and well-recognized professional golfer practicing numerous drives off the tee. This would be an endorsement by the golfer even though she makes no verbal statement in the advertisement.

Example 6: An infomercial for a home fitness system is hosted by a well-known entertainer. During the infomercial, the entertainer demonstrates the machine and states that it is the most effective and easy-to-use home exercise machine that she has ever tried. Even if she is reading from a script, this statement would be an endorsement, because consumers are likely to believe it reflects the entertainer's views.

Example 7: A television advertisement for a housewares store features a well-known female comedian and a well-known male baseball player engaging in light-hearted banter about products each one intends to purchase for the other. The comedian says that she will buy him a Brand X, portable, high-definition television so he can finally see the strike zone. He says that he will get her a Brand Y juicer so she can make juice with all the fruit and vegetables thrown at her during her performances. The comedian and baseball player are not likely to be deemed endorsers because consumers will likely realize that the individuals are not expressing their own views.

Example 8: A consumer who regularly purchases a particular brand of dog food decides one day to purchase a new, more expensive brand made by the same manufacturer. She writes in her personal blog that the change in diet has made her dog's fur noticeably softer and shinier, and that in her opinion, the new food definitely is worth the extra money. This posting would not be deemed an endorsement under the Guides.

Assume that rather than purchase the dog food with her own money, the consumer gets it for free because the store routinely tracks her purchases and its computer has generated a coupon for a free trial bag of this new brand. Again, her posting would not be deemed an endorsement under the Guides.

Assume now that the consumer joins a network marketing program under which she periodically receives various products about which she can write reviews if she wants to do so. If she receives a free bag of the new dog food through this program, her positive review would be considered an endorsement under the Guides.

§255.1 General Considerations.

Example 1: A building contractor states in an advertisement that he uses the advertiser's exterior house paint because of its remarkable quick drying properties and durability. This endorsement must comply with the pertinent requirements of Section 255.3 (Expert Endorsements). Subsequently, the advertiser reformulates its paint to enable it to cover exterior surfaces with only one coat. Prior to continued use of the contractor's endorsement, the advertiser must contact the contractor in order to determine whether the contractor would continue to specify the paint and to subscribe to the views presented previously.

Example 2: A television advertisement portrays a woman seated at a desk on which rest five unmarked computer keyboards. An announcer says, "We asked X, an administrative assistant for over ten years, to try these five unmarked keyboards and tell us which one she liked best." The advertisement portrays X typing on each keyboard and then picking the advertiser's brand. The announcer asks her why, and X gives her reasons. This endorsement would probably not represent that X actually uses the advertiser's keyboard at work. In addition, the endorsement also may be required to meet the standards of Section 255.3 (expert endorsements).

Example 3: An ad for an acne treatment features a dermatologist who claims that the product is "clinically proven" to work. Before giving the endorsement, she received a write-up of the clinical study in question, which indicates flaws in the design and conduct of the study that are so serious that they preclude any conclusions about the efficacy of the product. The dermatologist is subject to liability for the false statements she made in the advertisement. The advertiser is

also liable for misrepresentations made through the endorsement. [*See* 16 C.F.R. §255.3 regarding the product evaluation
that an expert endorser must conduct.]

Example 4: A well-known celebrity appears in an infomercial for an oven roasting bag that purportedly cooks every
chicken perfectly in thirty minutes. During the shooting of
the infomercial, the celebrity watches five attempts to cook
chickens using the bag. In each attempt, the chicken is
undercooked after thirty minutes and requires sixty minutes
of cooking time. In the commercial, the celebrity places an
uncooked chicken in the oven roasting bag and places the
bag in one oven. He then takes a chicken roasting bag from
a second oven, removes from the bag what appears to be a
perfectly cooked chicken, tastes the chicken, and says that if
you want perfect chicken every time, in just thirty minutes,
this is the product you need. A significant percentage of consumers are likely to believe the celebrity's statements represent his own views even though he is reading from a script.
The celebrity is subject to liability for his statement about the
product. The advertiser is also liable for misrepresentations
made through the endorsement.

Example 5: A skin care products advertiser participates in a
blog advertising service. The service matches up advertisers
with bloggers who will promote the advertiser's products on
their personal blogs. The advertiser requests that a blogger
try a new body lotion and write a review of the product on
her blog. Although the advertiser does not make any specific claims about the lotion's ability to cure skin conditions
and the blogger does not ask the advertiser whether there is
substantiation for the claim, in her review the blogger writes
that the lotion cures eczema and recommends the product to her blog readers who suffer from this condition. The
advertiser is subject to liability for misleading or unsubstantiated representations made through the blogger's endorsement. The blogger also is subject to liability for misleading
or unsubstantiated representations made in the course of
her endorsement. The blogger is also liable if she fails to

disclose clearly and conspicuously that she is being paid for her services. [*See* 16 C.F.R. §255.5.]

In order to limit its potential liability, the advertiser should ensure that the advertising service provides guidance and training to its bloggers concerning the need to ensure that statements they make are truthful and substantiated. The advertiser should also monitor bloggers who are being paid to promote its products and take steps necessary to halt the continued publication of deceptive representations when they are discovered.

§255.2 Consumer Endorsements.

Example 1: A brochure for a baldness treatment consists entirely of testimonials from satisfied customers who say that after using the product, they had amazing hair growth and their hair is as thick and strong as it was when they were teenagers. The advertiser must have competent and reliable scientific evidence that its product is effective in producing new hair growth. The ad will also likely communicate that the endorsers' experiences are representative of what new users of the product can generally expect. Therefore, even if the advertiser includes a disclaimer such as, "Notice: These testimonials do not prove our product works. You should not expect to have similar results," the ad is likely to be deceptive unless the advertiser has adequate substantiation that new users typically will experience results similar to those experienced by the testimonial givers.

Example 2: An advertisement disseminated by a company that sells heat pumps presents endorsements from three individuals who state that after installing the company's heat pump in their homes, their monthly utility bills went down by $100, $125, and $150, respectively. The ad will likely be interpreted as conveying that such savings are representative of what consumers who buy the company's heat pump can generally expect. The advertiser does not have substantiation for that representation because, in fact, less than 20% of purchasers will save $100 or more. A disclosure such as, "Results not typical" or, "These testimonials are based on the experiences of a few people and you are not likely to have similar results" is insufficient to prevent this ad from being deceptive because consumers will still interpret the ad as conveying that the specified savings are representative of what consumers can generally expect. The ad is less likely to be deceptive if it clearly and conspicuously discloses the generally expected savings and the advertiser has adequate substantiation that homeowners can achieve those results. There are multiple ways that such a disclosure could be phrased, e.g., "the average homeowner saves $35 per month," "the typical family saves $50 per month during cold months and $20 per month in warm months," or "most families save 10% on their utility bills."

Example 3: An advertisement for a cholesterol-lowering product features an individual who claims that his serum cholesterol went down by 120 points and does not mention having made any lifestyle changes. A well-conducted clinical study shows that the product reduces the cholesterol levels of individuals with elevated cholesterol by an average of 15% and the advertisement clearly and conspicuously discloses this fact. Despite the presence of this disclosure, the advertisement would be deceptive if the advertiser does not have adequate substantiation that the product can produce the specific results claimed by the endorser (i.e., a 120-point drop in serum cholesterol without any lifestyle changes).

Example 4: An advertisement for a weight-loss product features a formerly obese woman. She says in the ad, "Every day, I drank 2 WeightAway shakes, ate only raw vegetables, and exercised vigorously for six hours at the gym. By the end of six months, I had gone from 250 pounds to 140 pounds." The advertisement accurately describes the woman's experience, and such a result is within the range that would be generally experienced by an extremely overweight individual who consumed WeightAway shakes, only ate raw vegetables, and exercised as the endorser did. Because the endorser clearly describes the limited and truly exceptional circumstances under which she achieved her results, the ad is not likely to convey that consumers who weigh substantially less or use WeightAway under less extreme circumstances will lose 110 pounds in six months. (If the advertisement simply says that the endorser lost 110 pounds in six months using WeightAway together with diet and exercise, however, this description would not adequately alert consumers to the truly remarkable circumstances leading to her weight loss.) The advertiser must have substantiation, however, for any performance claims conveyed by the endorsement (e.g., that WeightAway is an effective weight loss product). If, in the alternative, the advertisement simply features "before" and "after" pictures of a woman who says "I lost 50 pounds in 6 months with WeightAway," the ad is likely to convey that her experience is representative of what consumers will generally achieve. Therefore, if consumers cannot generally expect to achieve such results, the ad should clearly and conspicuously disclose what they can expect to lose in the depicted circumstances (e.g., "most women who use Weight-Away for six months lose at least 15 pounds"). If the ad features the same pictures but the testimonial giver simply says, "I lost 50 pounds with WeightAway," and WeightAway users generally do not lose 50 pounds, the ad should disclose what results they do generally achieve (e.g., "most women who use WeightAway lose 15 pounds").

Example 5: An advertisement presents the results of a poll of consumers who have used the advertiser's cake mixes as well as their own recipes. The results purport to show that the majority believed that their families could not tell the difference between the advertised mix and their own cakes baked from scratch. Many of the consumers are actually pictured in the advertisement along with relevant, quoted portions of their statements endorsing the product. This use of the results of a poll or survey of consumers represents that this is the typical result that ordinary consumers can expect from the advertiser's cake mix.

Example 6: An advertisement purports to portray a "hidden camera" situation in a crowded cafeteria at breakfast time. A spokesperson for the advertiser asks a series of actual patrons of the cafeteria for their spontaneous, honest opinions of the advertiser's recently introduced breakfast cereal. Even though the words "hidden camera" are not displayed on the screen, and even though none of the actual patrons is specifically identified during the advertisement, the net impression conveyed to consumers may well be that these are actual customers, and not actors. If actors have been employed, this fact should be clearly and conspicuously disclosed.

Example 7: An advertisement for a recently released motion picture shows three individuals coming out of a theater, each of whom gives a positive statement about the movie. These individuals are actual consumers expressing their personal views about the movie. The advertiser does not need to have substantiation that their views are representative of the opinions that most consumers will have about the movie. Because the consumers' statements would be understood to be the subjective opinions of only three people, this advertisement is not likely to convey a typicality message. If the motion picture studio had approached these individuals outside the theater and offered them free tickets if they would talk about the movie on camera afterwards, that arrangement should be clearly and conspicuously disclosed. [See 16 C.F.R. §255.5.]

§255.3 Expert Endorsements.

Example 1: An endorsement of a particular automobile by one described as an "engineer" implies that the endorser's professional training and experience are such that he is well acquainted with the design and performance of automobiles.

If the endorser's field is, for example, chemical engineering, the endorsement would be deceptive.

Example 2: An endorser of a hearing aid is simply referred to as "Doctor" during the course of an advertisement. The ad likely implies that the endorser is a medical doctor with substantial experience in the area of hearing. If the endorser is not a medical doctor with substantial experience in audiology, the endorsement would likely be deceptive. A non-medical "doctor" (e.g., an individual with a Ph.D. in exercise physiology) or a physician without substantial experience in the area of hearing can endorse the product, but if the endorser is referred to as "doctor," the advertisement must make clear the nature and limits of the endorser's expertise.

Example 3: A manufacturer of automobile parts advertises that its products are approved by the "American Institute of Science." From its name, consumers would infer that the "American Institute of Science" is a bona fide independent testing organization with expertise in judging automobile parts and that, as such, it would not approve any automobile part without first testing its efficacy by means of valid scientific methods. If the American Institute of Science is not such a bona fide independent testing organization (e.g., if it was established and operated by an automotive parts manufacturer), the endorsement would be deceptive. Even if the American Institute of Science is an independent bona fide expert testing organization, the endorsement may nevertheless be deceptive unless the Institute has conducted valid scientific tests of the advertised products and the test results support the endorsement message.

Example 4: A manufacturer of a non-prescription drug product represents that its product has been selected over competing products by a large metropolitan hospital. The hospital has selected the product because the manufacturer, unlike its competitors, has packaged each dose of the product separately. This package form is not generally available to the public. Under the circumstances, the endorsement would be deceptive because the basis for the hospital's choice—convenience of packaging—is neither relevant nor available to consumers, and the basis for the hospital's decision is not disclosed to consumers.

Example 5: A woman who is identified as the president of a commercial "home cleaning service" states in a television advertisement that the service uses a particular brand of cleanser, instead of leading competitors it has tried, because of this brand's performance. Because cleaning services extensively use cleansers in the course of their business, the ad likely conveys that the president has knowledge superior to that of ordinary consumers. Accordingly, the president's statement will be deemed to be an expert endorsement. The service must, of course, actually use the endorsed cleanser. In addition, because the advertisement implies that the cleaning service has experience with a reasonable number of leading competitors to the advertised cleanser, the service must, in fact, have such experience, and, on the basis of its expertise, it must have determined that the cleaning ability of the endorsed cleanser is at least equal (or superior, if such is the net impression conveyed by the advertisement) to that of leading competitors' products with which the service has had experience and which remain reasonably available to it. Because in this example the cleaning service's president makes no mention that the endorsed cleanser was "chosen," "selected," or otherwise evaluated in side-by-side comparisons against its competitors, it is sufficient if the service has relied solely upon its accumulated experience in evaluating cleansers without having performed side-by-side or scientific comparisons.

Example 6: A medical doctor states in an advertisement for a drug that the product will safely allow consumers to lower their cholesterol by 50 points. If the materials the doctor reviewed were merely letters from satisfied consumers or the results of a rodent study, the endorsement would likely be deceptive because those materials are not what others with the same degree of expertise would consider adequate to support this conclusion about the product's safety and efficacy.

§255.4 Endorsements by Organizations.

Example: A mattress seller advertises that its product is endorsed by a chiropractic association. Because the association would be regarded as expert with respect to judging mattresses, its endorsement must be supported by an evaluation by an expert or experts recognized as such by the organization, or by compliance with standards previously adopted by the organization and aimed at measuring the performance of mattresses in general and not designed with the unique features of the advertised mattress in mind.

§255.5 Disclosure of Material Connections.

Example 1: A drug company commissions research on its product by an outside organization. The drug company determines the overall subject of the research (e.g., to test the efficacy of a newly developed product) and pays a substantial share of the expenses of the research project, but the research organization determines the protocol for the study and is responsible for conducting it. A subsequent advertisement by the drug company mentions the research results as the "findings" of that research organization. Although the design and conduct of the research project are controlled by the outside research organization, the weight consumers place on the reported results could be materially affected by knowing that the advertiser had funded the project. Therefore, the advertiser's payment of expenses to the research organization should be disclosed in this advertisement.

Example 2: A film star endorses a particular food product. The endorsement regards only points of taste and individual preference. This endorsement must, of course, comply with §255.1; but regardless of whether the star's compensation for the commercial is a $1 million cash payment or a royalty for each product sold by the advertiser during the next year, no disclosure is required because such payments likely are ordinarily expected by viewers.

Example 3: During an appearance by a well-known professional tennis player on a television talk show, the host comments that the past few months have been the best of her career and during this time she has risen to her highest level ever in the rankings. She responds by attributing the improvement in her game to the fact that she is seeing the ball better than she used to, ever since having laser vision correction surgery at a clinic that she identifies by name. She continues talking about the ease of the procedure, the kindness of the clinic's doctors, her speedy recovery, and how she can now engage in a variety of activities without glasses, including driving at night. The athlete does not disclose that, even though she does not appear in commercials for the clinic, she has a contractual relationship with it, and her contract pays her for speaking publicly about her surgery when she can do so. Consumers might not realize that a celebrity discussing a medical procedure in a television interview has been paid for doing so, and knowledge of such payments would likely affect the weight or credibility consumers give to the celebrity's endorsement. Without a clear and conspicuous disclosure that the athlete has been engaged as a spokesperson for the clinic, this endorsement is likely to be deceptive. Furthermore, if consumers are likely to take away from her story that her experience was typical of those who undergo the same procedure at the clinic, the advertiser must have substantiation for that claim. Assume that instead of speaking about the clinic in a television interview, the tennis player touts the results of her surgery—mentioning the clinic by name—on a social networking site that allows her fans to read in real time what is happening in her life. Given the nature of the medium in which her endorsement is disseminated, consumers might not realize that she is a paid endorser. Because that information might affect the weight consumers give to her endorsement, her relationship with the clinic should be disclosed. Assume that during that same television interview, the tennis player is wearing clothes bearing the insignia of an athletic wear company with whom she also has an endorsement contract. Although this contract requires that she wear the company's clothes not only on the court but also in public appearances, when possible, she does not mention them or the company during her appearance on the show. No disclosure is required because no representation is being made about the clothes in this context.

Example 4: An ad for an anti-snoring product features a physician who says that he has seen dozens of products come on the market over the years and, in his opinion, this is the best ever. Consumers would expect the physician to be reasonably compensated for his appearance in the ad. Consumers are unlikely, however, to expect that the physician receives a percentage of gross product sales or that he owns part of the company, and either of these facts would likely materially affect the credibility that consumers attach to the endorsement. Accordingly, the advertisement should clearly and conspicuously disclose such a connection between the company and the physician.

Example 5: An actual patron of a restaurant, who is neither known to the public nor presented as an expert, is shown seated at the counter. He is asked for his "spontaneous" opinion of a new food product served in the restaurant. Assume, first, that the advertiser had posted a sign on the door of the restaurant informing all who entered that day that patrons would be interviewed by the advertiser as part of its TV promotion of its new soy protein "steak." This notification would materially affect the weight or credibility of the patron's endorsement, and, therefore, viewers of the advertisement should be clearly and conspicuously informed of the circumstances under which the endorsement was obtained. Assume, in the alternative, that the advertiser had not posted a sign on the door of the restaurant, but had informed all interviewed customers of the "hidden camera" only after interviews were completed and the customers had no reason to know or believe that their response was being recorded for use in an advertisement. Even if patrons were also told that they would be paid for allowing the use of their opinions in advertising, these facts need not be disclosed.

Example 6: An infomercial producer wants to include consumer endorsements for an automotive additive product featured in her commercial, but because the product has not yet been sold, there are no consumer users. The producer's staff reviews the profiles of individuals interested in working as "extras" in commercials and identifies several who are interested in automobiles. The extras are asked to use the product for several weeks and then report back to the producer. They are told that if they are selected to endorse the product in the producer's infomercial, they will receive a small payment. Viewers would not expect that these "consumer endorsers" are actors who were asked to use the product so that they could appear in the commercial or that they were compensated. Because the advertisement fails to disclose these facts, it is deceptive.

Example 7: A college student who has earned a reputation as a video game expert maintains a personal weblog or "blog" where he posts entries about his gaming experiences. Readers of his blog frequently seek his opinions about video game hardware and software. As it has done in the past, the manufacturer of a newly released video game system sends the student a free copy of the system and asks him to write about it on his blog. He tests the new gaming system and writes a favorable review. Because his review is disseminated via a form of consumer-generated media in which his relationship to the advertiser is not inherently obvious, readers are unlikely to know that he has received the video game system free of charge in exchange for his review of the product, and given the value of the video game system, this fact likely would materially affect the credibility they attach to his endorsement. Accordingly, the blogger should clearly and conspicuously disclose that he received the gaming system free of charge. The manufacturer should advise him at the time it provides the gaming system that this connection should be disclosed, and it should have procedures in place to try to monitor his postings for compliance.

Example 8: An online message board designated for discussions of new music download technology is frequented by MP3 player enthusiasts. They exchange information about new products, utilities, and the functionality of numerous playback devices. Unbeknownst to the message board community, an employee of a leading playback device manufacturer has been posting messages on the discussion board promoting the manufacturer's product. Knowledge of this poster's employment likely would affect the weight or credibility of her endorsement. Therefore, the poster should clearly and conspicuously disclose her relationship to the manufacturer to members and readers of the message board.

Example 9: A young man signs up to be part of a "street team" program in which points are awarded each time a team member talks to his or her friends about a particular advertiser's products. Team members can then exchange their points for prizes, such as concert tickets or electronics. These incentives would materially affect the weight or credibility of the team member's endorsements. They should be clearly and conspicuously disclosed, and the advertiser should take steps to ensure that these disclosures are being provided.

Example 10: When an endorser who appears in a television commercial is neither represented in the advertisement as an expert nor is known to a significant portion of the viewing public, then the advertiser should clearly and conspicuously disclose either the payment or promise of compensation prior to and in exchange for the endorsement or the fact that the endorser knew or had reason to know or to believe that if the endorsement favored the advertised product some benefit, such as an appearance on television, would be extended to the endorser.

RECORD RETENTION SUMMARY LISTING

1. Records regarding customer identity must be kept for five years after the closing of the account
2. Extension of credit in excess of $10,000 (nonreal estate) (This must include the name and address of the borrower, the amount of credit, loan purpose, the date of transaction.)
3. International transactions in excess of $10,000 Signature cards
4. Account statements
5. Checks in excess of $100
6. Deposits in excess of $100
7. Records to reconstruct demand deposit accounts
8. Certificates of deposit purchased or presented (These records must contain name and address of customer, customer taxpayer identification number, description, method of payment, and date of transaction.)
9. Purchase of monetary instruments of $3,000 or more
   If the purchaser has a deposit account with the bank, this record shall contain:
   - Name of purchaser
   - Date of purchase
   - Type(s) of instrument
   - Amount of each of the instrument(s) purchased
   - Serial number(s) of the instrument(s) purchased

Source: Adapted from FED. FIN. INST. EXAMINATION COUNCIL, BANK SECRECY ACT ANTI-MONEY LAUNDERING EXAMINATION MANUAL (2004).

If the purchaser does not have a deposit account with the bank, this record shall contain:

- Name and address of purchaser
- Social security number of purchaser or alien identification number
- Date of birth of purchaser
- Date of purchase
- Type(s) of instrument purchased
- Amount each of the instrument(s) purchased
- Serial number(s) of the instrument(s) purchased
- Method used to verify the name and address of the purchaser

10. Funds transfers of $3,000 or more

Bank acting as an originator's bank. For each payment order that a bank accepts as the originator's bank, the bank must obtain and retain a record of the following information:

- Name and address of originator
- Amount of the payment order
- Execution date of the payment order
- Any payment instruction received from the originator with the payment order
- Identity of the beneficiary's bank
- As many of the following items as are received with the payment order:
  — Name and address of the beneficiary
  — Account number of the beneficiary
  — Any other specific identifier of the beneficiary

For each payment order that a bank accepts for an originator that is not an established customer of the bank, in addition to the information listed above, a bank must obtain additional information as required under 31 C.F.R. §103.33(e)(2).

Bank acting as an intermediary bank or a beneficiary's bank. For each payment order that a bank accepts as an intermediary bank, or a beneficiary's bank, the bank must retain a record of the payment order.

For each payment order that a bank accepts for a beneficiary that is not an established customer of the bank, the bank must also obtain additional information as required under 31 C.F.R. §103.33(e)(3).

Exceptions. Banks are not required to maintain records for the following: (1) funds transfers where both the originator and beneficiary are the same person and that originator's bank and the beneficiary's bank are the same bank; and (2) transfers where the originator and beneficiary are any of the following:

- A bank
- A wholly owned domestic subsidiary of a bank chartered in the United States
- A broker or dealer in securities
- A wholly owned domestic subsidiary of a broker or dealer in securities
- The United States
- A state or local government
- A federal, state, or local government agency or instrumentality

11. Taxpayer identification number

Exceptions. FFIEC regulated institutions do not need to maintain TINs for the following:

- Agencies and instrumentalities of federal, state, local, or foreign governments.
- Judges, public officials, or clerks of courts of record as custodians of funds in controversy or under the control of the court.
- Certain aliens as specified in 31 C.F.R. §103.34(a)(3)(iii)–(vi).
- Certain tax exempt organizations and units of tax-exempt organizations (31 C.F.R. §103.34(a)(3)(vii)).
- A person under 18 years of age with respect to an account opened as a part of a school thrift savings program, provided the annual dividend is less than $10.
- A person opening a Christmas club, vacation club, and similar installment savings programs, provided the annual dividend is less than $10.

- Non-resident aliens who are not engaged in a trade or business in the United States.

12. Suspicious activity report and supporting documentation
13. Currency transaction report
14. Designation of exempt person
15. Customer identification program

A bank must maintain the following:

- All identifying information about a customer (e.g., name, date of birth, address, and TIN).
- A description of the document that the bank relied upon to identity of the customer.
- A description of the non-documentary methods and results of any measures the bank took to verify the identity of the customer.
- A description of the bank's resolution of any substantive discrepancy discovered when verifying the identifying information obtained.

DATA BREACHES

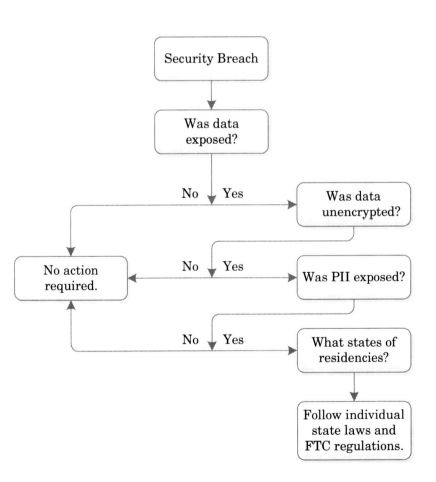

APPENDIX D

FINRA ANTI–MONEY LAUNDERING RULES

Two important regulatory developments relate to obtaining customer information: the Anti-Money Laundering Customer Identification Rule and the SEC's Books and Records Customer Account Records Rule. These rules require that important customer identification be obtained. However, these rules have critical differences including their purposes, their definitions, and their timing requirements. FINRA created this document to assist its member firms. It contains brief summaries of the rules' relevant provisions. Please check the rules and related NASD guidance for more information.

Anti–Money Laundering:	SEC Books and Records Amendments:
Customer Identification Final Rule Implementing Section 326 of the PATRIOT Act	Customer Account Record Information—SEC Rule 17a-3(a)(17)

Source: FIN. INDUS. REGULATORY AUTH., COMPARISON OF THE AML CUSTOMER IDENTIFICATION RULE AND THE SEC'S BOOKS & RECORDS CUSTOMER ACCOUNT RECORDS RULE (Sept. 2003).

PURPOSE:	**PURPOSE:**
To establish that a firm knows its customers' identities to the extent reasonable and practicable.	To provide regulators with access to books and records, which enables them to review for compliance with suitability rules.[1] Also, this information can assist firms and customers by ensuring that the firm has the correct information about customers in order to fulfill suitable obligations.
Required Information: (Minimum) ☐ Name; ☐ Date of Birth, for an individual; ☐ An address ☐ for an individual, a residential or business street address, or for an individual who does not have a residential or business street address, an Army Post Office or Fleet Post Office box number, or the residential or business street address of a next of kin or another contact individual; or ☐ for persons other than individuals, a principal place of business, local office, or other physical location; ☐ An identification number.[2]	**Required Information:** ☐ Name; ☐ Date of Birth, for an individual; ☐ An address; ☐ Tax identification number; ☐ Telephone number; ☐ Employment status (including occupation and whether the customer is an associated person of a broker/dealer); ☐ Annual income; ☐ Net worth (excluding value of a primary residence); ☐ The account's investment objectives; ☐ An indication of whether the record has been signed by the associated person responsible for the account, if any, and approved

---

[1] The rule states that the account record and furnishing requirements will only apply to accounts for which a firm is, or has within the past 36 months (of the effective date) been, required to make a suitability determination under the federal securities laws or under the requirements of a self-regulatory organization of which it is a member. *See* NASD Rules 2310 and 2860(b)(16)(B), NYSE Rule 723, Chicago Board Options Exchange Rule 9.9 and the MSRB Rule G-19.

[2] An identification number includes, for a U.S. person, a taxpayer identification number; or for a non-U.S. person, one or more of the following: a taxpayer identification number; a passport number and country of issuance; an alien identification card number; or the number and country of issuance of any other government-issued document evidencing nationality or residence and bearing a photograph or similar safeguard. Please note

	or accepted by a principal of the firm; and if the account is a discretionary account, the dated signature of each customer or owner granting the authority and the dated signature of each natural person to whom discretionary authority was granted.
When does the information have to be obtained? Prior to opening an account.[3]	**When does the information have to be obtained?** At the account opening stage.
What happens if the firm is unable to get the required information? The firm cannot open the account.	**What happens if the firm is unable to get the required information?** The broker/dealer is excused from obtaining the required information if a customer refuses, neglects or is unable to provide or update any account record information required. The rule does not require that the broker/dealer include an explanation of the customer's neglect, refusal or inability to provide the information; however, the broker/dealer is required to make a good faith effort to collect the information

that there is an exception in the final rule for natural persons who have applied for, but not received, a taxpayer identification number. Therefore, instead of obtaining a taxpayer identification number from a customer (either natural or non-natural) prior to opening an account, a CIP may include procedures for opening an account for a customer that has applied for, but has not received, a taxpayer identification number. In this case, the CIP must include procedures to confirm that the application was filed before the customer opens the account and to obtain the taxpayer identification number within a reasonable period time after the account is opened. *See NASD Notice to Members 03-34*. For more information about the Final Rule, please see *NASD Notice to Members 03-34* and NASD's AML Web Page at www.nasdr.com/money.asp.

[3] Please note that while the identification information must be obtained prior to opening an account, verification must occur within a reasonable time before or after the account is opened.

	and would bear the burden of explaining why the information is not available. Note: This is limited to Rule 17a-3(a)(17). It does not apply to other federal or SRO rules regarding the collection of information (e.g., Rule 17a-3(a)(9)).
How is "customer" defined? The "accountholder": ☐ the person that opens a new account and ☐ an individual who opens a new account for an individual who lacks legal capacity or for an entity that is not a legal person.	**How is "customer" defined?** The "accountholder" is a "natural person."
Trust Accounts: A broker/dealer is not required to look through a trust or similar account to its beneficiaries, and is required only to verify the identity of the named accountholder.	**Trust Accounts:** The account record requirement does not apply to an account where the account is owned by the trustees of the trust or a trust that is a legal entity separate from the holders of its beneficial interests (which may be natural persons). The requirement does not apply to a bank trust account where the bank has established an omnibus account at the broker/dealer holding the comingled assets of the bank's customers and the bank's customers are not aware that their assets are held by the broker/dealer.

Retirement Accounts:	**Retirement Accounts:**
The final rule excludes from the definition of "account" an account opened for the purpose of participating in an employee benefit plan established under the Employee Retirement Income Security Act of 1974 ("ERISA").	Rule 17a-3(a)(17) does not apply to a 401k account where the employer has established an omnibus account at the broker/dealer holding the assets of all its employees. The term "owner" in Rule 17a-3(a)(17) generally applies to an IRA account and a 401k account where the beneficiary of the account is a natural person.
Record Retention:	**Record Retention:**
For records of all of the identification information obtained from the customer: *Five years after the account is closed.* For records of information that verify a customer's identity: *Five years after the record is made. In all other respects, the records must be maintained pursuant to the provisions of SEC Rule 17a-4.*	Six years after the closing of the account or on which the information was replaced or updated, whichever is earlier.

FFIEC ANTI–MONEY LAUNDERING CHECKLIST

BANK SECRECY ACT/ ANTI–MONEY LAUNDERING CHECKLIST

	Yes/No	Comments
Bank Secrecy Act (BSA) [12 C.F.R. §21.21]		
BSA Compliance Program [12 C.F.R. §21.21(b)(1), (2)] • A written program. • Board approved. • Documented within Board minutes. Includes Customer Identification Program (CIP) (Does program address all BSA related areas (e.g. CTRs, SAR) and high money-laundering risk areas?)		
1. Internal Controls [12 C.F.R. §21.21(c)(1)] • Comprehensive (account opening, suspicious activity monitoring and reporting, currency reporting, and other BSA record keeping policies and procedures). • Management/Board reporting to ensure ongoing compliance. • Dual control and segregation of duties. • Risk-based customer due diligence.		

	Yes/No	Comments
2. Independent Testing (internal or external) [12 C.F.R. §21.21(c)(2)] • Attests to overall integrity/effectiveness of management systems and controls, and BSA technical compliance (31 C.F.R. pt. 103). • Tests transactions in all areas with emphasis on high-risk areas, products, services, customers, and geographic locations. • Assesses employees' knowledge of regulations and procedures. • Assesses adequacy, accuracy, and completeness of training programs. • Assesses adequacy of the bank's process for identifying suspicious activity. • Assesses timely reporting of appropriate issues to Board and senior management. • Ensures the development of effective corrective action programs, as necessary.		
3. Designated BSA Officer responsible for coordinating and monitoring day-to-day compliance [12 C.F.R. §21.21(c)(3)] • Designated by the Board. • Qualified/fully knowledgeable of BSA. • Reports BSA/AML compliance issues to senior managers and Board of Directors. • Given sufficient authority and resources.		

4. Training [12 C.F.R. §21.21(c)(4)]
 	
• The training program includes:
  — Content.
  — Employee coverage.
  — Attendance.
  — Frequency.		

	Yes/No	Comments
Bank Secrecy Act (BSA) [31 C.F.R. pt. 103]		
BSA REPORTING REQUIREMENTS:		
Suspicious Activity Reports (SARs)—Form 90-22.47 [31 C.F.R. §103.18/12 C.F.R. §21.11]		
• File SARs with FinCEN in the following circumstances: — Insider abuse involving any amount. — Violations aggregating $5,000 or more where a suspect can be identified. — Violations aggregating $25,000 or more regardless of potential suspects. — Transactions aggregating $5,000 or more that involve potential money laundering or violate the BSA. • File a SAR no later than 30 days after the date of *initial* detection of facts that constitute a basis for filing. If no suspect is identified, a NB may delay in filing an additional 30 days. In no case delay filing greater than 60 days. [31 C.F.R. §103.18(b)(3)/12 C.F.R. §21.11(d)] • Record Retention—maintain a copy of the original SAR filed and the supporting documentation for 5 years. [31 C.F.R. §103.18(d)/12 C.F.R. §21.11(g)] • Notification to Board of Directors. [12 C.F.R. §21.11(h)]		
Currency Transactions Reports (CTRs)— FinCEN Form 104 [31 C.F.R. §103.22] • System in place for identifying cash transactions aggregating more than $10,000 on the same day by (or on behalf of) the same individual or by account to ensure that a CTR is filed within the required time frame. — Manual System — Automated System • File CTRs within required timeframes (15 days).		

	Yes/No	Comments
Designation of Exempt Person—Form TDF 90-22.53 [31 C.F.R. §103.22(d)] • Exempt customers are designated in accordance with the requirements. [31 C.F.R. §103.22(d)(2) and 31 C.F.R. §103.22(d)(3)] • Bank reviews and verifies information concerning exemptions at least annually [31 C.F.R. 103.22(d)(4)] and biennial filings are performed on required accounts. [31 C.F.R. §103.22 (d)(5)] • Bank adequately monitors exempt persons for suspicious activity. [31 C.F.R. 103.22(d)(9)(ii)] • Exemptions are revoked when they no longer meet the regulatory criteria. [31 C.F.R. §103.22(d)(8)]		
Report of International Transportation of Currency or Monetary Instruments (CMIR)—FinCEN Form 105 Formerly Customs Form 4790 [31 C.F.R. §103.23] • Bank files a CMIR for each shipment, except by common carrier, of currency or other monetary instrument(s) in excess of $10,000 from the U.S. or into the U.S., by, or to the bank. [31 C.F.R. §103.23(a) and (b)] (In most cases, this refers to the bank's cash shipments.)		
Report of Foreign Bank and Financial Accounts (FBAR) TD F 90-22.1 [31 C.F.R. §103.24] • Report by persons having a financial interest in, or signature or other authority over, a bank, securities or other financial account in a foreign country to IRS each year of its existence. • Persons having a financial interest in 25 or more financial accounts need only note this fact on form. • Bank files report within the required timeframe.		

	Yes/No	Comments
BSA REGULATORY REQUIREMENTS		
Information Sharing between Law Enforcement and Financial Institutions—[31 C.F.R. §103.100] • Ability to receive information requests. • Policies and procedures are in place to process information requests. Procedures should include: — Guidance on reporting to FinCEN if the bank identifies an account or transaction requested [31 C.F.R. §103.100(b)(2)(ii)]; — The designation of a contact person. [31 C.F.R. §103.100(b)(2)(iii)]; and — Protects the security and confidentiality of requests from FinCEN [31 C.F.R. §103.100(b)(2)(iv)(C)]. • Bank systems are capable to perform record searches on: — Current accounts [31 C.F.R. §103.100(b)(2)(i)(A)]; — Accounts maintained during the preceding 12 months [31 C.F.R. §103.100(b)(2)(i)(B)]; and, — Any transaction or transmittal in which a named suspect was either the transmitter or recipient during the preceding six months [31 C.F.R. §103.100(b)(2)(i)(C)].		
Voluntary Information sharing—[31 C.F.R. §103.110] • Policies and procedures in place to process information shared among institutions, including procedures to safeguard the security and confidentiality of such information. [31 C.F.R. §103.110(b)(1)–(5)] • The bank has submitted an annual notice to FinCEN. [31 C.F.R. §103.110(b)(2)] • The bank has verified the financial institution it intends to share information with has filed notice with FinCEN. [31 C.F.R. §103.110(b)(3)]		

	Yes/No	Comments
Foreign correspondent account record keeping and due diligence [31 C.F.R. §§103.177, 103.185] • Prohibit dealings with foreign shell banks. • Sufficient internal controls.		
Customer Identification Program (CIP) [31 C.F.R. §103.121] • CIP implemented as part of the BSA compliance program. [12 C.F.R. §21.21(b)(2)] • The CIP has account opening procedures that include: — Obtaining the minimum information. [31 C.F.R. §103.121(b)(2)(i)] — Customer verification. [31 C.F.R. §103.121(b)(2)(ii)] — Record keeping requirements and retention. [31 C.F.R. §103.121(b)(3)] — Comparison with government lists. [31 C.F.R. §103.121(b)(4)] — Adequate customer notice. [31 C.F.R. §103.121(b)(5)] — Reliance on another financial institution. [31 C.F.R. §103.121(b)(6)]		
Suspicious Activity Reporting Requirements and Anti–Money Laundering Practices		
Suspicious Activity Monitoring: • Systems to identify, research, and report suspicious activity. • Assigns accountability for identification, research, and reporting suspicious activity. • Appropriate guidance for monitoring and identifying unusual activity. • An adequate transaction monitoring system is in place for the risk in the bank. • Procedures contain adequate guidance for law enforcement request. • Adequacy of SAR decision making process in place: — SAR decisions are documented. — The process ensures all applicable information is evaluated.		

	Yes/No	Comments
• Adequacy of ongoing monitoring on continuing activity. Quality of SARs filed.		
Monitoring Tools If the bank has an automated system, the bank generates a comprehensive report that details all applicable large currency transactions (i.e., all large cash-ins and cash-outs are reflected on the report).		
If the bank does not use an automated system, the bank, focusing on high cash volume locations, ensures that transactions are reviewed from all deposit-taking areas of the bank (e.g., mortgage banking department, private banking department, fiduciary, brokerage department, commercial loan department). Customer Due Diligence • CDD Guidelines are commensurate with the bank's BSA/AML risk profile. • Account opening policies, procedures, and processes are sufficient to develop an understanding of normal and expected activities. • Policies, procedures, and processes include guidance for enhanced due diligence for high-risk customers. • CDD Guidance ensures current customer information is maintained.		
OFFICE OF FOREIGN ASSETS CONTROL (OFAC) [31 C.F.R. pt. 3500]		
Bank has performed an adequate OFAC risk assessment.		
Bank maintains an accurate, current listing of prohibited countries, entities, and individuals.		
Bank ensures OFAC information is disseminated to all appropriate employees, including foreign country offices.		

	Yes/No	Comments
Prior to opening an account, or conducting a transaction, the bank compares new accounts (e.g., deposit, loan private banking, trust, discount, or other securities brokerage transactions), funds transfers, or other new bank transactions with the OFAC listings.		
The bank periodically compares established accounts and other customer transactions with the current OFAC listing.		
The bank's independent testing of its OFAC program is adequate.		

FFIEC ANTI–MONEY LAUNDERING
RED FLAGS

The following are examples of potentially suspicious activities, or "red flags" for both money laundering and terrorist financing. Although these lists are not all-inclusive, they may help banks and examiners recognize possible money laundering and terrorist financing schemes. Management's primary focus should be on reporting suspicious activities, rather than on determining whether the transactions are in fact linked to money laundering, terrorist financing, or a particular crime.

The following examples are red flags that, when encountered, may warrant additional scrutiny. The mere presence of a red flag is not by itself evidence of criminal activity. Closer scrutiny should help to determine whether the activity is suspicious or one for which there does not appear to be a reasonable business or legal purpose.

Source: FED. FIN. INST. EXAMINATION COUNCIL, BANK SECRECY ACT ANTI-MONEY LAUN-DERING EXAMINATION MANUAL (2004).

Potentially Suspicious Activity That May Indicate Money Laundering

Customers Who Provide Insufficient or Suspicious Information

- A customer uses unusual or suspicious identification documents that cannot be readily verified.
- A customer provides an individual tax identification number after having previously used a Social Security number.
- A customer uses different tax identification numbers with variations of his or her name.
- A business is reluctant, when establishing a new account, to provide complete information about the nature and purpose of its business, anticipated account activity, prior banking relationships, the names of its officers and directors, or information on its business location.
- A customer's home or business telephone is disconnected.
- The customer's background differs from that which would be expected on the basis of his or her business activities.
- A customer makes frequent or large transactions and has no record of past or present employment experience.
- A customer is a trust, shell company, or Private Investment Company that is reluctant to provide information on controlling parties and underlying beneficiaries. Beneficial owners may hire nominee incorporation services to establish shell companies and open bank accounts for those shell companies while shielding the owner's identity.

Efforts to Avoid Reporting or Record Keeping Requirement

- A customer or group tries to persuade a bank employee not to file required reports or maintain required records.
- A customer is reluctant to provide information needed to file a mandatory report, to have the report filed, or to

proceed with a transaction after being informed that the report must be filed.

- A customer is reluctant to furnish identification when purchasing negotiable instruments in recordable amounts.
- A business or customer asks to be exempted from reporting or record keeping requirements.
- A person customarily uses the automated teller machine to make several bank deposits below a specified threshold.
- A customer deposits funds into several accounts, usually in amounts of less than $3,000, which are subsequently consolidated into a master account and transferred outside of the country, particularly to or through a location of specific concern (e.g., countries designated by national authorities and Financial Action Task Force on Money Laundering (FATF) as non-cooperative countries and territories).
- A customer accesses a safe deposit box after completing a transaction involving a large withdrawal of currency, or accesses a safe deposit box before making currency deposits structured at or just under $10,000, to evade CTR filing requirements.

Funds Transfers

- Many funds transfers are sent in large, round dollar, hundred-dollar, or thousand-dollar amounts.
- Funds transfer activity occurs to or from a financial secrecy haven, or to or from a higher-risk geographic location without an apparent business reason or when the activity is inconsistent with the customer's business or history.
- Many small, incoming transfers of funds are received, or deposits are made using checks and money orders. Almost immediately, all or most of the transfers or deposits are wired to another city or country in a manner inconsistent with the customer's business or history.
- Large, incoming funds transfers are received on behalf of a foreign client, with little or no explicit reason.

- Funds transfer activity is unexplained, is repetitive, or shows unusual patterns.
- Payments or receipts with no apparent links to legitimate contracts, goods, or services are received.
- Funds transfers are sent or received from the same person to or from different accounts.
- Funds transfers contain limited content and lack related party information.

Automated Clearing House Transactions

- Large-value, automated clearing house (ACH) transactions are frequently initiated through third-party service providers (TPSP) by originators that are not bank customers and for which the bank has no or insufficient due diligence.
- TPSPs have a history of violating ACH network rules or generating illegal transactions, or processing manipulated or fraudulent transactions on behalf of their customers.
- Multiple layers of TPSPs appear to be unnecessarily involved in transactions.
- An unusually high level of transactions are initiated over the Internet or by telephone.
- NACHA—The Electronic Payments Association (NACHA) information requests indicate potential concerns with the bank's usage of the ACH system.

Activity Inconsistent with the Customer's Business

- The currency transaction patterns of a business show a sudden change inconsistent with normal activities.
- A large volume of cashier's checks, money orders, or funds transfers is deposited into, or purchased through, an account when the nature of the accountholder's business would not appear to justify such activity.

- A retail business has dramatically different patterns of currency deposits from similar businesses in the same general location.
- Unusual transfers of funds occur among related accounts or among accounts that involve the same or related principals.
- The owner of both a retail business and a check-cashing service does not ask for currency when depositing checks, possibly indicating the availability of another source of currency.
- Goods or services purchased by the business do not match the customer's stated line of business.
- Payments for goods or services are made by checks, money orders, or bank drafts not drawn from the account of the entity that made the purchase.

Lending Activity

- Loans are secured by pledged assets held by third parties unrelated to the borrower.
- Loans are secured by deposits or other readily marketable assets, such as securities, particularly when owned by apparently unrelated third parties.
- Borrower defaults on a cash-secured loan or any loan that is secured by assets that are readily convertible into currency.
- Loans are made for, or are paid on behalf of, a third party with no reasonable explanation.
- To secure a loan, the customer purchases a certificate of deposit using an unknown source of funds, particularly when funds are provided via currency or multiple monetary instruments.
- Loans lack a legitimate business purpose, provide the bank with significant fees for assuming little or no risk, or tend to obscure the movement of funds (e.g., loans made to a borrower and immediately sold to an entity related to the borrower).

Changes in Bank-to-Bank Transactions

- The size and frequency of currency deposits increases rapidly with no corresponding increase in non-currency deposits.
- A bank is unable to track the true accountholder of correspondent or concentration account transactions.
- The turnover in large-denomination bills is significant and appears uncharacteristic, given the bank's location.
- Changes in currency-shipment patterns between correspondent banks are significant.

Cross-Border Financial Institution Transactions[1]

- U.S. bank increases sales or exchanges of large denomination U.S. bank notes to Mexican financial institution(s).
- Large volumes of small denomination U.S. banknotes being sent from Mexican *casas de cambio* to their U.S. accounts via armored transport or sold directly to U.S. banks. These sales or exchanges may involve jurisdictions outside of Mexico.
- *Casas de cambio* direct the remittance of funds via multiple funds transfers to jurisdictions outside of Mexico that bear no apparent business relationship with the *casas de cambio*. Funds transfer recipients may include individuals, businesses, and other entities in free trade zones.
- *Casas de cambio* deposit numerous third-party items, including sequentially numbered monetary instruments, to their accounts at U.S. banks.
- *Casas de cambio* direct the remittance of funds transfers from their accounts at Mexican financial institutions to accounts at U.S. banks. These funds transfers follow the deposit of currency and third-party items by the *casas de cambio* into their Mexican financial institution.

---

[1] FinCEN Advisory FIN-2006-A003, "Guidance to Financial Institutions on the Repatriation of Currency Smuggled into Mexico from the United States," Apr. 28, 2006. [Original note 268.]

Bulk Currency Shipments

- An increase in the sale of large denomination U.S. bank notes to foreign financial institutions by U.S. banks.
- Large volumes of small denomination U.S. bank notes being sent from foreign nonbank financial institutions to their accounts in the United States via armored transport, or sold directly to U.S. banks.
- Multiple wire transfers initiated by foreign nonbank financial institutions that direct U.S. banks to remit funds to other jurisdictions that bear no apparent business relationship with that foreign nonbank financial institution. Recipients may include individuals, businesses, and other entities in free trade zones and other locations.
- The exchange of small-denomination U.S. bank notes for large-denomination U.S. bank notes that may be sent to foreign countries.
- Deposits by foreign nonbank financial institutions to their accounts at U.S. banks that include third-party items, including sequentially numbered monetary instruments.
- Deposits of currency and third-party items by foreign nonbank financial institutions to their accounts at foreign financial institutions and thereafter direct wire transfers to the foreign nonbank financial institution's accounts at U.S. banks.

Trade Finance

- Items shipped that are inconsistent with the nature of the customer's business (e.g., a steel company that starts dealing in paper products, or an information technology company that starts dealing in bulk pharmaceuticals).
- Customers conducting business in higher-risk jurisdictions.
- Customers shipping items through higher-risk jurisdictions, including transit through non-cooperative countries.
- Customers involved in potentially higher-risk activities, including activities that may be subject to export/import

restrictions (e g , equipment for military or police orga-nizations of foreign governments, weapons, ammunition, chemical mixtures, classified defense articles, sensitive technical data, nuclear materials, precious gems, or cer-tain natural resources such as metals, ore, and crude oil).

- Obvious over- or under-pricing of goods and services.
- Obvious misrepresentation of quantity or type of goods imported or exported.
- Transaction structure appears unnecessarily complex and designed to obscure the true nature of the transaction.
- Customer requests payment of proceeds to an unrelated third party.
- Shipment locations or description of goods not consistent with letter of credit.
- Significantly amended letters of credit without reason-able justification or changes to the beneficiary or location of payment. Any changes in the names of parties should prompt additional OFAC review.

Privately Owned Automated Teller Machines

- Automated teller machine (ATM) activity levels are high in comparison with other privately owned or bank-owned ATMs in comparable geographic and demographic locations.
- Sources of currency for the ATM cannot be identified or confirmed through withdrawals from account, armored car contracts, lending arrangements, or other appropri-ate documentation.

Insurance

- A customer purchases products with termination fea-tures without concern for the product's investment performance.

- A customer purchases insurance products using a single, large premium payment, particularly when payment is made through unusual methods such as currency or currency equivalents.
- A customer purchases a product that appears outside the customer's normal range of financial wealth or estate planning needs.
- A customer borrows against the cash surrender value of permanent life insurance policies, particularly when payments are made to apparently unrelated third parties.
- Policies are purchased that allow for the transfer of beneficial ownership interests without the knowledge and consent of the insurance issuer. This would include secondhand endowment and bearer insurance policies.
- A customer is known to purchase several insurance products and uses the proceeds from an early policy surrender to purchase other financial assets.
- A customer uses multiple currency equivalents (e.g., cashier's checks and money orders) from different banks and money services businesses to make insurance policy or annuity payments.

Shell Company Activity

- A bank is unable to obtain sufficient information or information is unavailable to positively identify originators or beneficiaries of accounts or other banking activity (using Internet, commercial database searches, or direct inquiries to a respondent bank).
- Payments to or from the company have no stated purpose, do not reference goods or services, or identify only a contract or invoice number.
- Goods or services, if identified, do not match profile of company provided by respondent bank or character of the financial activity; a company references remarkably dissimilar goods and services in related funds transfers;

explanation given by foreign respondent bank is inconsistent with observed funds transfer activity.
- Transacting businesses share the same address, provide only a registered agent's address, or have other address inconsistencies.
- Unusually large number and variety of beneficiaries are receiving funds transfers from one company.
- Frequent involvement of multiple jurisdictions or beneficiaries located in higher-risk offshore financial centers.
- A foreign correspondent bank exceeds the expected volume in its client profile for funds transfers, or an individual company exhibits a high volume and pattern of funds transfers that is inconsistent with its normal business activity.
- Multiple high-value payments or transfers between shell companies with no apparent legitimate business purpose.
- Purpose of the shell company is unknown or unclear.

Embassy and Foreign Consulate Accounts

- Official embassy business is conducted through personal accounts.
- Account activity is not consistent with the purpose of the account, such as pouch activity or payable upon proper identification transactions.
- Accounts are funded through substantial currency transactions.
- Accounts directly fund personal expenses of foreign nationals without appropriate controls, including, but not limited to, expenses for college students.

Employees

- Employee exhibits a lavish lifestyle that cannot be supported by his or her salary.
- Employee fails to conform to recognized policies, procedures, and processes, particularly in private banking.

- Employee is reluctant to take a vacation.

Other Unusual or Suspicious Customer Activity

- Customer frequently exchanges small-dollar denominations for large-dollar denominations.
- Customer frequently deposits currency wrapped in currency straps or currency wrapped in rubber bands that is disorganized and does not balance when counted.
- Customer purchases a number of cashier's checks, money orders, or traveler's checks for large amounts under a specified threshold.
- Customer purchases a number of open-end prepaid cards for large amounts. Purchases of prepaid cards are not commensurate with normal business activities.
- Customer receives large and frequent deposits from online payments systems, yet has no apparent online or auction business.
- Monetary instruments deposited by mail are numbered sequentially or have unusual symbols or stamps on them.
- Suspicious movements of funds occur from one bank to another, and then funds are moved back to the first bank.
- Deposits are structured through multiple branches of the same bank or by groups of people who enter a single branch at the same time.
- Currency is deposited or withdrawn in amounts just below identification or reporting thresholds.
- Customer visits a safe deposit box or uses a safe custody account on an unusually frequent basis.
- Safe deposit boxes or safe custody accounts opened by individuals who do not reside or work in the institution's service area, despite the availability of such services at an institution closer to them.
- Customer repeatedly uses a bank or branch location that is geographically distant from the customer's home or office without sufficient business purpose.
- Customer exhibits unusual traffic patterns in the safe deposit box area or unusual use of safe custody accounts.

For example, several individuals arrive together, enter frequently, or carry bags or other containers that could conceal large amounts of currency, monetary instruments, or small valuable items.

- Customer rents multiple safe deposit boxes to store large amounts of currency, monetary instruments, or high-value assets awaiting conversion to currency, for placement into the banking system. Similarly, a customer establishes multiple safe custody accounts to park large amounts of securities awaiting sale and conversion into currency, monetary instruments, outgoing funds transfers, or a combination thereof, for placement into the banking system.
- Unusual use of trust funds in business transactions or other financial activity.
- Customer uses a personal account for business purposes.
- Customer has established multiple accounts in various corporate or individual names that lack sufficient business purpose for the account complexities or appear to be an effort to hide the beneficial ownership from the bank.
- Customer makes multiple and frequent currency deposits to various accounts that are purportedly unrelated.
- Customer conducts large deposits and withdrawals during a short time period after opening and then subsequently closes the account or the account becomes dormant. Conversely, an account with little activity may suddenly experience large deposit and withdrawal activity.
- Customer makes high-value transactions not commensurate with the customer's known incomes.

POTENTIALLY SUSPICIOUS ACTIVITY THAT MAY INDICATE TERRORIST FINANCING

The following examples of potentially suspicious activity that may indicate terrorist financing are primarily based on "Guidance for Financial Institutions in Detecting Terrorist Financing" provided by the FATF. FATF is an intergovernmental body whose purpose is the development and promotion of policies, both at national and international levels, to combat money laundering and terrorist financing.

Activity Inconsistent with the Customer's Business

- Funds are generated by a business owned by persons of the same origin or by a business that involves persons of the same origin from higher-risk countries (e.g., countries designated by national authorities and FATF as non-cooperative countries and territories).
- The stated occupation of the customer is not commensurate with the type or level of activity.
- Persons involved in currency transactions share an address or phone number, particularly when the address is also a business location or does not seem to correspond to the stated occupation (e.g., student, unemployed, or self-employed).
- Regarding nonprofit or charitable organizations, financial transactions occur for which there appears to be no logical economic purpose or in which there appears to be no link between the stated activity of the organization and the other parties in the transaction.
- A safe deposit box opened on behalf of a commercial entity when the business activity of the customer is unknown or such activity does not appear to justify the use of a safe deposit box.

Funds Transfers

- A large number of incoming or outgoing funds transfers take place through a business account, and there appears to be no logical business or other economic purpose for the transfers, particularly when this activity involves higher-risk locations.
- Funds transfers are ordered in small amounts in an apparent effort to avoid triggering identification or reporting requirements.

- Funds transfers do not include information on the originator, or the person on whose behalf the transaction is conducted, when the inclusion of such information would be expected.
- Multiple personal and business accounts or the accounts of nonprofit organizations or charities are used to collect and funnel funds to a small number of foreign beneficiaries.
- Foreign exchange transactions are performed on behalf of a customer by a third party, followed by funds transfers to locations having no apparent business connection with the customer or to higher-risk countries.

Other Transactions That Appear Unusual or Suspicious

- Transactions involving foreign currency exchanges are followed within a short time by funds transfers to higher-risk locations.
- Multiple accounts are used to collect and funnel funds to a small number of foreign beneficiaries, both persons and businesses, particularly in higher-risk locations.
- A customer obtains a credit instrument or engages in commercial financial transactions involving the movement of funds to or from higher-risk locations when there appear to be no logical business reasons for dealing with those locations.
- Banks from higher-risk locations open accounts.
- Funds are sent or received via international transfers from or to higher-risk locations.
- Insurance policy loans or policy surrender values that are subject to a substantial surrender charge.

EXAMPLES OF IDENTITY THEFT RED FLAGS

Alerts, Notifications or Warnings from a Consumer Reporting Agency

1. A fraud or active duty alert is included with a consumer report.
2. A consumer reporting agency provides a notice of credit freeze in response to a request for a consumer report.
3. A consumer reporting agency provides a notice of address discrepancy, as referenced in Sec. 605(h) of the Fair Credit Reporting Act (15 U.S.C. §1681c(h)).
4. A consumer report indicates a pattern of activity that is inconsistent with the history and usual pattern of activity of an applicant or customer, such as:
   a. A recent and significant increase in the volume of inquiries;
   b. An unusual number of recently established credit relationships;
   c. A material change in the use of credit, especially with respect to recently established credit relationships; or

---

Source: Sec. Exch. Comm'n & Commodity Futures Trading Comm'n, Joint Final Rules on Red Flag Rules (2013).

d. An account that was closed for cause or identified for abuse of account privileges by a financial institution or creditor.

SUSPICIOUS DOCUMENTS

5. Documents provided for identification appear to have been altered or forged.
6. The photograph or physical description on the identification is not consistent with the appearance of the applicant or customer presenting the identification.
7. Other information on the identification is not consistent with information provided by the person opening a new covered account or customer presenting the identification.
8. Other information on the identification is not consistent with readily accessible information that is on file with the financial institution or creditor, such as a signature card or a recent check.
9. An application appears to have been altered or forged, or gives the appearance of having been destroyed and reassembled.

SUSPICIOUS PERSONAL IDENTIFYING INFORMATION

10. Personal identifying information provided is inconsistent when compared against external information sources used by the financial institution or creditor. For example:
    a. The address does not match any address in the consumer report; or
    b. The Social Security Number (SSN) has not been issued, or is listed on the Social Security Administration's Death Master File.

11. Personal identifying information provided by the customer is not consistent with other personal identifying information provided by the customer. For example, there is a lack of correlation between the SSN range and date of birth.
12. Personal identifying information provided is associated with known fraudulent activity as indicated by internal or third-party sources used by the financial institution or creditor. For example:
    a. The address on an application is the same as the address provided on a fraudulent application; or
    b. The phone number on an application is the same as the number provided on a fraudulent application.
13. Personal identifying information provided is of a type commonly associated with fraudulent activity as indicated by internal or third-party sources used by the financial institution or creditor. For example:
    a. The address on an application is fictitious, a mail drop, or a prison; or
    b. The phone number is invalid, or is associated with a pager or answering service.
14. The SSN provided is the same as that submitted by other persons opening an account or other customers.
15. The address or telephone number provided is the same as or similar to the address or telephone number submitted by an unusually large number of other persons opening accounts or by other customers.
16. The person opening the covered account or the customer fails to provide all required personal identifying information on an application or in response to notification that the application is incomplete.
17. Personal identifying information provided is not consistent with personal identifying information that is on file with the financial institution or creditor.
18. For financial institutions and creditors that use challenge questions, the person opening the covered account or the customer cannot provide authenticating information

beyond that which generally would be available from a wallet or consumer report.

UNUSUAL USE OF, OR SUSPICIOUS ACTIVITY RELATED TO, THE COVERED ACCOUNT

19. Shortly following the notice of a change of address for a covered account, the institution or creditor receives a request for a new, additional, or replacement means of accessing the account or for the addition of an authorized user on the account.
20. A covered account is used in a manner that is not consistent with established patterns of activity on the account. There is, for example:
    a. Nonpayment when there is no history of late or missed payments;
    b. A material increase in the use of available credit;
    c. A material change in purchasing or spending patterns; or
    d. A material change in electronic fund transfer patterns in connection with a deposit account.
21. A covered account that has been inactive for a reasonably lengthy period of time is used (taking into consideration the type of account, the expected pattern of usage and other relevant factors).
22. Mail sent to the customer is returned repeatedly as undeliverable although transactions continue to be conducted in connection with the customer's covered account.
23. The financial institution or creditor is notified that the customer is not receiving paper account statements.
24. The financial institution or creditor is notified of unauthorized charges or transactions in connection with a customer's covered account.

Notice from Customers, Victims of Identity Theft, Law Enforcement Authorities, or Other Persons Regarding Possible Identity Theft in Connection with Covered Accounts Held by the Financial Institution or Creditor

25. The financial institution or creditor is notified by a customer, a victim of identity theft, a law enforcement authority, or any other person that it has opened a fraudulent account for a person engaged in identity theft.

TABLE OF CASES

INDEX

*References are to chapters and section numbers (e.g., **8:** IV.C.4 indicates the index entry appears in Chapter 8 under section IV.C.4). The back-of-the-book appendixes are indicated by their letter designation (e.g., App. D). Alphabetization is letter-by-letter (e.g., "Banking Act" precedes "Bank of England").*